H. Wiley Hitchcock, editor

Prentice-Hall
History of Music Series

MUSIC IN THE MEDIEVAL WORLD, *Albert Seay*

RENAISSANCE MUSIC, *Joel Newman*

BAROQUE MUSIC, *Claude V. Palisca*

MUSIC IN THE CLASSIC PERIOD, *Reinhard G. Pauly*

NINETEENTH-CENTURY ROMANTICISM IN MUSIC, *Rey M. Longyear*

TWENTIETH-CENTURY MUSIC: AN INTRODUCTION, *Eric Salzman*

FOLK AND TRADITIONAL MUSIC OF THE WESTERN CONTINENTS, *Bruno Nettl*

MUSIC CULTURES OF THE PACIFIC, THE NEAR EAST, AND ASIA, *William P. Malm*

MUSIC OF LATIN AMERICA, *Gilbert Chase*

MUSIC IN THE UNITED STATES: A HISTORICAL INTRODUCTION, *H. Wiley Hitchcock*

TWO HUNDRED YEARS OF RUSSIAN MUSIC, 1770–1970, *Boris Schwarz*

Music in the United States: A Historical Introduction

H. WILEY HITCHCOCK

Professor of Music
Hunter College
City University of New York

PRENTICE-HALL, INC., ENGLEWOOD CLIFFS, NEW JERSEY

PRENTICE-HALL INTERNATIONAL, INC., *London*
PRENTICE-HALL OF AUSTRALIA, PTY. LTD., *Sydney*
PRENTICE-HALL OF CANADA, LTD., *Toronto*
PRENTICE-HALL OF INDIA PRIVATE LTD., *New Delhi*
PRENTICE-HALL OF JAPAN, INC., *Tokyo*

to my mother,
and to the memory of my father

Foreword

Students and informed amateurs of the history of music have long needed a series of books that are comprehensive, authoritative, and engagingly written. They have needed books written by specialists—but specialists interested in communicating vividly. The Prentice-Hall History of Music Series aims at filling these needs.

Six books in the series present a panoramic view of the history of Western music, divided among the major historical periods— Medieval, Renaissance, Baroque, Classic, Romantic, and Contemporary. The musical cultures of the United States, Latin America, and Russia, viewed historically as independent developments within the larger Western tradition, are discussed in three other books. In yet another pair, the rich yet neglected folk and traditional music of

Foreword continued

both hemispheres is treated. Taken together, the eleven volumes of the series are a distinctive and, we hope, distinguished contribution to the history of the music of the world's peoples. Each volume, moreover, may be read singly as a substantial account of the music of its period or area.

The authors of the series are scholars of national and international repute—musicologists, critics, and teachers of acknowledged stature in their respective fields of specialization. In their contributions to the Prentice-Hall History of Music Series their goal has been to present works of solid scholarship that are eminently readable, with significant insights into music as a part of the general intellectual and cultural life of man.

H. WILEY HITCHCOCK, *Editor*

Preface

Surely no lengthy justification is needed for a historical survey of American music and musical life. For reasons suggested in Chapter 3 of this book, we know less about our own music than about that of western Europe. Many of us have cared less, but that attitude is changing as we begin to take a less oblique view of our own musical past. My own attempt has been to view it head-on, to measure it in its own terms, and to seek the "why" behind the "what" in American music. I have also attempted to view it in the round, believing that pop songs as well as art songs, player-pianos as well as piano players, are important parts of the American musical experience.

I have dealt at somewhat less length than I should have liked with the Colonial and Federal periods; but these have been explored more thoroughly than our music of the nineteenth and twentieth centuries. My approach to nineteenth-century American music has been in terms of what I call our "cultivated" and "vernacular" traditions. In dealing with the latter I touch occasionally on folk music, but only at the point where it becomes "popular," a part of the broad musical experience of the nation at large. In discussing American music since the First World War, I have emphasized the principal stylistic trends and the predominant musical attitudes. Many fine composers have thereby gone unmentioned; they have had to make way, with my apologies, for the few who seem to me to have been the ones in whose work the major themes of twentieth-century American music have been expressed most clearly, boldly, and influentially. I make no apologies for devoting an entire chapter of a rather brief book to Charles Ives: both his thought and his music stand as continuing, fertile challenges to American musical evolution.

Scholarly apparatus is used sparingly in this book. However, bibliographical notes follow each chapter, and other works cited in footnotes constitute a further roster of sources. Among the books and periodicals listed in the table of abbreviations below, a special word is in order about "*MinA*": the reader is advised to have close at hand a copy of this sole anthology of earlier American music, as I often refer to the music in it.

I express with pleasure my gratitude to the two teachers who, many years ago, awakened my interest in the history of American music: Glenn McGeoch and Raymond Kendall. My greatest debt is to those who have shaped my attitudes about American music; I have been influenced most by the ideas of Charles Seeger and of Gilbert Chase, particularly his *America's Music*, and by the American

Preface continued

music scholar (and friend) Irving Lowens. Others who have aided me include Henry Leland Clarke, Richard Crawford, Paul Echols, Leonard Feist, John Kirkpatrick, Josef Marx, Kenneth Roberts, Howard Shanet, Brooks Shepard, Frank Tirro, Margaret Bostwick Vaill, and Charles Wuorinen. Many libraries have served beyond the call of duty, especially the Music Research Division of the New York Public Library, and its chief, Frank Campbell; the Music Division of the Library of Congress, and two of its scholar-librarians, William Lichtenwanger and Carroll Wade; and the library of the Union Theological Seminary. For her extrasensory perception in transferring my manuscript to typescript I thank Judy Kanazawa. As a teacher, I can hardly over-emphasize the role my students have played in shaping my thought—greater, perhaps, than mine in shaping theirs—and I am ever grateful.

The main themes of the book were sketched in an essay written for *American Civilisation: An Introduction,* edited by A. N. J. den Hollander and Sigmund Skard (London: Longmans, Green & Co., 1968); others were developed from articles published in *The Musical Quarterly* and *Hi Fi/Stereo Review.* To these I am appreciative for permission to expand on ideas they were the first to publish. And for their patience and care in seeing the book into print I thank my editors at Prentice-Hall, Alan Lesure and Raeia Maes.

To my wife, Janet, I am grateful for many things, among them the model of her own impeccable scholarship; her contribution to whatever accuracy and grace of expression may be found herein; and her cheerful sufferance, for several years, of my imperfect humming, singing, whistling, and playing through three and a half centuries of American music.

H. W. H.

Contents

Table of Abbreviations

PART ONE

To 1820

I

Sacred Music in New England and Other Colonies

The musical world left behind by the earliest English-speaking American colonists was a rich one, perhaps the richest England has ever known. At Court and in the mansions of the British peerage was heard elegant and sophisticated music of many kinds—madrigals, balletts, ayres, canzonets, and other part-songs by such Renaissance masters as William Byrd, Thomas Morley, Thomas Weelkes, and John Dowland; variations, dance pieces, preludes, and other fanciful works for harpsichord by Elizabethan virginalists like Orlando Gibbons, John Bull, and Giles Farnaby; fantasies and suites for ensembles of viols and other instruments. The music at the Chapel Royal and in the great cathedrals was no less elaborate and magnificent: both Catholic and Anglican services were permitted under Elizabeth I, and choirs of good size performed intricate and resonant motets and Mass-settings in the one, anthems and great Services in the other.

The American colonists, however, could hardly maintain such kinds of music in the New World. Most of them were not of the wealthy aristocracy that had created and supported such music in England. The leisure necessary to enjoy such purely artistic music was, needless to say, not their lot. Cargo space was at a premium on the tiny colonial ships, and large instruments like organs or harpsichords could not be accommodated.

So far as we know, the colonists could and did enjoy only music that was quite simple and fully functional: social music and worship music. Of the former we have few specific details; of the latter we know more. The history of "American music," in the first century of British colonization, must begin with New England worship music, specifically the psalmody, sung in religious meetings and at home, that had originated in mid-sixteenth-century Protestant sects of Western Europe.

Protestant backgrounds

John Calvin, austere leader of the Swiss-French Protestant movement, believed that the only proper music for the church had to be based on the lyric poetry of the Bible, the Psalms. Like Martin Luther, Calvin encouraged a congregational music in the language of the people, not a choral music in the ecclesiastical Latin of the Roman Catholic Church. But, unlike Luther, Calvin thought that polyphonic music, instruments, hymns, and other non-biblical texts were too much associated with Catholicism; he replaced them with the unaccompanied congregational unison singing of psalms, translated into metrical French verse. By 1562 the Calvinists had published in their center at Geneva the complete psalter in translations by Clément Marot and Théodore de Bèze (Beza, in Latin), with melodies composed or adapted by Louis Bourgeois.[1] Similar psalters for congregational use were prepared by Dutch Protestants, and, in the same year as the Geneva psalter, the London printer

[1] Two French psalms are printed in *MinA*, Nos. 1a, 5a.

John Day published a complete English psalter, with translations of the psalms by Thomas Sternhold and John Hopkins and with melodies partly of English origin, partly of continental, the latter brought back, after Queen Elizabeth's ascendancy, by English Protestants who had sought asylum in Geneva during the reign (1550–58) of Mary, a Catholic (see *MinA*, Nos. 7–11).

The music of these Protestant psalters was adapted from a variety of sources. Some melodies were derived from popular songs of the day; some were older hymn tunes; some were altered versions of Catholic chants. They must have been sung with fervor and gusto: apparently because of their sprightliness, the French Huguenot psalms were dubbed "Geneva jigs" and "Beza ballads"; Shakespeare, in *The Winter's Tale* (Act IV, scene 3), has the clown say, "Three-man song men all [i.e., singers of part-songs], and very good ones . . . but one Puritan amongst them, and he sings psalms to hornpipes!"

In view of the character of this music and considering the popularity of part-songs in the sixteenth century, it should not surprise us that polyphonic arrangements of psalm tunes, for enjoyment at home, were soon forthcoming. In England, Damon's psalter of 1579 contained four-part settings, and in 1592 Michael East (Este) enlisted the aid of prominent composers of the day (John Dowland, Giles Farnaby, Michael Cavendish, and others) to provide polyphonic settings for his psalter. Two later and very popular collections of harmonized psalm tunes were Richard Alison's of 1599 and Thomas Ravenscroft's of 1621 (see *MinA*, No. 6).

Early New England psalmody

That the fiercely devout New England colonists regarded the singing of psalms as an integral part of life is suggested by a comment of one of the little group of Pilgrims that sailed from Delftshaven, Holland, in 1620:

They that stayed at Leyden feasted us that were to go at our pastor's house, [it] being large; where we refreshed ourselves, after tears, with singing of Psalms, making joyful melody in our hearts as well as with the voice, there being many of our congregation very expert in music; and indeed it was the sweetest melody that ever mine ears heard.[2]

The "joyful melody" sung by "many . . . very expert in music" was doubtless a group of the psalms collected, translated, and published in 1612 for his congregation by the pastor of the English Separatists at Amsterdam, Rev. Henry Ainsworth. Ainsworth's psalter included both prose and poetic translations, copiously annotated, of the entire Book of Psalms; it also included 39 melodies borrowed by Ainsworth from "our former Englished Psalms [and from] the French and Dutch Psalms" (see *MinA*, Nos. 1–5). In variety of length, meter, and rhythm Ainsworth's choices were remarkable: compare, for example, the lilting asymmetry of Psalm 21, which is of English origin and which Ainsworth probably got from Damon's psalter, with the powerful, stomping regularity of Psalm 44, a Huguenot tune first printed in Genevan psalters, then taken over in the Sternhold-Hopkins English psalter (Example 1-1).

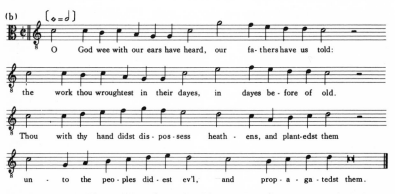

EXAMPLE 1-1. Two psalms from the Ainsworth psalter (1612), after the Amsterdam edition of 1618.

[2] Edward Winslow, *Hypocrisie Unmasked* (1646), quoted in Waldo Selden Pratt, *The Music of the Pilgrims* (Boston: Oliver Ditson Company, 1921), p. 6.

Used by the Pilgrims of the Plymouth colony and also by settlers at Ipswich and Salem, Ainsworth's psalter was finally replaced in 1692 by another, the so-called *Bay Psalm Book*. This psalter, famous as the first real book to be published in the British colonies, was a product of the Massachusetts Bay Colony. The committee of thirty which compiled it sought not only to make "a plain and familiar translation" of the psalter more accurate than the Sternhold-Hopkins version they had brought with them from England, but also to differentiate their Puritan, Bay Colony psalter from that of the Pilgrims at Plymouth. First printed in 1640, the *Bay Psalm Book* (or "New England version") originally included no music, but directed that most of its verses could be sung either to Ravenscroft's tunes or those of "our english psalm books"—i.e., Sternhold-Hopkins. Enormously popular, the Bay psalter was published in nine editions in the seventeenth century alone. To the ninth edition of 1698 (or possibly to an earlier, missing one) were appended thirteen melodies, with basses as well (see *MinA*, Nos. 12–17), which the unknown compiler had borrowed from various editions of John Playford's *Introduction to the Skill of Music* (London, 1667 and later).

That only thirteen melodies could suffice for all 150 psalms suggests that the psalms of the Bay psalter were less diverse metrically than those of earlier psalters, and perhaps that the New England congregations of the late seventeenth century were less "expert in music" than their forebears. Indeed, "almost all this whole book of psalmes," declared the preface of the 1640 edition, was composed in three meters: Common Meter (8, 6, 8, and 6 syllables for the four-line verses); Long Meter (8, 8, 8, 8); and an irregular meter of 6, 6, 8, 6. The decline in the number of psalm tunes regularly sung was a reflection of a general decline in the quality of psalmody in the colonies. By the early eighteenth century, Puritan ministers were raising horrified outcries at the poor singing in their churches; one complained in 1721 that "the tunes are now miserably tortured, and twisted, and quavered . . . into an horrid Medly of confused and disorderly Noises." Precentors, who were appointed to "line out" the psalms for their congregations—that is, to set the pitch and remind their fellows of a psalm tune by chanting it, line by line, echoed by the congregation—were altering the melodies at will: "every Leading-Singer would take the Liberty of raising any Note of the Tune, or lowering of it, as best pleas'd his Ear, and add such Turns and Flourishes as were grateful to him," wrote Rev. Thomas Symmes of Bradford, Massachusetts in 1720.

Like clergymen before and after them, the Puritan ministers of New England set out to reform music in their churches. In so doing, they created the first music instruction books in America, established a unique kind of musical education, and paved the way for our first school of composers.

First came sermons, pleading for a return to "regular" singing, by note instead of by rote; one such plea was Symmes's sermon on "The Reasonableness of Regular Singing" (1720). The earliest practical attempt to improve matters, and the first American music textbook, was a small volume by the Rev. John Tufts of Newbury, *An Introduction to the Singing of Psalm-Tunes*, first published in 1721. Tufts wrote a brief preface explaining the rudiments of music and a new method of musical notation (by letter rather than by note) that he had devised (see the reproduction of one page in *MinA*, plate [5]) and followed these with a collection of English psalm tunes. The fifth edition of 1726, the earliest extant, included 37 such tunes, with two other harmonizing parts (see *MinA*, Nos. 21–23). Among them is one, *100 Psalm Tune New*, which has not been found in earlier publications and which may perhaps be claimed as the first American composition; whether Tufts wrote it himself we do not know. The little piece (Example 1-2) is worth a brief look: not ungraceful, it has nevertheless an angularity of melody (the Cantus is the principal air) and a predilection for unisons, octaves, and bare fifths—not to mention the parallel fifths at the end of the second phrase—which distinguish it

EXAMPLE 1-2. J. Tufts, *100 Psalm Tune New, An Introduction to the Singing of Psalm-Tunes . . . The Fifth Edition* (Boston: Printed for Samuel Gerrish, 1726), p. 10.

EXAMPLE 1-2 continued.

from British psalm tunes of the period. As we shall see, it was precisely such features of style that would characterize native American music of the later eighteenth century.

At almost the same time that Tufts first published his *Introduction*, another manual appeared, also including a number of psalm
tunes with accompanying parts. This was *The Grounds and Rules
of Music Explained* (Boston, 1721), by Rev. Thomas Walter of
Roxbury, a nephew of the well-known Cotton Mather and, like
Tufts, a graduate of Harvard College (see *MinA*, Nos. 24–26).
These two "tunebooks," as such works came to be known, were
the first of many hundreds that were published in the eighteenth
century. They marked the beginning of a significant movement in
American music, the singing-school movement, to which I shall
return shortly. Meanwhile, I should mention briefly the expansion
of New England worship music by the addition of hymns to the
traditional psalmodic repertory.

Calvin had limited the texts of church song to biblical psalms
in metrical vernacular translations. The other great leader of the
Protestant Reformation, Luther, had not been so restrictive; from
the beginning he had permitted, and even composed himself, original
hymns. Hymnody flourished under Lutheranism, and by the early
eighteenth century it found its way into the English Puritan services.
The first significant writer of English hymns was the Rev. Dr.
Isaac Watts. From 1707 he published "hymns and spiritual songs"
as well as paraphrases of psalms, and for a century or more his works
were the most popular source of texts for English and American
hymnody. A further impetus to hymnody was provided, from the
1730's on, by the evangelical movement of Wesleyanism and by
the series of "awakenings" and "revivals" which, beginning with the
"Great Awakening" of 1735, studded the evolution of American
Protestantism.

The singing-school movement

As we have seen, agitation among Puritan ministers for better singing in their churches resulted in the first American music instruction books. At their call too was instituted the first kind of American music school. Rev. Symmes asked in 1720:

> Would it not greatly tend to promote singing of psalms if singing schools were promoted? . . . Where would be the difficulty, or what the disadvantages, if people who want skill in singing, would procure a skillful person to instruct them, and meet two or three evenings in the week, from five or six o'clock to eight, and spend their time in learning to sing?

That is precisely what happened. As early as March, 1722, Boston had a Society for Promoting Regular Singing, with a core of about ninety who had learned to read music. From that time on, the singing school, convened to learn, practice, and demonstrate the skill of reading music at sight, became an important institution in the colonies, social as well as musical. Although originally begun in an attempt to improve church music, and although their music was for the most part religious, the singing schools were as much secular institutions as sacred, as much social outlets as pious assemblies. One student at Yale, for example, wrote to a friend with characteristic undergraduate querulousness:

> At present I have no inclination for anything, for I am almost sick of the World & were it not for the Hopes of going to the singing-meeting tonight & indulging myself a little in some of the carnal Delights of the Flesh, such as kissing, squeezing &c. &c. I should willingly leave it now.[3]

In a society that recognized no split between religion and everyday life, the singing school was a popular meeting-ground for both. Not only in New England but in the more southerly colonies, singing-school instruction became popular in the eighteenth century: we hear of it in South Carolina by 1730, in New York by 1754, in Pennsylvania from the late 1750's, and in Maryland by 1765.

A broadside or a newspaper advertisement would alert a community that a singing school was to be organized. Arriving on the scene, the singing master would enroll students for classes once

[3] Quoted in *MMEA*, p. 282.

or twice a week for a month or more. Their text was usually a tunebook of the singing master's compilation, if not wholly of his own composition. Characteristically oblong, an "end-opener," the tunebook contained an introduction to the rudiments of music theory and notation and a sizable number of psalm tunes (and, later in the century, of hymn tunes, anthems, and even secular songs) harmonized in three or four parts. The singing school culminated in a "singing lecture"—essentially a choral concert embellished by a sermon from the local minister—or a "singing assembly," without the sermon. Having taught his pupils to sing accurately by note, having enlarged his reputation and the use of his tunebooks, and perhaps having got in a few licks for some other business interest (many of the singing masters were veritable prototypes of the Yankee peddler), the singing master would move on to another community to begin a new singing school.

In this way the first group of American composers developed. Perhaps "tunesmiths" is the better word, for most of the itinerant singing masters regarded themselves unpretentiously as artisans, not artists. They forged a distinctive style of music, awkward and archaic-sounding to later, more genteel ears, but rugged, powerful, and homogeneous.

Yankee tunesmiths: the First New England School

It was some time before the efforts of Tufts, Walter, and others in the 1720's bore fruit. Singing schools of the middle decades of the eighteenth century must have relied mainly on English psalters and hymnals, for not until 1761 was another important colonial one published. This was *Urania*, "a choice Collection of Psalm-tunes, Anthems, and Hymns" compiled by the New Jersey-born James Lyon (1735–1794) and published at Philadelphia. Lyon apparently culled most of the 96 compositions in the work from various English tunebooks in circulation at the time (see *MinA*, No. 40). Among the 70 psalm settings are some of special interest to us: they are "fuging psalm tunes" with a form and texture that were to be taken up lustily by the Yankee tunesmiths. *The V Psalm Tune* (Example 1-3), borrowed by Lyon from the English composer Aaron Williams (1731–1776), is characteristic: beginning with a four-part setting of the tune (in the tenor voice), it reaches a cadence (here on the dominant) in measure 12; then it starts afresh with imitative entries for the individual voices—the so-called "fuge" (fugue) or "fuging section"—which soon lead to a final cadence. Aside from some peculiarities in harmony—for instance, the characteristically British use of cross-relations (F♯ vs. F♮) in measures 1 and 2 and the clash of soprano and alto in measure 16—there is a smoothness about the little piece that betrays its transatlantic origin; American fuging tunes would tend to be simpler in rhythm, more angular in melody, less chromatic in harmony, and in some ways stronger in general effect.

EXAMPLE 1-3. [A. Williams,] *The V Psalm Tune*, in J. Lyon, *Urania* (Philadelphia: William Bradford, 1761), pp. 42–43.

The Yankee tunesmiths—our "First New England School" of composers—made their appearance in the 1770's, beginning with *The New-England Psalm-Singer: or, American Chorister*, engraved at Boston in 1770 by Paul Revere. Its composer was William Billings (1746–1800), a Boston tanner turned tunesmith, and one of the most picturesque personalities in American music. In his prefatory "Thoughts on Music" (portions reprinted in *ACS*, pp. 29–31), Billings proclaimed with a splendid show of individualism that "I don't think myself confined to any rules for composition laid down by any that went before me." Nevertheless, like the other tunebook writers he went on to instruct the reader in the rudiments of music, following them with 108 psalm and hymn settings and 15 anthems and canons, all of his own composition. The four-part canon "When Jesus Wept"[4] is one of Billings's loveliest melodic inspirations; similar to it in style is another *Canon 4 in 1*, "Thus saith the high, the lofty one" (Example 1-4).

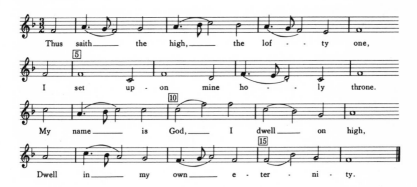

EXAMPLE 1-4. W. Billings, *Canon 4 in 1, The New-England Psalm-Singer* (Boston: Edes and Gill, 1770); original a whole-tone higher.

Eight years later, at the height of the Revolutionary War, Billings published his second tunebook, *The Singing Master's Assistant* (Boston, 1778), which came to be known as "Billings' Best." Among some fervently patriotic pieces in it was an expansion of Billings's earlier *Chester*, whose incendiary text (by the composer himself) and powerful melody became virtually the Revolutionary hymn:

> *Let tyrants shake their iron rod,*
> *And Slav'ry clank her galling chaines.*
> *We fear them not, we trust in God,*
> *New-england's God for ever reigns.*
>
> . . .
>
> *The foe comes on with haughty stride,*
> *Our troops advance with martial noise.*
> *Their Vet'rans flee before our Youth,*
> *And Gen'rals yield to beardless Boys.*[5]

---

[4] Reprinted in *AM*, p. 132, and in *MinA*, No. 42.

[5] The music and complete text in *MinA*, No. 43. In stanza 3, correct the word "Shelter'd" to "Shatter'd."

The Singing Master's Assistant also included Billings's notoriously dissonant *Jargon* (*MinA*, No. 44), apparently offered, along with wildly humorous instructions for performance, in response to criticisms of his earlier collection. Fuging tunes, the first composed by an American, also make their appearance in *The Singing Master's Assistant*, with the excited comment of the composer that they were "twenty times as powerful as the old slow tunes; each part striving for mastery and victory." Following *Music in Miniature* (1779), which was largely a reprinting of successful items from the two earlier tunebooks, Billings published *The Psalm-Singer's Amusement* in 1781. This included the clever *Modern Music* (*MinA*, No. 45), a secular piece instructive to singers and listeners alike, and a song in praise of music, *Consonance*. Billings's last publications were *The Suffolk Harmony* (1786) and *The Continental Harmony* (1794).

Billings has captured the imagination of American music historians by virtue of his colorful personality, his apostleship of artistic freedom and individuality, his sense of humor, and his flair for tuneful melody. If he was not, as some have implied, the most original, the most typical, or the most popular of the First New England School, he does symbolize perfectly the cheerful, unselfconscious pride, the honest journeyman excellence of our nation's first composers.

It was mainly Connecticut and central Massachusetts that produced the majority of the Yankee tunesmiths. Here flourished such popular composers and compilers of music for the singing schools as Daniel Read (1757–1836), Samuel Holyoke (1762–1820), Stephen Jenks (1772–1856), Jacob French (1754–18?), Oliver Holden (1765–1844), Timothy Swan (1758–1842), Justin Morgan (1747–1798), Jeremiah Ingalls (1764–1828), Supply Belcher (1751–1836), Andrew Law (1749–1821), Jacob Kimball (1761–1826), and many others.[6] For most of these singing masters, music was a part-time occupation: Daniel Read was a New Haven merchant; Timothy Swan was apprenticed to a merchant, then to a hatter (in later life, he was termed "poor, proud, and indolent" by his neighbors); Supply Belcher was a tavernkeeper in Stoughton, Massachusetts be-

---

[6] Pieces by most of these composers are reprinted in *MinA*, Nos. 50ff. *Bunker Hill* (No. 47), attributed to Andrew Law, is probably not of Law's composition. Lowens, in a review of *MinA* (*MQ*, L [1964], 393–98), has pointed out other inaccuracies in this section of *MinA*.

fore he moved to the northern frontier to become known as the "Handel of Maine"; Justin Morgan is better known as breeder of the famous Morgan horse than as a composer; Andrew Law was a minister with several college degrees.

The kind of piece which the New Englanders liked best was the fuging tune; about one-quarter of their total production is made up of this characteristic type which, as we have seen, was modeled on English fuging psalm tunes of the sort Lyon had borrowed for *Urania*. Some psalms and hymns were composed in three-part or four-part settings throughout, without fuging sections. Anthems and other "set pieces" attempted longer formal spans in varied textures. The music was usually composed for four voices, with the principal air in the tenor part. Some women usually doubled the tenor in a higher octave; conversely, some men doubled the soprano part. Thus the New England style resulted in an organ-like sonority of six parts. Women generally outnumbered the men; on the other hand, the singing masters favored a very strong bass, which was often doubled by a 'cello.

The melodies of the Yankee tunesmiths have a folkish quality, now simple and flowing, now angular and rhythmically powerful, if somewhat rigid. One of the most striking airs is that of Swan's *China (MinA,* No. 53), a piece that so caught the fancy of New England that it was sung at funerals "down East" for about a century after it first appeared in 1790 (Example 1-5).

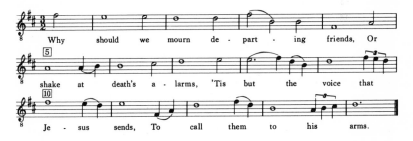

EXAMPLE 1-5. T. Swan, *China* (1790), as printed in William Little and William Smith, *The Easy Instructor* (Albany: Websters & Skinner and Daniel Steele, [1809]), p. 99; tenor part only.

The harmony of the Yankee fuging tunes and other works was perhaps the most characteristic feature of their style. Abounding in open fifths, parallel fifths and octaves, modal inflections, surprising dissonances, it seems almost a throwback to an earlier style of European music, long before the development of the highly organized tonal syntax of the century of Handel and Haydn. Yet the Americans were consistent in their taste, and their music is perfectly homogeneous stylistically; in its own terms, it is as "stylish" as the more complex and sophisticated European music of its time. Exemplary of the New England style is Daniel Read's fuging tune *Sherburne*, first published in *The American Singing Book* (1785) and later reprinted many times (Figure 1-1). Other fuging tunes whose popularity can be measured by the number of times they were reprinted (usually without permission) were Lewis Edson's *Greenfield* (first published in Simeon Jocelin's *Chorister's Companion*, 1782), Read's *Stafford* (*Chorister's Companion*) and his *Russia* (Read's *American Singing Book*, 1785), Billings's *Maryland* (*Singing Master's Assistant*, 1778), and Morgan's *Montgomery* (Law's *Rudiments of Music*, 2nd ed., 1786; reprinted in *MinA*, No. 58).

The diffusion of the New England idiom was aided not only by the peripatetic singing masters—Andrew Law, for instance, held singing schools throughout his native New England and in New

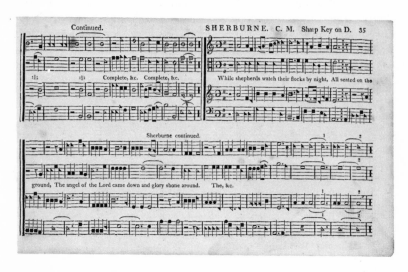

FIGURE 1-1. Daniel Read's fuging tune *Sherburne* (1785), as printed in shape-notes in an 1809 edition of *The Easy Instructor*.

York, New Jersey, Pennsylvania, Maryland, and even the Carolinas —but also by the evangelistic revival movements, like the "Great Revival" of 1800. It may also have been encouraged by the development of new systems of music notation, especially the "shape-note" notation of William Smith and William Little, in whose *Easy Instructor* (Albany, 1798) the musical notes were shaped differently according to their position in the scale (see Figure 1-1). At that time, instead of *do, re, mi, fa, sol, la, ti, do* the syllables *fa, sol, la, fa, sol, la, mi, fa* were used; hence, four shapes sufficed to distinguish the syllables: ◁ (*fa*), ○ (*sol*), □ (*la*), ◇ (*mi*). Little and Smith's invention, reminiscent of other less successful American attempts (e.g., Tufts's) both earlier and later to make easier the task of learning to read music, had the simplicity of genius. Their four-shape notation was widely adopted in other tunebooks: it would seem that Andrew Law, who claimed shape notes as his own idea, borrowed them from *The Easy Instructor* for his *Art Of Singing* (4th ed., 1803), and other tunebook compilers followed suit, especially those who favored the New England style of music.

But not every post-colonial American did favor it. With the new wave of immigration that followed the successful establishment and consolidation of the United States of America came a new wave of foreign influence in American music. The story of the submersion of the native American idiom of the Yankee tunesmiths beneath this wave belongs to a later chapter. Here, let me simply acknowledge it with words from two composers who witnessed the change in taste. Andrew Law, after a lengthy career as partisan of the native style, turned his back on it completely. Increasingly, as his knowledge of the "sublime and beautiful compositions of the great Masters of Music" grew, he sought to substitute "serious, animated, and devout" music for "that lifeless and insipid, or that frivolous and frolicksome succession and combination of sounds" which the New Englanders had created. Daniel Read never became a self-styled reformer, but he too felt the impact of the new wave. Oddly touching are some words written by Read in his old age, with which he confessed to changed musical values but proudly refused to disavow entirely his older ones:

> Since studying the writings of such men as D'Alembert [and others], since carefully examining the system of harmony practically

exhibited in Handel's *Messiah,* Haydn's *Creation,* and other similar works . . . my ideas on the subject of music have been considerably altered; I will not say improved.[7]

South of New England

If the British colonists of the New World must, because of their predominance among the early settlers, be considered the mainstream of early American culture, there were nevertheless important minority groups very early. In general, these groups—notably German Pietists in Pennsylvania and Moravian brethren in Pennsylvania and the Carolinas—were culturally insular; their communities tended to remain "foreign" enclaves even in a land of immigrants. Nevertheless, their musical cultures deserve brief mention.

The Pennsylvania Germans

A number of Protestant German sects settled in Pennsylvania for religious motives. Each differed in its worship-music practice, but all were alike in their emphasis on congregational song, especially chorales. To Germantown in 1694 came a group of Pietists under the leadership of Johannes Kelpius (1673–1708). Known as the Hermits of the Ridge (or Wissahickon Mystics, or True Rosicrucians), they sang hymns, psalms, and anthems and apparently used instrumental accompaniment. Kelpius compiled for his flock a hymn book with the Pietist title *The Lamenting Voice of the Hidden Love at the Time when She Lay in Misery and forsaken* (the manuscript is now at the Historical Society of Pennsylvania), containing ten hymn tunes, some with basses, of a harmonic richness unknown to the New England Puritans.

Conrad Beissel (1690–1768), who emigrated to Pennsylvania in 1720, founded in 1732 a semi-monastic community at Ephrata, in what is now Lancaster County, sixty-five miles from Philadelphia. Urging on his band an active musical seventh-day observance, Beissel turned from Pietist hymns and traditional chorales to original compositions, some of great length and in as many as eight voices. In

[7] Quoted in *MMEA,* p. 175.

1747 he published at Ephrata a massive collection of sacred choral pieces, *The Song of the Lonely and Forsaken Turtle Dove, namely the Christian Church*, the pages of which give some idea of the uniquely mannered notation of Beissel, even better viewed in the beautifully illuminated manuscripts that emanated from the cloister.[8] Beissel's music is purposely ultra-consonant, avoiding any dissonant harmony on accented text syllables, which produces a monolithic if somewhat tedious result only slightly relieved by occasional antiphonal treatment of the choristers, who are said to have numbered twenty-five, fifteen women and ten men.

The Moravians

The richest and most sophisticated musical culture in colonial America was that of the Moravians in Pennsylvania and the Carolinas. They came from German-speaking Bohemia for the most part, members of the Unitas Fratrum, the first independent Protestant sect, founded in Bohemia and Moravia in the mid-fifteenth century. The first Moravians to reach America came to the West Indies in 1732; a sizable community settled in Bethlehem, Pennsylvania, in 1741. Other Moravian centers were created at Lititz and Nazareth and at Salem (now Winston-Salem) in North Carolina.

The musical life of the Moravian brethren was extraordinarily intense. Theirs was the first concerted sacred music in America: instruments joined soloists and choirs in anthems, sacred arias, motets, and chorales. At the major Moravian musical centers, Bethlehem and Salem, brass ensembles serenaded the communities of brethren and played for weddings, christenings, funerals, and other solemn occasions. Collegia Musica—groups meeting regularly to practice music, especially instrumental music—were organized and substantial libraries of European music of the seventeenth and eighteenth centuries accumulated. Some of this country's earliest and best instrument makers helped to supply the Collegia; especially notable is the Lititz organ builder David Tannenberg (1728–1804), who

[8] A reproduction of one page of the published version of the *Turtle Dove* is printed in *MinA;* No. 31 is a transcription. The largest and most stunning of the manuscript versions, once possessed by Benjamin Franklin, is in the Library of Congress.

designed and constructed almost fifty organs, for Lutheran and Roman Catholic as well as Moravian churches.

Like most of the Yankee tunesmiths to the north, many of the Moravian composers were occupied in other tasks for a living. Indeed, some might never have composed at all had not a demand for new music existed. Jeremias Dencke (1735–1795) arrived from Germany in 1760 as pastor and business manager in Bethlehem. He was the first to compose sacred music with instruments, notably three sets of sacred songs for soprano, strings, and organ, among them the lovely aria *Ich will singen von einem Könige*. Johannes Herbst (1734–1812) came to Pennsylvania in 1786, was pastor at Lancaster and later Lititz, and pastor and bishop at Salem in the last year of his life. The most prolific of the Moravian composers, Herbst wrote some 125 sacred songs and anthems. John Antes (1741–1811), American-born, was a string-instrument maker who was later ordained a pastor and sent to Egypt as a missionary. There, between 1779 and 1781, he composed three trios for two violins and 'cello, the earliest chamber music written by an American.[9] Johann Friedrich (John Frederick) Peter (1746–1813) was probably the most gifted of the Moravian composers: almost one hundred works, mostly anthems and arias but also six string quintets (Salem, 1789), reveal him as a sensitive and highly expressive minor master of the early Classic style.[10] David Moritz Michael (1751–1825), a German who was in Pennsylvania from 1795 to 1815 in various administrative posts, put his first-hand knowledge of woodwind instruments to good use in sixteen suite-like works for wind sextet;[11] he is also notable for having conducted a performance of Haydn's *Creation* in America as early as 1811.

The Moravian culture was essentially insular: although it was known and spoken of admiringly by other Americans in the eighteenth century, it had little influence outside the Moravian communities themselves. On the other hand, the music of the American

[9] Trio II, 1st movement, in *MinA*, No. 34. Antes's moving aria *Go, Congregation, Go!* and the choral anthem *Surely He has Borne our Griefs* (which some claim to be a companion piece for the aria) in *MinA*, Nos. 32, 33.

[10] Quintet V, 2nd movement, in *MinA*, No. 35; the sacred song *Ich will mit euch einigen ewigen Bund machen* in *MinA*, No. 36.

[11] The first movement of No. 1 of these, which were called *Parthien* by Michael, in *MinA*, No. 37.

Moravians had a special stamp, the result of the New World environment. One specialist in their music has cogently described the source of this "American" quality:

> The Moravians were devout people. Colonial life for them had a religious purpose and religious ideas dominated their activities. This gives their music a special character. In Europe, the average late 18th century composer wrote an occasional piece of church music between the symphonies, sonatas, operas, and other secular works which were his chief concern. To the Moravian musicians in America, however, church music was the most important expression of their inner lives. Their music therefore is better suited to the purpose and more touching than most religious music written in Europe during the same period.[12]

Philadelphia and South Carolina

The story of sacred music in the middle Atlantic and Southern British colonies is less well documented than in the German-speaking communities or in New England. The German immigrants maintained and even enriched their European musical life; thanks to the singing-school movement, the New Englanders created a whole repertory of published sacred-secular music. Little is known, however, of sacred music in the Quaker center of Philadelphia until the 1760's; Virginia, almost wholly an agricultural colony, has left us almost no colonial music; and South Carolina, especially its largest city Charleston (Charles Town at the time), had an active secular music life that has somewhat obscured its special activity in sacred music.

Two native-born composers (the first Americans securely identifiable as such) figured in the sacred music of Philadelphia in the early 1760's. These were James Lyon and Francis Hopkinson (1737–1791; see below, p. 33). Lyon began the history of Philadelphia music publishing in 1761 with *Urania* (see above, p. 9). He indicated in the index that six of the 96 pieces in it were "completely new"; some of these may have been by Lyon himself, but the setting of *The 23d Psalm* is by Hopkinson, better known as a cultivated dilettante specializing in secular music (Example 1-6).

---

[12] Hans T. David (ed.), *Ten Sacred Songs*. Music of the Moravians in America . . . , No. 1 (New York: New York Public Library, 1947), p. v.

EXAMPLE 1-6. F. Hopkinson, *The 23d Psalm Tune*, in J. Lyon, *Urania* (Philadelphia: William Bradford, 1761), p. 50; measures 1-12. The cut-time signature turned around indicates a quick tempo, $\frac{2}{2}$.

One of the hymns in *Urania*, *Whitefield's*, is a setting of a text from the 1757 *Hymn Collection* of the famous British Methodist revivalist George Whitefield; its music is the first American publication of the tune *God Save the King*, later (1831) to be used as the melody for Samuel Francis Smith's "My Country 'tis of Thee."[13]

Charleston, by 1775 the largest city south of Philadelphia, was a brilliant center of church music, as it was of secular. Free from the restrictions on instruments observed in Puritan New England, Charleston's Anglican churches of St. Philip's and St. Michael's allowed organs to be heard, and peals of bells. Organist at St. Philip's from 1737 to 1750 was Charles Theodore Pachelbel (1690–1750), son of the famous Nuremberg organist Johann Pachelbel. Of Charles Theodore's music we have a fine *Magnificat* for two choirs and organ, written, however, before the composer left Germany for America.

---

[13] The hymn is in *MinA*, No. 40. The tune has been put to various uses by Americans; one version from the Federal period begins with the words "God save great Washington," another with "God save America."

Bibliographical notes

Robert Stevenson's *Protestant Church Music in America* (New York: W. W. Norton & Company, Inc., 1966) is a rich reference source for material in this chapter.

The music of Ainsworth's psalter has been transcribed, not without errors, in Waldo Selden Pratt's *The Music of the Pilgrims* (Boston: Oliver Ditson Company, 1921). The most extensive study of the *Bay Psalm Book*, emphasizing textual rather than musical matters, is Zoltán Haraszti, *The Enigma of the Bay Psalm Book* (Chicago: University of Chicago Press, 1956), published together with a facsimile of the first edition of 1640.

"The Singing School Movement in the United States" was the subject of a round-table discussion at the Eighth Congress of the International Musicological Society; the illuminating paper by Allen P. Britton on which the discussion was based was printed in Volume I of the *I.M.S. Congress Report (1961)*, a summary of the discussion in Volume II (1962). Britton and Irving Lowens have collaborated on a number of articles in the *Journal of Research in Music Education* and the *Journal of the American Musicological Society;* Lowens's independent work, especially an invaluable series of bibliographical studies, has been revised and reprinted in *MMEA*. Tufts's *Introduction* (1726 edition) has been published in facsimile (Philadelphia: Musical Americana, 1954) with an introduction by Lowens.

I have written on "William Billings and the Yankee Tunesmiths" in Hi Fi/Stereo Review, XVI, 2 (February 1966), 55–65. Billings's *Continental Harmony* is available in a facsimile reprint, introduced by Hans Nathan (Cambridge: Harvard University Press, 1961).

The American Moravians have been exhaustively studied by researchers affiliated with the Moravian Music Foundation (Winston-Salem, N.C.), especially its former director Donald McCorkle. Professor McCorkle has also been instrumental in publishing Moravian music (Boosey & Hawkes; Brodt Music Co.), as have Clarence Dickinson (H. W. Gray Co.) and Hans David (C. F. Peters Corp.).

2
Secular Music
in the Urban Centers

Thus far I have been discussing early American sacred music or music which, although put to secular social use in the singing schools, was ostensibly sacred. The secular music of the German-speaking communities of Moravians I have mentioned too, but for the rise of secular music per se in the predominantly Anglo-American colonial culture we must look to the eastern seaboard cities. These developed remarkably in size and in wealth during the first three-quarters of the eighteenth century. If by 1690 substantial towns had been established at Boston, New York, Philadelphia, Charleston, and elsewhere, by 1774, on the eve of the Revolution, these had mushroomed into real cities which grew even more rapidly in the next quarter-century. The following table[1] shows the growth during this period.

	1690	1774	1800
New York (founded 1625)	3900	25–30,000	60,000
Boston (founded 1630)	7000	20,000	25,000
Charleston (founded 1672)	1100	10,000	18,000
Philadelphia (founded 1682)	4000	40,000	70,000

Other growing cities were Salem, Providence, New Haven, Perth Amboy, Baltimore, Richmond, and Savannah. Although the population of these cities was but a fraction of the total population of the colonies, their concentration of wealth and of social, political, and intellectual activity made them the cultural centers of the new land. As commercial cities, they tended to reflect the artistic life of similar European cities with which they had close contacts. Thus, among other kinds of art, art–music gained its first Anglo-American expression in the cities, where from the 1730's we have records of concerts, operas, and other secular music.

The rise of concerts and opera

The New World was hardly behind the Old in the establishment of a secular music culture based on public concerts. This would be a matter for nationalistic pride were it not for the fact that public concerts in Europe were a reflection of the rise of the middle class as patron of music, in contrast to the traditional aristocratic and churchly patronage; lacking a true aristocratic class, America's was basically a middle-class culture from the beginning, and it was natural that some of its musical energy was directed very early into public concerts. Thus, from the 1730's we hear of concerts in Boston, Charleston, New York, and other cities. The first of these we know about was announced in the *Boston Weekly News Letter* of December 16, 1731 as a forthcoming *"Concert of Music* on sundry Instruments at Mr. Pelham's great Room. . . . Tickets to

---

[1] Adapted from Charles A. and Mary R. Beard, *A Basic History of the United States* (Philadelphia: The Blakiston Company, 1944), p. 44, and from Russell B. Nye, *The Cultural Life of the New Nation, 1776–1830* (New York: Harper & Brothers, 1960), p. 124.

be delivered at the place of performance at *Five shillings* each. The concert to begin exactly at Six o'clock. . . ."[2]

Opera too was heard in America from the 1730's, not of course the lavish, costly, and aristocratic Baroque opera but English ballad operas, those plays-with-songs which had captivated London's public with the immensely successful run in 1728 of John Gay's *The Beggar's Opera*. To Gay's text, which satirized the social, political, and musical establishment, John Christopher Pepusch adapted well-known popular songs and ballad airs (and, with tongue in cheek, some music from Handel's Italian operas). The result was a vernacular musical play that appealed immediately to the middle-class public of London. New York audiences heard *The Beggar's Opera* in 1750 and 1751, as produced by a company of "comedians from Philadelphia," but the record of ballad opera in America had begun even before that with *Flora, or Hob in the Well* (London, 1729), produced at Charleston in 1735 (both the libretto and the music lost), and Coffey's *The Devil to Pay* (adapted in Germany as one of the first *Singspiele* under the title *Der Teufel ist los*) in 1736, also at Charleston. The operatic centers of America in the eighteenth century were the cities from New York south: at Boston, the anti-theater blue law of 1750 had put an effective check on the establishment of ballad opera there. By the end of the eighteenth century two major opera companies were renowned. One was William Hallam's London troupe, which started its American career in 1752 at Williamsburg, moved to New York, named itself the American Company (and later the Old American), went back to England during the Revolution, then returned after the war to New York. The Old American Company's rival was the New Company founded in 1792 at Philadelphia by Thomas Wignell, English actor and singer, and Alexander Reinagle (see below, p. 28). The Wignell-Reinagle company played in the celebrated New Theatre on Chestnut Street, a handsome hall with a stage 36 feet wide and 71 deep and with some 2000 seats, 900 of them in two tiers of boxes, above which was a large gallery.

Early American concerts and ballad operas were understandably

---

[2] Quoted in O. G. T. Sonneck, *Early Concert Life in America* (Leipzig: Breitkopf & Härtel, 1907), p. 251.

dominated by emigrant professional musicians, unlike the singing schools which, arising from a long native tradition, were led by American-born journeyman composers. The cities could support these emigré "professors" of music, particularly in the post-Revolutionary period of economic and commercial consolidation between 1783 and 1812, and indeed their standards and taste were to have a shaping influence on American musical culture in general. They were aided by, in fact they led, the remarkable development in the late eighteenth century of music publishing in America. In little more than a half-century before 1820, American publishers issued an estimated 15,000 separate works in sheet-music editions, plus more than 500 different "songsters"—pocket-size collections of song texts. Instrument manufacture was also on the rise: the simpler instruments had probably been made in America almost from the beginning, but as early as the 1740's we learn of a harpsichord builder, Gustav Hesselius of the Old Swedes' Church in Philadelphia, and of piano builders from 1775, when John Behrent of Philadelphia announced the manufacture of "an extraordinary instrument, by the name of the pianoforte, in mahogany in the manner of a harpsichord."[3]

Concerts and opera performances in the cities were paralleled by a dramatic rise of secular music in the urban home. "Almost every young lady and gentleman, from the children of the judge, the banker, and the general, down to those of the constable, the huckster and the drummer, can make a noise upon some instrument or other, and charm their neighbors with something which courtesy calls music," wrote a correspondent in the Philadelphia *Mirror of Taste and Dramatic Censor* in 1810.[4] Even if professional musicians could not make a living solely by performing, they could eke out an existence by hanging out a shingle as teachers or as proprietors of music stores—"magazines" or "repositories," as they were more often called. In short, secular music was becoming a real business in America as the eighteenth century closed and the nineteenth opened.

We should not, however, expect to find in the secular music

[3] Arthur Loesser, *Men, Women and Pianos* (New York: Simon & Schuster, 1954), pp. 442–43.

[4] Quoted *ibid.*, pp. 456–57.

of eighteenth-century America anything to match the scope or seriousness of purpose of, say, the music of Vienna, Rome, or Paris. The American ballad opera was an unpretentious entertainment with simple songs, enjoyable to all. The American concert was a mixture of short instrumental pieces delivered by a few performers and songs or duets of no great dimensions. The American music publishers addressed themselves mainly to amateurs: like the singing-school tunebooks, the thousands of music sheets and songsters aimed to satisfy the modest abilities of music-makers at home, to offer them practical or topical sources of mild diversion. It would remain for a later generation to distinguish between such "popular" music and a more selfconsciously high-flown "classical" music with serious artistic pretentions.

Representative of the socially useful and surprisingly diversified output of our early publishers is a collection of the 1790's with the informative title page *Evening Amusement. Containing fifty airs, song's, duett's, dances, hornpipe's, reels', marches, minuett's, &c., &c., for 1 and 2 German flutes or violins. Price 75 cents. Printed & sold at B[enjamin] Carr's Musical repositories, Philadelphia and New York, & J[oseph] Carr's, Baltimore.* Published in 1796, this potpourri of pieces designed for "evening amusement" typifies the kinds of secular music enjoyed by American townspeople of the early Federal period.

Traditional popular songs (we would call them folk songs today) of the English, Scottish, and Irish past are well represented, among them *Soldier's Joy, The Irish Washerwoman,* and *O Dear, What Can the Matter Be?* Newer songs, many of them from ballad operas, are present, like *What a Beau your Granny Was, Thou Softly Flowing Avon,* and *How Happily My Life I Led* (the last taken from the ballad opera *No Song No Supper* of British composer Stephen Storace). Patriotic songs furnished tunes for several of the items: *God Save Great Washington, Yankee Doodle,* Reinagle's *America, Commerce, and Freedom,* and *The Marseilles Hymn.* A variety of dance tunes appears—several hornpipes, a highland reel, a "minuet de la cour," *Mrs. Fraser's Strathspey*—and so do marches, including *General Washington's March, The Duke of York's March,* and a march from *The Battle of Prague* by the Czech-English composer Franz Kotzwara. Haydn is represented by a minuet and an "air" from two symphonies.

Here, then, is what our early urban secular music consisted of: martial and patriotic music, opera airs and traditional songs, dance tunes, and a smattering of programmatic or absolute instrumental music.

Marches and patriotic songs

As we might expect, both the Revolutionary and Federal periods produced their share of military music, including marches and patriotic songs. Sometimes both were combined, as in *Hail, Columbia!* The poem by Joseph Hopkinson (son of Francis) was written in 1798 to be sung to the tune of *The President's March;* the latter, a sturdy foursquare tune, was the work of Philip Phile, who may have composed it after George Washington's inauguration as President of the new United States in 1789, but did not publish it until 1793 or 1794. It was very popular: arrangements for two flutes and for piano duet appeared, as well as many other versions adapted from Phile's original piano setting. *Hail, Columbia!* was first published in Philadelphia by Benjamin Carr "for the Voice, Piano Forte, Guittar and Clarinet" (*MinA*, No. 111).

Yankee Doodle has all the earmarks of a march, too, and in fact the earliest known separate edition of the song, published in England in the 1780's, carries the mocking title *Yankee Doodle, or (as now Christened by the Saints of New England) The Lexington March.* A subtitle instructs: "NB. The Words to be Sung thro' the Nose, & in the West Country drawl & dialect"—a jibe at the rural, plebeian backgrounds of most English emigrants to America. Popular here even before the Revolution,[5] *Yankee Doodle* appeared in 1797 or 1798 with bold new words from the press of James Hewitt, leading New York composer in the post-Revolutionary period (*MinA*, No. 110).

The song destined to become the national anthem was anything but patriotic to begin with. Addressed "to Anacreon in Heav'n," the tune later sung as *The Star-Spangled Banner* originated as a British drinking song, celebrating the twin delights of Venus and

---

[5] It is mentioned in the libretto of *The Disappointment: or, the Force of Credulity* (New York, 1767), where its tune is to be sung to Air IV of that ballad opera (which seems to have been the first actually written in America).

Bacchus. Taken up by Americans, it was given new patriotic words in 1798 by a (not *the*) Thomas Paine, who sang of "Ye sons of Columbia, who bravely have fought/For those rights, which unstained from your Sires had descended." The *Star-Spangled Banner* text, which was composed in 1814 by Francis Scott Key after the bombardment of Fort McHenry by the British, was applied to the old tune, and the resulting song was made the national anthem in 1931 (all three versions, among many variants, printed in *MinA*, Nos. 113–115).

Opera airs and other songs

The song *America, Commerce, and Freedom* found in *Evening Amusement* has a patriotic text, but it originated as a theater air. The composer was Alexander Reinagle (1756–1809), who came to New York in 1786 from his native England but soon moved to Philadelphia, where he dominated the musical scene for over two decades. An indefatigable composer, pianist, arranger, conductor, and impresario, Reinagle typified the emigrant professional musicians of the Federal period. A competent if not extraordinary composer, he wrote many of the airs for the ballad operas produced at the New Theatre on Chestnut Street, where he was musical director. (Its opening concert of February 2, 1793, offered an elaborate program of overtures, concertos, symphonies, songs, a quartet, and glees.) *America, Commerce, and Freedom* was composed for the "ballet pantomime" *The Sailor's Landlady;* lusty and virile, it is one of Reinagle's best songs. Example 2-1 gives the beginning of the verse and the sturdy refrain.

EXAMPLE 2-1. A. Reinagle, *America, Commerce, and Freedom* (Philadelphia: B. Carr, [1794]), measures 9–16, 29–42.

EXAMPLE 2-1 continued.

More characteristic of the American ballad opera air than *America, Commerce, and Freedom* was a tender, lyrical effusion in the tradition of English or Irish love songs, and modeled on the pleasant if somewhat effete airs of the middle and later eighteenth-century English composers for ballad opera like Thomas (1710–1778) and Michael (1741–1786) Arne, Charles Dibdin (1745–1814), William Shield (1748–1829), and Stephen Storace (1763–1796). Reinagle surely contributed many of this kind to Philadelphia productions, although surprisingly few of his airs are extant today.[6] The general nature of the "tender" airs, and of their usually vapid poetry, is well seen in *Why, Huntress, Why?*, composed by Benjamin Carr (1768–1831) for a ballad opera on the tale of William Tell (*The Archers; or, the Mountaineers of Switzerland*), produced by the Old American Company in New York in 1796 (*MinA*, No. 76). Carr, who came to New York from London in 1793, established with his brother and his father a chain of music stores in Philadelphia, New York, and Baltimore and was a prolific publisher as well. He also had a nice, if modest, talent as a composer of songs, as suggested by his *Hymn to the Virgin* ("Ave Maria"), No. 3 of *Six Ballads from the Poem of "The Lady of the Lake"* (Philadelphia, 1810), which is perhaps the most impressive American song before Foster's best, and, on a smaller scale, by his sensitive little setting of the "Willow Song" from Shakespeare's *Othello*. It is so inconclusive, however, as to suggest it was not intended as an independent work but as an interpolation in the play (Example 2-2).

EXAMPLE 2-2. B. Carr, "Shakespeare's 'Willow,'" *Musical Journal*, Vol. I, Vocal Section (Philadelphia: Carr and Schetky, [1800]), 22.

---

[6] One, *When I've got the ready rhino*, a humorous song to a hornpipe tune, printed in *AM*, 1st ed., pp. 115–16; omitted from 2nd ed.

O the green wil-low, O the green wil-low, O the green wil-low, must be my gar-land.

EXAMPLE 2-2 continued.

Lacking a lyric theater tradition, New England did not produce a large body of secular song in the eighteenth century, at least not of the sort I have been discussing. The Yankee singing-school tunebooks served, as noted above, for secular diversion even though their contents were mainly sacred; and into them, as the eighteenth century neared its close, secular texts crept more frequently. Supply Belcher's *The Harmony of Maine* (Boston, 1794) included no less than eight secular, nonpatriotic songs to texts in the English lyric tradition and was intended for use in both "singing schools and musical societies." Belcher meant by the latter term those urban rivals of the singing schools which were beginning to be organized in the cities—choral or instrumental groups established (usually under emigrant professional musicians) to perform the "new, scientific" music of Europe. The most famous of these was Boston's Handel and Haydn Society, organized in 1815 by Gottlieb Graupner (1767–1836), who had settled in Boston in 1797 to become an influential entrepreneur of concerts and musical organizations. The invitation to the organizational meeting of the Society was explicit about its aim: ". . . cultivating and improving a correct taste in the performance of sacred music, and also to introduce into more general practice the works of Handel, Haydn, and other eminent composers."

Organist of the Handel and Haydn Society was the corpulent Dr. George K. Jackson (1745–1823), deemed the most learned musician of Boston. Composer of an affecting *Dirge for General Washington* with a complementary *Dead March* for instruments, Jackson also wrote "songs, serenades, cantatas, canzonetts, canons, glees, &c. &c.," as we read in the subtitle of his undated collection *New Miscellaneous Musical Work*. One of its songs, *Cancherizante*, suggests he was indeed musically learned: planned as a demonstration of *cancrizans* or retrograde melodic technique, it is, as Dr. Jackson pedantically explains at the head of the music, "a song to be sung forwards & then backwards beginning at the last note & ending with the first." Pedantic or not, the little song comes off rather well, its music matching nicely the gentle pastoral text (Example 2-3).

EXAMPLE 2-3. G. K. Jackson, *Cancherizante, New Miscellaneous Musical Work* (n.p., n.d. [after 1800]), p. 9.

Gilbert Chase has neatly pinpointed (in *AM*, Chapters 5 and 6) the two kinds of musicians who fostered eighteenth-century urban secular music: emigrant professionals and "gentleman amateurs." Among the latter, best-known are Thomas Jefferson, who if not a practicing musician or composer was still an aristocratic patron of art music; Benjamin Franklin, who was a practicing musician on the guitar, harp, and musical glasses and who may have composed (although not the string quartet sometimes claimed to be his); and Francis Hopkinson. According to John Adams, Hopkinson was a "pretty, little, curious, ingenious" man, "genteel and well-bred." He was something of a poet (his *Battle of the Kegs* is well known) and a political figure (his signature is on the Declaration of Independence, and he was our first Secretary of the Navy). Hopkinson's interest in music extended beyond performance and composition to mechanical improvements for the harpsichord (somewhat belatedly since the instrument was already being superseded by the pianoforte).[7] In 1788 Hopkinson dedicated a set of *Seven Songs for the Harpsichord or Forte Piano* to George Washington (an eighth was added after the title page was set in type), remarking in the dedication (reprinted in *ACS*, pp. 39–40) that "I cannot, I believe, be refused the credit of being the first native of the United States who has produced a musical composition." Hopkinson probably knew the music of the New England Yankee tunesmiths, some of whom doubtless antedated him as native-born composers, but he must have adjudged his genteel songs for the "republican court circle" of Philadelphia as *real* music, compared to the folkish singing-school tunes of his northern contemporaries. Nevertheless, the first composition we can unequivocally attribute to a native American is a manuscript song by Hopkinson dated 1759, *My Days Have Been So Wondrous Free*. The music does not quite live up to the charm of its first verse line; it is a bit stiff, if innocuously pleasant (*MinA*, No. 38). The *Seven Songs*, written (or at least published) almost thirty years later, show hardly any advance in style or technique, although one of them, *My Gen'rous Heart Disdains*, is a lilting rondo of considerable verve and wit; Example 2-4 is its refrain.

Song and instrumental music were combined in a special way in a few turn-of-the-century theater works which mingled the English ballad-opera tradition with the descriptive incidental music of French and German "melodrama," a term at that time denoting a play with background music. Such a mélange was the historically interesting

---

[7] In March, 1771, Jefferson wrote to his agent in Philadelphia, sending a list of purchases to be made in Europe. Nine weeks later he wrote again to the agent, who was by then in England, correcting the list to include a piano: "I have since seen a Piano-forte and am charmed with it. Send me this instrument instead. . . ." Quoted in Loesser, *op. cit.*, p. 441.

EXAMPLE 2-4. F. Hopkinson, *My Gen'rous Heart Disdains, Seven Songs
. . .* (Philadelphia: Thomas Dobson, 1788), No. 7, measures 21–48.

"operatic melo-drame" *The Indian Princess* by the American play-wright James Nelson Barker and the British-born actor-composer John Bray (1782–1822), produced at the Chestnut Street Theatre in Philadelphia in 1808. The first surviving play on the story of Captain John Smith and Pocahontas, *The Indian Princess; or, La Belle Sauvage* contains an overture, solo airs, choruses, and vocal ensemble numbers in the manner of ballad opera; it also has snippets of instru-mental music sounding in the background of the spoken dialogue to underscore the drama and heighten its emotional impact. Open-ended, to be repeated as many times as needed during a given scene, these mood-music miniatures are the precursors of later American background music for drama and films, and they point to the dawn-ing Romantic era's impulse to exaggerated emotionalism (to "melo-drama" in the later sense) and to a programmatic, narrative musical aesthetic.

Dance music

One of the least-studied areas of early American music is that of the dance. Yet the colonists, even the earliest ones, were great dancers. Hawthorne's tale of *The Maypole of Merry Mount* is partly legendary, but its essence is confirmed by William Bradford's contemporary account (1647) of the revels at the Merry Mount settlement, where ". . . they also set up a May-pole, drinking and dancing about it many days together." Throughout the colonial and Federal periods, journals and letters are full of mention of dancing. The eminent justice Samuel Sewall of Boston refers in his diary in 1685 to "a Dancing Master who seeks to set up here and hath mixt dances"; by 1716 the *Boston News-Letter* was advertising instruments, instrumental instruction books, and ruled (music) paper "to be sold at the Dancing School of Mr. Enstone." Eighteenth-century concerts often concluded with a march, which served then to introduce a post-concert ball.

The main reason, of course, that the actual music of early American dances is not better known is that little of it was published or even written down: like most of the world's dance music, it was not transcribed but improvised by musicians according to the needs of the moment, elaborating upon, extending or shortening, repeating or varying the current repertory of dance tunes. Popular dancing, moreover, is traditionally done to the accompaniment of whatever instruments and/or voices are at hand. Thus when dance music *is* written down, it usually appears as a bare-boned skeleton, to be given flesh and blood in actual performance; the written music is often merely a cue-sheet for the musicians. Ultimately, a composer may base a fully-realized work on a well-known tune, a dance rhythm, or a typical dance form; but his music presents a somewhat flossy and stylized, if artistically valid, image of a particular dance.

By the late eighteenth century, American dance music found its way into manuscript and even printed music-sheets. Some of the pieces are stylized versions for pianoforte of well-known dance types, e.g., the "Tempo di Menuetto" movement of a *Sonata for the Pianoforte with an Accompaniment for the Violin* (1797? in *MinA*, No. 75) by Raynor Taylor (1747–1825), a teacher of Alexander Reinagle and active in Philadelphia's musical life from 1793. Many, however, are practical dances written out usually in abstract format on treble and bass staves (although often just the treble tune is given), to be fleshed out by actual instrumentation and improvisation on the spot.

The dances in the *Evening Amusement* collection of 1796 mentioned earlier suggest the types favored by the late eighteenth century: hornpipes, reels, minuets, strathspeys, and marches. To these might be added the gavotte, the allemande, the country dance, the cotillion, the quadrille, and (the great novelty of the period) the waltz. The music of a "line dance" like the country dance (or "contra dance") was often the same as for a "square dance" like the cotillion or the quadrille: hornpipes, reels, cotillions, strathspeys served equally well for these dances of British origin. On the other hand, the minuet, gavotte, and allemande, introduced from France, each had its own tempo, steps, and rhythmic character.

Cotillions and country dances were the most popular in the late eighteenth-century American cities. The music comes as a surprise to the twentieth-century listener, since it is obviously the forerunner of square-dance music that he considers rural, not urban. It is not hard to hear *Harriet's Birthday* or *Jefferson's Hornpipe* (Example 2-5), both published by James Hewitt about 1802 in *A Collection of the Most Favorite Country Dances*, as lusty, ongoing fiddle tunes, pattering along in running eighth-notes until, at the phrase endings, they land stompingly on repeated cadence chords.

EXAMPLE 2-5. Two country dances, from James Hewitt (compiler), *A Collection of the Most Favorite Country Dances* (Philadelphia: J. Hewitt, [1802?]), pp. 5, 17. (a) *Harriet's Birthday.* (b) *Jefferson's Hornpipe.*

EXAMPLE 2-5b continued.

Fitz James (Example 2-6) is a lively dance tune from a collection of "the most favorite cotillions" published at Philadelphia about 1804. The collection is interesting not only for the verve and unpretentious excellence of the tunes in it but for its arrangement in "sets" showing the actual order that the dances followed, and for the "figures" (directions for the dances) which follow each tune. *Fitz James* turns out to be a miniature group of variations on its first strain, which then returns at the end to round out the form neatly. The "figure" for this dance is:

> GRAND ROUND—NB. The Change must be danced at the beginning of every Cottillion—
>
> The leading couples chassez to the right—back again—chassez across each couple with your partners and back again—right and left.

EXAMPLE 2-6. *Fitz James* ("First Set, No. 1"), from *A Collection of the most favorite Cotillions* . . . (Philadelphia: G. E. Blake, [1804?]), p. 2.

EXAMPLE 2-6 continued.

Simple as such dance music is, it has a vitality, an infectious appeal, and a kind of rawboned integrity that transcend much other music of the period.

Other instrumental music

Aside from marches, dances, and some overtures for ballad operas, colonial America produced little instrumental music. The Federal period saw more extensive publication of independent instrumental music, mostly by European composers: by 1825, American presses had issued some 170 works by Mozart, almost 80 by Haydn, over 50 by Handel, and about 30 each by Beethoven and Weber. More highly favored than sonatas or even the flowery sets of variations coming into favor in the late eighteenth century were programmatic pieces of all kinds, especially "battle" pieces. The prototype among these, at least in terms of the number of American editions published, was *The Battle of Prague* by Franz Kotzwara (d. 1791), described as late as 1879 by Mark Twain as "that venerable shivaree" in a hilarious account of its performance by one young lady (*A Tramp Abroad*, Volume II, Chapter 3). Originally a piano work, *The Battle of Prague* (1789) was re-

arranged constantly by American musicians to fit their instrumental resources; one Boston program in 1810 proudly announced
that its version would include "double-basses, cymbals, French
horns, kettle drums, trumpets, cannon, etc." Other battle pieces were
popular: Bernard Vignerie's *Battle of Maringo* [sic] came out in an
American edition (1802) as "a military and historical piece for the
piano forte," with cannon shots (expressed by the symbol ⊗) to be
produced "by stretching the two hands flat on the three lower
octaves in order to sound indistinctly every note." Like other battle
pieces, *The Battle of Maringo* is an episodic work, its various sections
titled "March," "Word of command," "Trumpet call," "Cries of the
wounded," and such. The whole work ends with a gigantic ⊗ .

One American composer of battle pieces was James Hewitt
(1770–1827), who came to New York in 1792 as "leader of the
band" for the Old American Company. The first concert he organized in New York included an overture by Haydn, a quartet by
Pleyel, and a flute quartet by Stamitz, plus Hewitt's own *Overture
in 9 movements, expressive of a battle* and an *Overture in 12 movements, expressive of a voyage from England to America* by Jean
Gehot (b. ca. 1756), who had come to America with Hewitt.
Hewitt also composed a *Battle of Trenton* (1797), duly dedicated
to General Washington and enlivened with quotations from *Washington's March* and *Yankee Doodle*. This was not the first American
publication of *Yankee Doodle* in instrumental guise, for three years
earlier Benjamin Carr had included it along with the *Marseillaise*,
Ça ira, O Dear What Can the Matter Be and other popular tunes in
a patriotic potpourri called *The Federal Overture*. Carr, whom we
have met as an able songwriter, could when he wished write a grace-
ful Haydnesque miniature for keyboard, if the six sonatas in *A New
Assistant for the Piano-Forte or Harpsichord* (Baltimore and Philadelphia, 1796) attributed to him are indeed his (Example 2-7).

EXAMPLE 2-7. B. Carr (?), *Sonata I, A New Assistant for the Piano-Forte
or Harpsichord* (Baltimore, Philadelphia: B. Carr, 1796), second movement.

EXAMPLE 2-7 continued.

Carr's tiny sonata movements were aimed to instruct (the fingerings of Example 2-7 are those of the original edition). Much more lengthy and probably written for his own performance are four sonatas left in manuscript by Alexander Reinagle. One of these may have been played by Reinagle at a concert in June, 1787, heard and noted in his diary for June 12 by George Washington, then in Philadelphia as a delegate to the Constitutional Convention. Example 2-8 shows the beginnings of the first two movements of Sonata III, a charming if somewhat over-extended essay in the style of C. P. E. Bach (the second and third movements of Sonata II printed in *MinA*, No. 74).

EXAMPLE 2-8. A. Reinagle, Sonata III, beginnings of first and second movements (after Library of Congress manuscript).

EXAMPLE 2-8 continued.

Bibliographical notes

The two basic sources on the development of concert music and opera in eighteenth-century America are by O. G. T. Sonneck: *Early Concert Life in America* (Leipzig: Breitkopf & Härtel, 1907; reprinted New York, 1949) and *Early Opera in America* (New York: G. Schirmer, Inc., 1915; reprinted New York, 1963). Sonneck also produced a monumental *Bibliography of Early Secular American Music* (Washington: Library of Congress, 1905; revised and enlarged by W. T. Upton, Washington, 1945; the latter edition reprinted New York, 1964). Taking up where Sonneck-Upton left off is Richard J. Wolfe's three-volume bibliography, *Secular Music in America 1801–1825* (New York: New York Public Library, 1964); the informative introduction to this is by Carleton Sprague Smith.

H. Earle Johnson's *Musical Interludes in Boston, 1795–1830* (New York: Columbia University Press, 1943) is a model of what can (and should) be done by way of regional studies. Charles Haywood's *Bibliography of North American Folk Lore and Folk Song* (2nd ed.; New York: Dover Publications, 1961) is a basic source for what was once "popular" and is now "folk" music. Hopkinson's *Seven Songs* have been reprinted in facsimile by Musical Americana (Philadelphia, 1954). I have discussed Barker and Bray's *The Indian Princess* in *Notes*, XIII (1955), 375–88. Irving Lowens has contributed an essay on Carr's *Federal Overture* (*MMEA*, pp. 89–114).

3

Cultivated and Vernacular Traditions and the Impact of Romanticism

Americans distinguish colloquially between two broad categories of music: they speak of "classical" music and "popular" music. The terms may be poor ones, especially the former, but they bespeak a common realization of the existence of two major traditions in American music. These I shall call the "cultivated" and "vernacular" traditions. I mean by the term "cultivated tradition" a body of music that America had to cultivate consciously, music faintly exotic, to be approached with some effort, and to be appreciated for its edification, its moral, spiritual or aesthetic values. By the "vernacular tradition" I mean a body of music more plebeian, native, not approached selfconsciously but simply grown into as one grows into one's vernacular tongue; music understood and appreciated simply for its utilitarian or entertainment value.[1]

As America entered the nineteenth century, a distinction between cultivated and vernacular traditions was hardly visible. The music of the ballad operas at New York and Philadelphia was also the music of broadsides and songsters, as it was of the popular products of sheet-music publishers. The fuging tunes of the New England Yankees aimed to improve church singing and thus to be spiritually edifying, but they served also as a popular social music for secular entertainment. The Alexander Reinagles of the late eighteenth century brought a cultivated professionalism to the New World, but they wrote and played and sang to the populace at large as well as to the gentlemen and gentlewomen.

However, as the nineteenth century unfolds we can distinguish with increasing clarity two bodies of American music, two attitudes toward music: cultivated and vernacular traditions become visible; an eventually profound schism in American musical culture begins to open up. On the one hand there continues a vernacular tradition of utilitarian and entertainment music, essentially unconcerned with artistic or philosophical idealism; a music based on established or newly diffused American raw materials; a "popular" music in the largest sense, broadly based, widespread, naive, and unselfconscious. On the other hand there grows a cultivated tradition of fine-art music significantly concerned with moral, artistic, or cultural idealism; a music almost exclusively based on continental European raw materials and models, looked to rather selfconsciously; an essentially transatlantic music of the pretenders to gentility; hopefully sophisticated and by no means widespread throughout all segments of the populace.

Many factors worked to create this dualistic musical culture in nineteenth-century America, among them the rapid geographical expansion of the nation and distinctive new immigration patterns.

---

[1] There is yet another great category of American music, of course, somewhat too loosely called "folk music." This body of music, whether in its form of a legacy of older musical tradition still to be found in cultural backwaters (or taken up selfconsciously by the more sophisticated) or in its form of traditional communal music among various immigrant or ethnic minorities, is not my concern in this book. It has been dealt with by Bruno Nettl in a companion volume in this series: *Folk and Traditional Music of the Western Continents* (Englewood Cliffs: Prentice-Hall, Inc., 1965).

Perhaps most significant were the impact of Romanticism's attitudes and ideals and the continued development of public concerts as a primary source of musical experience.

The extraordinary territorial growth of the United States in the nineteenth century accelerated a split between cultivated and vernacular traditions in American music because it diversified the cultural possibilities of American society. Dominating the entire social and cultural situation was the moving frontier, constantly being pushed westward and leaving behind it an ever-widening area of newly settled towns, with the old urban centers of the eastern seaboard behind *them*. Necessarily, musical life was vastly different in a pioneer settlement like Horse Creek, Nebraska, on the Mormon and Oregon Trails; in a relatively new but substantial and growing town like Pittsburgh, just beyond the Allegheny Mountains, which increased in population between 1810 and 1840 from less than 5,000 to more than 20,000; and in an old established urban center like New York or Boston. Music of cultivated taste was taken up first in the older eastern cities, which were closest in spirit and space to Europe's centers of an art-music tradition. The music formerly enjoyed in such cities by all levels of society then tended to become both a slightly déclassé "popular" music and part of a vernacular tradition accompanying the westerly push of Americans across the land. By 1853, for instance, a Boston writer remarked of the Yankee singing-school tunebooks, once enjoyed by Bostonians great and small, that "if used at all, [they] have been crowded to the far West, out of sight and hearing."[2]

The frontier settlements had virtually no contact with the developing cultivated tradition of the eastern urban centers. However, the newly established towns in between, rapidly growing in numbers, in population, in stability and ease of life, did have some contact and sought still more. But, lacking the urbanity, wealth, leisure, and comforting traditions of the eastern seaboard cities they were at once envious, fearful, and resentful of the culture "down East." The men, only one step removed from pioneering, viewed any time spent on non-productive, inutile art as wasteful or effete. Land and money needed cultivation, not their sensibilities. Music,

[2] Nathaniel Gould, *History of Church Music in America* (Boston: A. N. Johnson, 1853), p. 55.

the most intangible and "useless" among the arts, had their special disdain and hostility. Leave music to the women, or to the immigrant "professors." Thus crystallized an American view of fine-art music as essentially the province of females, foreigners, or effeminates, a view still common in the twentieth century although it weakened rapidly after World War I.

New immigration patterns during the nineteenth century were also of great importance in shaping America's music, particularly that of the cultivated tradition. The flow of immigrants was immense: some 16,000,000 between 1840 and 1900, spurred on by the land-rich, broadening nation and by its manpower-hungry industrialization. Until the 1880's the main influx of immigrants continued to be from Great Britain, but from the 1830's came also, in roughly chronological order, Germans, Scandinavians, Italians, and eastern Europeans. The arrival of these continental Europeans was critical in the moulding of cultivated American taste because it diluted the traditional mainstream of Anglo-American culture and especially because it occurred at the peak of the Romantic movement in Europe. Early nineteenth-century America was ripe for Romanticism: indeed, someone has said that the American Revolution itself was perhaps the first and greatest example of Romanticism and, as Lewis Mumford has written, "pioneering may in part be described as the Romantic movement in action."[3] The ordinary American may not have been aware of the philosophic concepts of Romanticism—idealism, imagination, boundlessness, personal freedom, individualism—but his whole way of life and thought reflected them. And his musical attitudes were no less ready to be shaped along Romantic lines.

Romanticism had its earliest and strongest flourishing in Germany and, although springing initially from poets and novelists, it found its highest expression and made its greatest impact through German music and musicians. Outside the field of opera, in which Italy maintained a national identity, hardly any kind of nineteenth-century music escaped being touched by German influence; hardly any musician could avoid the impact of Beethoven, Schubert, Schumann, Mendelssohn, Liszt, Wagner. Essentially, the centers of nineteenth-century musical thought were Berlin, Leipzig, Munich,

[3] *The Golden Day* (2nd ed.; Boston: Beacon Press, 1957), p. 20.

and Vienna; essentially, the ultimate in fine-art music was considered to be German music.

Even before massive crop failures and the 1848 revolutions brought a huge wave of Germans to the United States, some Americans were shifting their musical allegiance from England to Germany. The influential hymnodist Thomas Hastings spoke for his generation, poised on the brink of submission to German rather than English models, when he wrote in 1822 in his *Dissertation on Musical Taste:*

> We are the decided admirers of *German* musick. We delight to study and to listen to it. The science, genius, the taste, that every where pervade it, are truly captivating to those who have learned to appreciate it: but such, we presume, are not yet the *majority* of American or English auditors or executants.[4]

Hastings was writing as one of the first spokesmen for the cultivated tradition of American music. Terms like "science," "genius," and "taste" bespeak special standards, not for all music but for the *art* of music; not for music as a utilitarian part of everyday life or a pleasant diversion on the surface of life but as an art whose holy mission it was to edify and uplift. "Appreciation" of such music required cultivation. As expressed by the highly respected and pontifical editor and critic of the later nineteenth century, John Sullivan Dwight, the aim of such music and of the other arts was to remedy the defects of a materialistic society by "familiarizing men with the beautiful and the infinite." This was the credo of the cultivated tradition. As the exponents of this attitude saw it, German music more than any other achieved the desired goals. One significant result of this view was a rejection of the American musical past, dominated as it had been not only by popular, "unscientific" taste but by British backgrounds. Both the friendly, folkish music of the Yankee tunesmiths and the great melodic reservoir of Anglo-American song were spurned as bases for the new "scientific" music of the cultivated tradition.

In their self-conscious, unself-confident striving toward a transatlantic taste for cultivated music, Americans also tended to reject

---

[4] *Dissertation on Musical Taste* (Albany: Websters and Skinner, 1822), p. 194.

the American *present* as a source of musical subject-matter. The very aspects of American civilization that were unique had of course no models in Europe; they found scant celebration in American art-music. Europeans of the early nineteenth century were, after all, infinitely disparaging of American culture: "Who, in the four quarters of the globe, reads an American book, or goes to an American play, or looks at an American painting or statue?" asked the British author-minister Sydney Smith in 1820.[5] The European might grudgingly admit to American achievements in industry, technology, and science but considered them, if anything, inimical to art and edification. When the Philadelphia journalist-composer William Fry asked the director of the Paris opera if he might present at his own expense an open rehearsal of his opera *Leonora*, he was refused with the remark: "In Europe we look upon America as an industrial country—excellent for electric telegraphs, but not for art."[6] The American pianist Louis Moreau Gottschalk had a similar experience: "Zimmerman, director of the piano classes at the Paris Conservatoire, . . . without hearing me refused to receive me because 'l'Amérique n'était qu'un pays de machines à vapeur'."[7] Cowed by such attitudes, American musicians of the cultivated tradition were not about to celebrate their electric telegraphs or their steam engines, their reapers or railroads. (Vernacular-tradition composers, of popular songs for instance, did indeed celebrate them, as they did American steamboats and streetcars, balloons, baseball, and the Brooklyn Bridge.)

With the European music of Romanticism their main model, and with German music held up as the ideal, Americans welcomed German musicians. They came in large numbers. Gottschalk heard a volunteer military band in Williamsport in 1863: "Is it necessary," he wrote in his journal, "to say that it is composed of Germans (all the musicians in the United States are Germans)?" A year earlier he had only half facetiously noted that, "It is remarkable that almost all the Russians in America are counts, just as almost all the musicians

---

[5] Quoted from the *Edinburgh Review* by J. B. McMaster, *History of the People of the United States* (New York: D. Appleton and Company), I (1883), 82.

[6] Quoted in *OAM*, p. 245.

[7] Louis Moreau Gottschalk, *Notes of a Pianist*, ed. Jeanne Behrend (New York: Alfred A. Knopf, 1964), p. 52.

who abound in the United State are nephews of Spohr and Mendelssohn." The figure of the German music teacher came to be a familiar
one in American towns; Gottschalk, Paris-trained and something of
a Germanophobe (but with a perceptive eye and a sharp pen),
wickedly described one:

> I was introduced [in St. Louis in 1862] to an old German musician
> with uncombed hair, bushy beard, in constitution like a bear, in
> disposition the amenity of a boar at bay to a pack of hounds. I
> know this type; it is found everywhere.[8]

It was inevitable that as the cultivated tradition of American
music developed momentum in the nineteenth century, under the
sway of European music and musicians here at home, young American musicians affluent enough to do so would go to the source, to
Europe, for training. Not surprisingly, when they went, it was to
Germany.

Some aspects of Romanticism, working in combination with
a new domination of the economics of music by the middle class,
confirmed the dichotomy between cultivated and vernacular traditions in American music.

Romantic art-music put a premium on the individuality of the
composer and on an apparent subjectivity of artistic expression. One
result was a broadening of the vocabulary of art-music, for to the
degree that a composer used a vocabulary different from others' he
could be viewed as unique, as one who was expressing his innermost
thoughts as only he felt and knew them, a sort of extraordinary culture hero. Romanticism encouraged the virtuoso composer. But if
individuality and novelty were most highly prized assets of the
composer, they also collided with the fundamentally conservative
tastes of the mass public which had become the principal patron of
music. The agents of the new patronage were the public concert
and the public opera, which had replaced the aristocratic soirée
musicale and the cathedral service as the principal forums for
musical performance. Public concerts depended for their existence
on the approbation of a large, heterogeneous audience. Such an
audience, with collective ears less finely tuned, less carefully cultivated than those of the earlier aristocratic patrons of music, tended

[8] This, and the previous two quotations, from *Notes of a Pianist;* in
order, pp. 127, 102, 63.

to resist complexity and innovation in the musical language, just what the Romantic-era composer was striving for. The composer was trapped between the conflicting demands of Romantic individualism and the mass audience. Precisely to the degree that he spoke in a uniquely personal language, his communication with the public—which liked what it knew and knew what it liked—was attenuated. Inevitably, a fissure appeared between the taste of the composer of art-music and that of his ostensible patron, the public. Inevitably, the fissure widened as the nineteenth century wore on. Ultimately, the fissure now a chasm, the public concert would virtually exclude the contemporary composer; the public concert hall and the public opera house would virtually become musical museums. The composer would be forced to find other sources of patronage, or at least other sources of income than musical composition. The vernacular-tradition composer might be paid to exercise his craft, but not the cultivated-tradition composer his art.

If the virtuoso composer's lot was a problematic one, the virtuoso performer's was not. Not only was he a critical success for his unique gifts, which made him appear the inspired Romantic individualist par excellence; he was a popular success as well. Technical brilliance is confused with musical profundity in direct ratio to the naiveté of the listener, and the mass-public concert audience of the Romantic era tended to be naive. American concert audiences welcomed the virtuosos, equated virtuosity with artistry, mistook virtuosity for talent. European virtuosos appeared regularly in America. Robert Schumann commented:

> The [European] public has lately begun to weary of virtuosos, and . . . we have too. The virtuosos themselves seem to feel this, if we may judge from a recently awakened fancy among them for emigrating to America; and many of their enemies secretly hope they will remain over there; for, taken all in all, modern virtuosity has benefited art very little.[9]

To America came the Norwegian violinist Ole Bull (five American visits beginning in 1843); the "Swedish Nightingale," soprano Jenny Lind, brought over in 1850 by the notorious impresario P. T. Barnum; mezzo-soprano Maria Malibran, 1825 to 1827; Henriette

[9] *Gesammelte Schriften über Musik und Musiker* (5th ed.; Leipzig, 1914), II, 134, as trans. by Paul Rosenfeld, *Robert Schumann on Music and Musicians* (New York: Pantheon Books Inc., 1946), p. 81.

Sontag, celebrated German soprano, in the United States from 1852 to 1854; the pianists Henri Herz (1845 to 1851) and Sigismond Thalberg (1856 through 1857).

One result of the adulation of virtuosos was an emphasis on the performer of music rather than on the composer or even the music itself; that is to say, on the means rather than the end. Did it matter *what* Paganini or Liszt or Jenny Lind performed, so long as they performed? Symbolic of this view of the musical experience (and still common today) was the listing in announcements of a forthcoming concert not of the music to be heard but only its performer. In earlier eras, when the virtuoso was primarily an improviser, virtually composing the music as he performed, such an attitude was hardly peculiar and posed no threat to progressive trends in the musical vocabulary. But in the Romantic era, when the art of improvisation was dying under the effect of the composer-as-culture-hero idea and when at the same time the conservatism of the mass audience meant resistance to innovation, this attitude tended to freeze the concert repertory and to block any change in the musical vocabulary. In this sense the nineteenth-century virtuoso became the real musical hero while only lip-service was paid to the living composer, whose heroism often had to await posthumous recognition after the slowly changing taste of the concert public, finally catching up with the composer's vocabulary, allowed a change in the performance repertory.

The virtuoso conductor, a new kind of virtuoso, was born during the Romantic era. He was no longer merely *primus inter pares*, a musical chronometer keeping time for a group of co-equal instrumentalists, but a kind of super-performer playing a super-instrument, the Romantically expansive symphony orchestra. America welcomed increasingly this kind of virtuoso, as was reflected in a number of visiting orchestras and the development of American orchestras themselves, with a parade of European conductors to lead them, further emphasizing the faint exoticism, the "foreignness" from an American standpoint, of the cultivated tradition.

The premium put on virtuosity tended to create higher performance standards in general, thus to increase professionalism in music of the cultivated tradition. This was mirrored in the establishment of America's first musical conservatories. Perhaps more significant in terms of musical attitudes were the increasingly common attempts through private music lessons to train amateurs up to professional levels of accomplishment, often with futile and musically disenchanting results, and always with an affirmation of the distinction between cultivated and vernacular music traditions. A similar educative aim, but one hoping to train people up to "professional" levels of musical understanding, lay behind the phenomenon of "music appreciation" lectures; the music in question, whose appreciation had to be cultivated, was of course exclusively cultivated-tradition music.

If the rise of the middle class altered the system of musical patronage and accelerated a musical professionalism, it also tended to create a vast new army of amateur performers of art-music, persons with the leisure time to spend on music-making and the aspiration to do so, but with only modest talent or artistic judgment. Symbolic of this aspect of middle-class musical culture was the rapid growth of the sheet-music publishing industry, which in America had reached impressive proportions even by the last decade of the eighteenth century and continued to expand throughout the nineteenth. The main output of the publishers was naturally music simple enough to be sold in quantity to amateur musicians across the land, music which in one sense of the word would be "popular." At first this published popular music was indistinguishable from the music to be heard on concert programs. This is true, for example, of late eighteenth-century American sheet music, which more often than not made an advertising pitch for its desirability by actually citing its use in concert or opera: Alexander Reinagle's opera air *Rosa* (1800), ". . . sung with great applause by Mrs. Merry in the comedy of *The Secret*," or Benjamin Carr's *Federal Overture* (1794) ". . . as performed at the theatres in Philadelphia and New York." But here too a fissure appeared—between the taste and capability of the amateur performer and the music of the professional concert and opera performers. As the latter became ever more professionalized and as virtuosity tended to increase, concert music outstripped amateur ability, and the "popular" music of the music sheets came to be a different thing from the "classical" music of the concerts.

Some of this sheet music was music of the vernacular tradition. But much of it (songs and piano pieces for the most part) had an aura of pretentious gentility about it; it derived from and lay within the cultivated tradition rather than the vernacular, although its accessibility to both performer and listener kept it near the latter. As composed by innumerable musical poetasters, it actually represented a subdivision of the cultivated tradition that might best be termed "household music," a term we find in the title of a collection of the 1850's: *Household Melodies, a Selection of Popular Songs, Duets, Trios & Quartettes, Arranged to Household Words,* issued first by W. C. Peters & Sons of Cincinnati and then by other publishers and distributors at St. Louis, Nashville, Cleveland, Pittsburgh, and Louisville. The term "household music" seems appropriate, for it suggests an analogy with the other household artifacts of the period like silverware, ceramics, glass, textiles, furniture which although utilitarian were never acquired solely for their utility but with an eye to their attractiveness and their reflection of fashionable cultivated taste. The early twentieth century would call such music "semi-classical" or "light classical," thus perfectly describing its ambiguous status.

By that time, the two main traditions of American music, cultivated and vernacular, came to be less independent, or at least the cultivated tradition began to draw on the vernacular. By the mid-twentieth century, "popular" music was even beginning to draw on "classical," and once again the lines were not so clearly drawn in American musical taste.

In the following three chapters, I shall discuss that period in American music when the two traditions diverge and remain more or less separate: from about 1820 until the end of World War I. It will be most convenient to speak first of the cultivated tradition (including the genteel household music) up to the Civil War; next of the vernacular-tradition music during the whole period; and finally, in Chapter 6, of the cultivated-tradition music from the Civil War to World War I.

4

The Cultivated
Tradition, 1820-1865

American music of the cultivated tradition between about
1820 and the end of the Civil War can perhaps best be approached
through a discussion of its main genres: church music, song, piano
music, orchestral music, and opera.

Church music

As we have seen (see above, p. 15), the New England school of
composers of psalm tunes, hymns, anthems, and patriotic pieces, of
fuging tunes and other sacred-secular works in a characteristic,

indigenous style, waned in popularity after the turn of the nineteenth century. As early as 1791, when Samuel Holyoke published at Boston a collection titled *Harmonia Americana*, he specifically called attention to his omission of "fuging pieces," claiming in his preface that "the principal reason why few were inserted was the trifling effect produced by that sort of music; for the parts, falling in, one after another, each conveying a different idea, confound the sense, and render the performance a mere jargon of words." But this argument, an old one against vocal counterpoint, was only part of the reason for the new disfavor in which the Yankee composers found themselves. More significant was the developing taste for "the sublime and beautiful compositions of the great Masters of Music," to recall Andrew Law's phrase—specifically the masters of continental Europe.

Symptomatic of the shift in taste are the collections of church music published by Thomas Hastings (1784–1872), whom we have met as a "decided admirer of German musick" and who was a major figure in nineteenth-century cultivated church music. In 1815 Hastings brought out his first compilation, *Musica Sacra: A Collection of Psalm Tunes, Hymns, and Set Pieces*. Along with original tunes and works by other Americans, he included adaptations from the following Europeans: Giardini (to whose melody the hymn "Come Thou, almighty King" is sung even today in Protestant American churches), Purcell, William Croft, Handel (*Messiah*), Burney, and Madan. The English bias is clear; Hastings had not yet submitted to "the science, genius, the taste" of "German musick." He turned to it increasingly, however, for tunes to include in later hymn collections. By 1849 he could even title one hymn book *The Mendelssohn Collection*. To its main body he added as a sort of appendix a group of older hymns and psalm settings, a concession, apparently, to those who still wanted to sing the old New England favorites. Among them we find Timothy Swan's *China* (see above, p. 13), but in a completely bowdlerized version. Hastings's condescending footnote reads: "Extensively sung in former times, at funerals. The original harmony was, of course, inadmissible."

Hastings's own output as a hymnodist was considerable: he is said to have written some 600 hymn texts and composed 1000 hymn tunes. Among the best known are "Gently, Lord, O gently lead us," "How calm and beautiful the morn," "Return, O wand'rer to thy home," and, most popular of all, "Rock of ages" (*MinA*, No. 86), which appeared as a setting for A. M. Toplady's text in *Spiritual Songs for Social Worship* (1832), a collection compiled jointly by Hastings and the other dominant figure in the cultivated tradition's church music, Lowell Mason.

Mason (1792–1872) has been conceded by even so unsympathetic a critic as Gilbert Chase (see *AM*, Chapter 8) to have had "the strongest, the widest, and the most lasting impress on the musical culture" of any nineteenth-century American musician. His first musical success came with sponsorship by the weighty Handel and Haydn Society of Boston, which aimed not only ". . . to introduce into more general practice the works of Handel, Haydn and other eminent composers" but to support the publication of approved church music. Upon the recommendation of its esteemed organist, Dr. Jackson, the society accepted a hymn collection assembled by Mason, then a young bank clerk working in Savannah, and in 1822 there appeared the first of many editions of *The Boston Handel and Haydn Society Collection of Church Music*.

Mason's father and grandfather were both musical, and by the time he went to Savannah from his native Massachusetts he was proficient on several instruments. In Savannah he was taught by a German musician, one F. L. Abel, who probably contributed to Mason's esteem for "scientific" music as opposed to the less suave and polished American style. Already in his collection of 1822 Mason was basing his style on continental European models and even included some six hymn tunes based on music of Beethoven. Other sources he was to tap included German chorales, Gregorian chants, and works of Gluck, Handel, Haydn, Mozart, Nägeli, and Pleyel.[1]

The Boston Handel and Haydn Society Collection was an immediate and continuing success: twenty-two editions were published between 1822 and 1858. Mason returned to Massachusetts in 1827, to become president of the Handel and Haydn Society and to found in 1832, together with George J. Webb (1803–1887) and other Boston musicians, the Boston Academy of Music; its purpose was to instruct children in music on principles based on the inductive

---

[1] See Henry L. Mason, *Hymn-Tunes of Lowell Mason: A Bibliography* (Cambridge: The University Press, 1944).

methods of the Swiss educator, Johann Pestalozzi. Mason continued to compose, compile, and adapt hymns: later successful collections were *The Choir; or Union Collection of Church Music* (1832); *The Boston Academy's Collection of Church Music* (1835); *The Modern Psalmist* (1839); and *Carmina Sacra: or Boston Collection of Church Music* (1841), among others. With the income from these four major publications and from his original 1822 collection, Mason's fortune was assured; along with it went extraordinary fame and influence.

The musical style of Mason's hymns, based on European Classic-era music, is one of genteel correctness, neat and tidy in harmony and form, bland in rhythm and melodic thrust. The airs are now in the tenor voice in the old manner, now in the treble; not infrequently, they are oddly awkward, perhaps because Mason's musical thought as a whole was dominated by considerations of harmony, and as a result even the air is sometimes made to accommodate the harmony rather than fulfilling its own directional impulse. Two of Mason's best-known hymns, *A Missionary Hymn* ("From Greenland's icy mountains"; *MinA*, No. 83) and *Olivet* ("My faith looks up to thee"; *MinA*, No. 84) share this trait. It hardly seems coincidental that Mason chose, among British sources, the century-old *St. Thomas* by Aaron Williams to arrange, alter, and expand (in *New Carmina Sacra*, 1852; *MinA*, No. 85), for its air too is of this type.

Mason was not only a composer of some 1200 original hymn tunes and adapter of almost 500 melodies from other composers. He was also a dedicated teacher: to him must go credit for getting music admitted into the public-school curriculum of Boston, and indirectly into public-school programs over the entire country. The beginning was the Boston Academy, which provided free extracurricular music classes for schoolchildren. In 1838, after years of propagandizing by Mason, the public schools of Boston began to include musical instruction as a part of the regular curriculum, with Mason appointed as superintendent of music for the city system. It was a historic moment in the history of American music and musical attitudes; for better or worse, Mason's ideals and tastes, and those of a huge circle of musicians and educators associated with him, could now be directed where they would have the greatest impact: among the children.

Song

The Anglo-American tradition of the genteel air was maintained during the entire nineteenth century. Songs were the staples
of the mid-nineteenth-century concert repertory; hardly any concert of exclusively instrumental music was to be heard, and the
majority of public concerts were essentially song recitals. Up to the
Civil War, at least, the songs of the public concerts were also heard
in the parlor, the very center of middle-class polite society; there,
beside horsehair-stuffed chairs and sofas and polite, instructive family magazines, could be found—ever more commonly as the century
wore on—a square or an upright piano or a reed organ. Here, in the
home, their cultural life dominated by the new breed of middle-
class woman, nineteenth-century Americans gathered to hear a
favorite daughter or bride sing the latest concert-household songs.

If eighteenth-century American songs only occasionally borrowed the sentimental tone and the high-flown language of Thomson's *Seasons* and Goldsmith's *Deserted Village*, nineteenth-century
songs went the whole way, reflecting the tastes of an age which
reveled in Scott's poems and Gothic romances, after a turn-of-the-
century preparation by way of Richardson's *Pamela* and Susanna
Rowson's *Charlotte Temple: A Tale of Truth*. Almost entirely
vanished were the sturdy unforced optimism of Reinagle's *America,
Commerce, and Freedom* or the lightly mocking bow to conventional love of Hopkinson's *My Gen'rous Heart Disdains the Slave
of Love to Be*. In their place were set texts of the most extreme
sentimentality, descending to bathos and ascending to manic ecstasy.

Models for American songs of the period were provided by the
English singers who barnstormed through the eastern half of the
country in the 1830's and '40's. One such was Henry Russell
(1812–1900; in America from 1833 to 1841), who left the organ
bench of Rochester's First Presbyterian Church to make a name for
himself as a baritone soloist and songwriter. Mining the vein of
sentiment for the aged that ran so deep in mid-nineteenth-century
America, Russell concentrated on "old" songs (*The Old Bell, The
Brave Old Oak, The Old Sexton*, and many others), for a total he
claimed to be over 800 songs. Among the most renowned were
Woodman, Spare That Tree (". . . Touch not a single bough,/In
youth it shelter'd me,/And I'll protect it now") and *The Old Arm
Chair* (*MinA*, No. 123). *The Old Arm Chair*, published in 1840 at

the peak of Russell's popularity, illustrates in every detail the genre of the household song. The text is embarrassingly maudlin: the poet gazes on the armchair "with quivering breath and throbbing brow"; religion and filial love are identified ("I almost worshipp'd her when she smiled,/And turn'd from her bible to bless her child"); the chair itself is an object of sentimental veneration ("I love it, I love it, and cannot tear/My soul from a mother's Old Arm Chair"). The cover page, with its lithograph showing Mother and the chair (reproduced in *MinA*), is characteristic: nineteenth-century song sheets aimed to be visually seductive as well as vocally attractive. The music is quite simple, the melodic style essentially declamatory, in easy $\frac{4}{4}$ rhythms, with an occasional touch of affective chromaticism and a climactic, shuddering diminished-seventh chord. The form is strophic. The most frequent harmonic progression is the gentle I-IV-I, often made even softer by a tonic pedalpoint. One of Russell's songwriting successors was John Hill Hewitt (1801–1890), composer of some three hundred songs, among them the Civil War ballad *All Quiet Along the Potomac Tonight* (1861; *MinA*, No. 118). He claimed that because of Russell's limited vocal range *The Old Arm Chair* has "but five notes in its melodic construction." This is untrue, but it is restricted to one octave and virtually sings itself, with a predictable curve of line and falling sequences. Most characteristic of the melodic method are the many sighing, drooping appoggiaturas, which strive to confirm the text's tone of deep emotion. One paradox of the song, typical of the genre, is that despite its lachrymose subject it is in the major rather than the minor mode; the latter must have been viewed as *too* potent a musical purveyor of sadness.

I have dwelt at this length on *The Old Arm Chair* not because it is either the best or the worst song of the period, but because it epitomizes so perfectly the concert-household song repertory. Far more extreme examples could be cited, and by composers highly thought-of: perhaps the nadir was reached in *The Lament of the Blind Orphan Girl* (1847) by W. B. Bradbury (1816–1868), who compiled hymn books in collaboration with Hastings and was thought of as a rival by Mason. In this song, the doubly afflicted heroine is made to voice her lament in skipping rhythms and a modest coloratura (derived in part, certainly, from the Donizetti and Rossini arias that Bradbury would have heard in New York in the 1840's). It is a remarkable lesson in how to turn sentiment into sentimentality (Example 4-1).

EXAMPLE 4-1. W. Bradbury, *The Lament of the Blind Orphan Girl* (New York: Atwill, 1847), measures 25–30, 73–84.

The Lament of the Blind Orphan Girl was published "as sung with distinguished Applause, by Abby Hutchinson." Abby was the female member of the most celebrated American "singing family" of the period from 1840 to 1860: the Hutchinsons. They were one of a number of American troupes formed in imitation of European family groups, like the Rainer family from the Tyrolean Alps, which toured the States during the 1840's and after. The Hutchinsons specialized not only in laments—*Oh! I'm in Sadness, Last Year's Flowers, Give That Wreath to Me, The Guardian of the Grave*—but in "Alpine" songs. Precisely at the moment (1846) when the Donner party battled to get to settlements in California across the mountain walls of the Rockies, Americans in the East were hearing about

> *The mountain top! the mountain top!*
> *Oh! that's the place for me;*
> *I love to mount each craggy steep*
> *With shout of joyful glee!*

And on an Albany program in 1842 the Hutchinsons sang *The Snowstorm*, its concluding verses a classic of American melodrama:

> *And colder still the wind did blow,*
> *And darker hours of night came on,*
> *And deeper grew the drifts of snow.*
> *Her limbs were chilled, her strength was gone.*
> *"Oh God!" she cried in accents wild,*
> *"If I must perish, save my child!"*

It is against this background, of the nostalgic sentimentality of *The Old Arm Chair*, the crocodile tears of *The Blind Orphan Girl*, the hysterical unreality of *The Mountain Top*, that one must view the household songs of Stephen Collins Foster, a few of which so sublimate or mitigate the conventions of the genre, and so transcend the songs of his contemporaries, that Foster must be adjudged America's first great songwriter.

Born in 1826 on the Fourth of July, fifty years to the day after the Declaration of Independence, near the still small but booming commercial and industrial town of Pittsburgh, Foster had a typical middle-class upbringing in a family to which household music was no stranger (his older sister played the piano, and his father fiddled a bit). Drawn to music from early childhood (his father commented when Foster was sixteen that "his leisure hours are all devoted to musick, for which he possesses a strange talent"), he nevertheless got scant encouragement. His brother later claimed that Foster "studied deeply, and burned much midnight oil over the works of the masters, especially Mozart, Beethoven, and Weber. They were his delight, and he struggled for years and sounded the profoundest depths of musical science."[2] But Foster's music itself leaves no room for illusions about the extent of his training: there is ineptitude and amateurishness on virtually every page. On the other hand, there is an obvious and undeniable natural gift for melody.

Foster's debut as a songwriter was with *Open Thy Lattice, Love* (1844). Text and music are both remarkably restrained for the period, and we seem to be back in the very early nineteenth century, with a typically cool if amorous air set to music that reflects Foster's Anglo-Irish descent (Example 4-2).

EXAMPLE 4-2. S. Foster, *Open Thy Lattice, Love* (Philadelphia: Willig, 1844), measures 5–8.

Within the next twenty years, until his death in New York in 1864, Foster was to publish about 150 such household songs. Most are love songs, but the sweetheart is usually unattainable, either dead or distant, and the poet (usually Foster himself) can dwell with her only in a dream of love. Nostalgic yearning for the irretrievably lost is the keynote, but the poet finds the mournful dream delicious. "I dream of Jeanie with the light brown hair," sang Foster in 1854—but Jeanie is gone:

> *Many were the wild notes her merry voice would pour,*
> *Many were the blithe birds that warbled them o'er.*
>
> .   .   .

and we see Jeanie only through a gentle haze of nostalgia, "floating like a vapor on the soft summer air." Gentle tenderness, or temperate gentility, characterizes the music as well as the texts of Foster's best household songs. *Gentle Annie* (1856) and *Gentle Lena Claire*

---

[2] Morrison Foster, *My Brother Stephen* (1896, privately printed; reprinted Indianapolis: Foster Hall, 1932), p. 32.

(1862) are stereotypes; but both heroines are depicted in memorable melodies (Example 4-3).

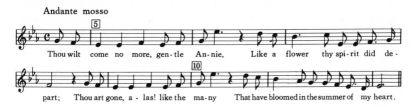

EXAMPLE 4-3a. S. Foster, *Gentle Annie* (New York: Firth, Pond & Co., 1856), measure 5–12 (piano part omitted).

EXAMPLE 4-3b. S. Foster, *Gentle Lena Claire* (New York: S. C. Gordon, 1862), measures 9–16 (piano part omitted).

In one of the most thoroughly "composed" love songs, *Come Where My Love Lies Dreaming* (1855), it is the sweetheart who is dreaming, hence asleep, hence for the moment unattainable. *Come Where My Love Lies Dreaming* is set, atypically for a household song, for vocal quartet, with the soprano part set in relief against three lower voices and given an arching line that just barely hints at the Italian opera to be heard in New York, where Foster had lived for most of 1854 (Example 4-4).

EXAMPLE 4-4. S. Foster, *Come Where My Love Lies Dreaming. Quartette* (New York: Firth, Pond & Co., 1855), measures 13–16 (piano part omitted).

The last love song written by Foster is one of the best, musically: *Beautiful Dreamer*, copyrighted shortly after his death (1864).

As in the love songs, nostalgia suffuses an extraordinary proportion of the other household songs of Foster. Perhaps from Henry Russell, whom he had heard in concert in Pittsburgh, comes the favorite adjective "old." But Russell's "old" usually means simply "aged"; Foster's usually means "of the past": *Old Memories* (1853), *When Old Friends Were Here* (1864), *Farewell, Old Cottage* (1851), *My Old Kentucky Home, Good Night* (1853). Beloved ones lost through death are mourned in *Bring My Brother Back to Me* (1863), *Our Willie Dear is Dying* (1861), and *Little Belle Blair* (1861). In *Ah! May the Red Rose Live Alway* (1850), one of Foster's richest works harmonically, the poet asks "Why should the beautiful die?" (Example 4-5).

EXAMPLE 4-5. S. Foster, *Ah! May the Red Rose Live Alway* (Baltimore: F. D. Benteen, 1850), measures 9–16.

There are, of course, some happy ones among Foster's household songs. *Fairy Belle* (1859); *If You've Only Got a Moustache* (1864), an Irish reel with coy advice to bachelors; and *There's a Good Time Coming* (1846) are a few. But for the most part a sense of loss and nostalgia for the lost are pervasive. An apostrophe to the family hound, *Old Dog Tray* (1853), leads Foster to mourn a "once happy day":

The morn of life is past
And evening comes at last;
It brings me a dream of a once happy day,
Of merry forms I've seen
Upon the village green. . . .

Some historians have seen more than simple sentimentality in the insistent nostalgia of the American mid-nineteenth century, so typified by Foster. The "once happy day," they say, was an unspoiled early America, fresh for clearing and settling, since, as Lewis Mumford has put it, "ruin and change lay in the wake of the pioneer, as he went westering." The sense of uneasiness, of dislocation, of transition and change must have permeated post-pioneer life. Mumford reminds us of the fascination the legend of Rip Van Winkle held for the period:

> The old landmarks have gone; the old faces have disappeared; all the outward aspects of life have changed. At the bottom, however, Rip himself has not changed; for he has been drunk and lost in a dream, and . . . he remains, mentally, a boy.[3]

Foster, too, perhaps remained mentally a boy; he did musically, for there is no essential stylistic difference between his early works and his late ones among the household songs. (There is, however, between his household songs and his minstrel-show songs, as we shall see.) But with his natural talent as melodist, despite his artlessness, Foster spoke for pre-Civil War America; not for the frontier or for the seaboard cities, perhaps, but for that broadening span in between, settled but unsettled, no longer a frontier to be pierced and conquered but an America to be made into something else, and perhaps frighteningly so.

Foster's last years coincided with the Civil War, which evoked as all wars have a spate of songs from American composers. Foster himself contributed a few (as a Northerner, though a Democrat)— *We are Coming, Father Abraham, 300,000 More*, a poem set by several composers; *We've a Million in the Field;* and others—but they are of no particular distinction. Two other composers seem to have caught in a few of their songs the militant spirit of the Civil War far better than did Foster: George Frederick Root (1820–1895) and Henry Clay Work (1832–1884). Work, an otherwise undistinguished composer incapable of sustained effort, produced in

---

[3] Both quotations from *The Golden Day*, pp. 32–33.

Marching Through Georgia (1865) a jaunty valedictory to the war, following on Sherman's unopposed march through Georgia to the sea (*MinA*, No. 121). Root, after an early association in Boston with Lowell Mason, enlisted Mason's cooperation in opening his own Musical Institute in New York in 1853 but then moved west to Chicago where, in the 1860's, he was music editor for the important music publishing firm of his brother, Root and Cady. Of his 200-odd songs, almost thirty are Civil War songs, among them *The Battle Cry of Freedom* (1863), *Just Before the Battle, Mother* (1863), and *Tramp! Tramp! Tramp!* (1864). An amusing and revealing footnote to Root's career: having decided to try for some of the popular household-song market occupied by Foster but taking a patronizing attitude toward it, Root sought a pseudonym; in view of the adulation of German musicians at the time, a German translation of his own name was the choice: Friedrich G. Wurzel.

Another kind of song, the glee, was also popular during the period and, like the solo song, was sung both in concerts and at home. A part-song for three or four unaccompanied male voices, the glee (from the Anglo-Saxon *gliw* or *gléo:* "entertainment, music") had been enormously popular in eighteenth-century England. Unpretentious, set to friendly doggerel, glees were written by most of the composers we have mentioned above (though not by Foster) for household use and for male singing societies (glee clubs) usually of amateur musicians.[4] The influence of this tradition is also often seen in the solo songs themselves, which not infrequently end with a three- or four-part "chorus." Male chorus singing in America, which preserved the tradition of the glee long after it had waned in England, was stimulated by the influence of the German *Männerchor;* a German singing society of this name was organized at Philadelphia in 1835, and similar groups were formed elsewhere, particularly in the Midwest where many German immigrants settled.

Pianos and piano music

If any single instrument can be called the Romantic-era instrument par excellence, it is the pianoforte. Indeed, its invention in

---

[4] Two glees by Isaac B. Woodbury (1819–1858) are printed in *MinA*, Nos. 89, 90.

early eighteenth-century Florence by Bartolomeo Cristofori, its gradual supersession of the harpsichord during that century, its triumphant hegemony among keyboard instruments during the nineteenth, and the decline in its importance during the twentieth reflect a whole cycle in Western musical history.[5] Unlike the harpsichord and organ, and more resoundingly than the clavichord, the piano responds directly to the player's touch: not only can it play *piano* and *forte* but all the dynamic levels above, below, and between. Not only is it appropriate for intimate music-making at home but, as enlarged and extended in range during the nineteenth century, it can rival an orchestra in power. Not only can it simulate the sustained, affective melodic curve of a single voice but it can produce dense polyphonic textures. In a period like the Romantic era, which viewed tonal flux as a musical mirror of life itself, whose centers of music were the parlor and the concert hall, and whose musical fabric was a blend of cantabile melody and rich harmony, the piano was the ideal instrument. If the organ was still viewed as the imperious king of instruments, the piano was a responsive and versatile queen.

Manufacture and sale of pianos in America boomed in the nineteenth century. It has been estimated that whereas in 1829 some 2500 instruments were built, or one for every 4800 persons in the nation, in 1851 more than 9000 were produced and sold. By 1860 the figures had risen again, to 21,000 pianos manufactured, one for every 1500 Americans, with sales across the country of thirty pianos every working day.[6] If we take into account the longevity of a sturdy pianoforte and its low depreciation and degeneration rates, even the last figures must be low as a reflection of the number of people who had access to a playable piano on the eve of the Civil War.

American piano builders (many of them immigrants, of course) were among the best in the world, making significant improvements

---

[5] And in social history as well, as has been shown with brilliance and wit by Arthur Loesser in *Men, Women and Pianos: A Social History*.

[6] See Loesser, *op. cit.*, pp. 469, 492, 511. The social necessity of a piano in a proper parlor is graphically shown in the design for an ideal *American Woman's Home* (New York, 1869) suggested by Catherin Beecher and Harriet Beecher Stowe. On their first-floor ground plan, they indicated only two pieces of furniture, both in the Drawing Room: one is a sofa, the other a piano. The design is reproduced in John A. Kouwenhoven, *Made in America* (New York: Doubleday, 1949), p. 77.

in the instrument during the period. From the 1820's through the '40's, Jonas Chickering (1798–1853) of Boston was pre-eminent. Like other manufacturers, he concentrated on the heavy, four-footed "square" (actually rectangular) piano that was most popular in America during the nineteenth century, but he and his sons made wing-shaped "grands" as well, and very grand they were: the virtuoso pianist Gottschalk commented in his journal in June, 1863 on "two mastodons, which [Thomas] Chickering made expressly for me. . . . The tails of these monster pianos measure three feet in width. Their length is ten feet; they have seven and a half octaves." Piano builders were among the German immigrants of the 1830's and later. Among them were William Knabe, who settled in Baltimore in 1837, and, most celebrated of all, Henry Steinway (*recte* Heinrich Steinweg, 1797–1871), who fled the revolutions of 1848, settled in New York in 1850, and with his sons established his own firm in 1853. America's own nineteenth-century dynasty of musicians, the Masons, figured in piano manufacturing through Lowell Mason's son Henry, a co-founder of the Mason & Hamlin Company in 1854. Initially the company built melodeons, the American term for small reed organs (harmoniums), which, because of their small size and price and their popularity mainly in rural America, Loesser has brightly called "the American piano's little country cousin."

The Romantic fondness for the piano, its versatility and its value both as cultural symbol and source of entertainment, resulted in an extraordinary output of piano music from American publishers. Most of it was frankly utilitarian, intended for household use as pleasant diversion and without pretensions to high artistic value, though with overt claims to cultivated gentility. Hundreds of dilettante composers appeared in print as writers of airy trifles; almost anyone, it seems, could gain publication in that era of a seller's market for parlor piano music. The nonentities are legion and need not detain us. One among them might be cited, however, partly because his music so completely typifies the kinds of piano music of the period and partly because of his fantastic prolixity: Charles Grobe.

We know next to nothing about Grobe; having served his purpose as composer of parlor pieces, he was promptly forgotten, all the more quickly since he seems not to have been a performer of any calibre. He is said to have been born in 1817 in Weimar and to have come to the United States in 1839. He was appointed music teacher in Wesleyan Female College (Wilmington) in 1841 and, according to John W. Moore (1807–1889), America's first musical lexicographer, "in 1842 his piano-forte publications became known, which are very numerous."[7] Moore was putting it mildly: Grobe's production of music, apparently all of it for piano, surpasses any other known composer's. By 1847, with *The Battle of Buena Vista* ("a descriptive Fantasie for the Piano"), he was up to Op. 101; six years later, he had trebled his output: the *Gothamite Quick Step* of 1853 is Op. 352. Another half-dozen years, and Grobe's extensive and thorough *New Method for the Piano-Forte* (Philadelphia, 1859) came out as Op. 1100. Practically in the same breath was issued an *Italian Medley*, Op. 1102, on opera airs by Rossini, Donizetti, Verdi, and others. The mid-century fad for the jog-trot rhythm of the polka was reflected in Grobe's *Tommy Polka* of 1860, Op. 1211, and the Civil War naturally elicited from him an "American Medley," *Music of the Union*, Op. 1348 (Boston, 1861). Over six hundred more opus-numbers were yet to come.

Programmatic and patriotic pieces, marches and dances, medleys of popular tunes and opera airs, and above all variation sets were the order of the day, pianistically speaking. When Grobe published in 1854 his *Buds and Blossoms: 60 Sacred Melodies with Brilliant Variations for the Piano* (among the melodies were Mason's *Missionary Hymn*, *Adeste Fideles*, Haydn's "The Heavens are Telling," an air from Rossini's *Stabat Mater*, another from "Mozart's 12th Mass"), the publisher obligingly printed on the back cover a catalogue of representative compositions by Grobe (Figure 4-1). One could write the history of early nineteenth-century America from the 215 titles listed. For our purposes, it is interesting to note that the 68 sets of variations outnumber any other type of piece; next come 52 waltzes, 28 duets (mostly dances: waltzes, polkas, and schottisches), 25 marches and quicksteps, 18 "gallops," 11 polkas, and a few each of "piano songs" and "rondos, etc."

The popularity of piano variations reveals several things about the era. One was its love of the imaginative and inventive: to the ordinary consumer-musician, what could be more delightfully titil-

---

[7] *Appendix to Encyclopaedia of Music* (Boston: Oliver Ditson Company, 1875), article "Grobe." Moore's *Complete Encyclopaedia of Music* (Boston, 1854) was the first comprehensive American music encyclopedia.

CATALOGUE
OF THE
COMPOSITIONS OF CHARLES GROBE,

Published by LEE & WALKER, (Successors to George Willig,) 188 Chestnut St., Philadelphia.

WALTZES.

A Home that I Love	12½
Alpine Rose	12½
L'Amarante	12½
Amusement de Salon	18¾
Barcarole	12½
Charity	12½
Chateau en Espagne	12½
Cologne Water	12½
La Confiance	12½
Court Ball	12½
L'Etoile du Matin	12½
Fillmore	25
Home of my Heart	12½
Snow Flake	12½
The Lone Star	12½
The Meteor	12½
Guadalquiver	12½
Hand in Hand	12½
Kate	12½
Ladies' Smile	12½
Mazeppa, (Grand)	25
Mnemosyne, (Valse Brillante)	12½
Monterey	12½
Night and Morning	12½
O Summer Night	12½
Queen of my Soul	12½
Ole Bull's Dream	12½
Orsini, (from Lucretia Borgia)	12½
Pet, (Call me pet names)	12½
Potpourri, (from the Bohemian Girl)	12½
Ray of Hope	12½
Rose Blanche	12½
Sans Souci	12½
Souvenir de Belleville	12½
Souvenir de Cape May	12½
Spring Flower	12½
'Tis Midnight Hour	12½
Ruby	12½
Don Pasquale	12½
Come to the Old Oak Tree	12½
By the Margin, etc	12½
Snails	12½
The Sky Lark	12½
The Magician	12½
Annie Laurie	12½
Couleur de Rose	12½
Thou art gone from my gaze	12½
True Love	12½
El Cabalera	12½
Metamores	12½
United States Grand Waltz	25
Sophie Waltz, (by Strauss)	12½

GALLOPS.

Banisher of Sadness	12½
Fausta	12½
Flying Cloud	12½
Homage aux Belles du Philadelphia	25
Hortensia	12½
Ice Cream	12½
Les plus beau de mes jours, etc	12½
Lucy Neal	12½
Maritana	12½
Pine Apple	12½
Ray of Joy	12½
Sentinel	12½
Strawberry	12½
Unassuming	12½
Ever be Happy	12½
Comet's Flight	12½
Short and Sweet	12½
Orlando	12½

DANCES, etc.

Mirror Dance	38
Les Nymphes	25

MARCHES AND QUICKSTEPS.

Adieu et Retour	12½
Brewer of Preston Grand March	12½
Capuletti i Montecchi	25
Captain Walker's Quickstep	12½
Clay Club Quickstep	12½
General Taylor's Grand March	12½
Les Amazones	12½
Lucrezia Borgia	12½
Old Rough and Ready Quickstep	12½
Philadelphia Gals' Quickstep	12½
Alpine Horn	25
Cuba	12½
March from Lucia	12½
Pestal Quickstep	12½
Spider and the Fly	12½
Virginia Rosebud Quickstep	12½
Mr. and Mrs. Jones's Quickstep	12½
March from "Il Crociato"	12½
Cuckoo Quickstep	12½
Swiss March	12½
Sixty Miles an Hour Quickstep	12½
Avant Courier Quickstep	12½
Going Ahead Quickstep	12½
Alpine March	12½
Gothamite Quickstep	25

DUETS FOR TWO PERFORMERS.

Flow gently, sweet Afton	12½
Venetian Gallop	12½
Louisville Gallop	12½
Elfin Waltz	12½
La Belle du Sud	12½
Baden-Baden Polka	12½
Affection Waltz	12½
Grand March from the Bohemian Girl	12½
Flower of America	12½
Hohnstock Polka	25
Mollie's Dream Waltz	25
Morning Star Waltz	25
Evening Star Waltz	25
National Schottisch	25
Redowa Waltz	25
Sounds from Home	25
Henriette Polka	25
Souvenir of Germany, (Schottisch)	25
Emerald Waltz	25
Gipsy March	25
Pet Waltz	25
Jenny Lind Polka	12½
Gertrude's Dream Waltz	12½
'Tis Midnight Hour, (Waltz)	12½
Les Vents, (No. 1, 2, 3, 4,) each	12½
London Polka Quadrilles	50
March Triumphale	25
Le Retour des Heroes	25

POLKAS.

Fidelia	12½
Lucilla	12½
La Mode	12½
My Heart and Lute	12½
Saratoga	12½
Rose Atherton	12½
Bona Fide	12½
Ne Plus Ultra	25
The White Violet	25
Fitzgerald's Gift Polka	25
Leap Year Polka	25

PIANO SONGS.

The heart, the heart, oh, let it be	12½
Kindred Hearts	25
Look how the Stars like jewels glisten	25
The Sabbath Bells	25

VARIATIONS.

L'Amitie, (La Fille du Regiment)	38
Amusement des Amateurs	50
Bachelor Polka	50
Les Bords du Hudson	50
Charity	38
Evening Song to the Virgin	38
Les Charmes de l'Amitie	38
Chasse d'Amour	50
Clochette Polka	62½
Dearest Mae	25
I dream of my Fatherland	38
The False Friend	38
Flow gently, sweet Afton	38
O Susanna	25
Oh! would I were a Boy again	50
Ravel Polka	50
Old Uncle Ned	25
Mary Blane	25
Rosa Lee	25
Virginia Rose Bud	25
Gipsy's Wild Chant	50
Hope and the Rose	50
Leonore	25
Les Ideals	50
Song of the Regiment	38
Salut a Philadelphie	25
Les Amoureux	25
Serenade March	38
Les Troubadours	62½
La Solitude	38
What's a' the Steer Kimmer	25
Come, ye Disconsolate	38
From Greenland's Icy Mountains	38
Jerusalem, my Happy Home	38
Henriette Polka	50
A Life on the Ocean Wave	50
Salut a Baltimore	25
La Liberte	50
Child of the Regiment	38
Song of the Drum	38
Rataplan	38
By the Sad Sea Waves	38
Love Not	25
Les Fleurs du Plaisir	50
Columbia the Gem of the Ocean	62½
Jenny Lind Polka	50
Vesper Hymn	38
I would not live alway	38
Strike the Cymbal	38
Peace, troubled Soul	38
Far, far, o'er Hill and Dell	38
Fading, still Fading	38
Messenger Bird	38
Widow of Nain	38
Adeste Fideles	38
There is nothing true but Heaven	38
Sicilian Hymn	38
Pleyel's German Hymn	38
Pilgrim Fathers	38
Prayer from Moses	38
Prayer from Zampa	38
Prayer from Tancredi	38
Watchman, tell us of the Night	38
Faith .... 38 Hope	38
Washington's March	38
Maretzek's Rondo Finale	50
Yes, I Remember, (answer to Ben Bolt)	38
Wings of a Dove	38

RONDOS, etc.

Bellone, (Polonaise á la Militaire)	38
Diane, (Rondeau de Chasse)	25
El Sinsonte de Camagne	25
La Tendresse, (Rondoletto)	12½
The Talisman, (Rondo Militaire)	50
Love's Influence, (Rondo)	25
Potpourri en forme de Rondeau	25

☞ Just Published, 1st and 2d Nos. of GROBE'S WORLD OF MUSIC, an unsurpassable Collection of Music, consisting of 100 of the most charming Melodies ever offered to the Musical World. ☜

☞ LEE & WALKER'S Publications may be had of the principal Music Dealers in N. York, Boston, Baltimore, N. Orleans, Cincinnati, St. Louis, Louisville, Charleston, Savannah, Pittsburg, Detroit, Chicago, and other Cities of the U. States and Canada.

FIGURE 4-1. A list of piano works (incomplete) by Charles Grobe, from the back cover of his *Wings of a Dove* (1854).

lating than to hear, through a shower of fanciful passagework, the hidden outlines of a familiar tune? what more suggestive of a composer's invention—tested, as it is in variation sets, against the given material of a theme? Another, closely related, was its love of the improvisatory in performance. The concert pianist at that time was still expected as a matter of course to improvise, sometimes on familiar tunes, often on themes called out to him by the audience. Almost by definition, such improvisations took the form of variations; and if not of variations, then of a "fantasy," less formally strict than variations but no less a matter of creating new shapes out of old. In a survey of New York piano concerts between 1849 and 1865, one researcher found that one out of every three works presented was a fantasy on popular themes.[8] Variations and fantasies were also the simplest and most foolproof substructure for virtuoso scaffolding, since neither form nor thematic content was problematic and all attention could be paid by both performer and listener to the treatment of the musical material. It is against this background that some comments made by Gottschalk toward the end of his career about the improved taste of American audiences must be read. He noted in his journal for December 8, 1864 that "at the time of my first return from Europe [1853] I was constantly deploring the want of public interest for pieces purely sentimental; the public listened with indifference; in order to arouse it, it became necessary to astound it; grand movements, tours de force, and noise had alone the privilege in piano music." Now, however, audiences were willing to listen to "pieces purely sentimental"—pieces which, in Gottschalk's terms, had real musical content and "feeling," not just spectacular fantasies and pyrotechnical variations.

If Grobe can represent for us the legion of minor composers of piano music for the household market, a few others of the period before the Civil War emerge as composers with higher aspirations and more carefully nurtured gifts. Most notable are Richard Hoffman, William Mason, and Gottschalk.

Hoffman (1831–1909) came to America from his native England as a boy of sixteen, having already studied with a constellation of German pianists, among them Liszt and Leopold de Meyer. (The latter, renowned as the "Lion of Pianists," had been, in 1845–47, the first great European pianist to tour in America.) Hoffman settled in New York, where beside teaching and composing he played concerts. Competent and agreeable ("a perfect musician, a distinguished and modest man . . . an artist and a *gentleman*," wrote Gottschalk with unusual generosity) Hoffman wrote a piano music of flowery grace through almost one hundred opus-numbers.

[8] Andrew C. Minor, "Piano Concerts in New York City 1849–1865" (unpublished Master's thesis, University of Michigan, 1947), p. 475.

La Gazelle (1858?) was a favorite, with its Lisztian arabesques (Example 4-6) and its fashionable French title evoking the image of Chopin.

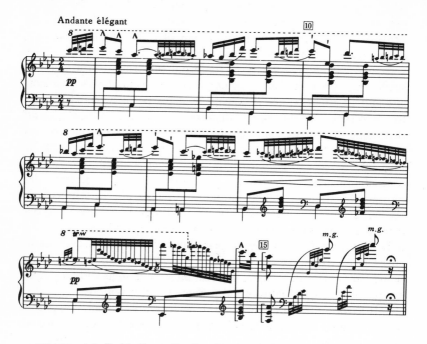

EXAMPLE 4-6. R. Hoffman, *La Gazelle* (Mainz, New York: B. Schott's Söhnen, [ca. 1858]), measures 8–15.

William Mason (1829–1908), the third son of Lowell Mason, was also a pupil of Liszt, during the last of his five years' study in Germany (1849–1854). His main role, like that of his father, was more that of tastemaker and teacher than composer; he was also a most competent performer. He concertized in the northern states from the east coast to Chicago, offering solo piano recitals without the usual interpolations of song from an "assisting vocalist"; he played music of high calibre, if almost exclusively Germanic, although his recital-closing improvisations might, because of audience demand, have to be based on *Yankee Doodle* counterpointed with *Old Hundred;* he formed an influential chamber music group and for thirteen years offered New York City its finest chamber music; he was also a renowned piano teacher. His own music seems proper but bloodless, without even Hoffman's airy Lisztian flair, although Liszt politely called Mason's *Amitié pour Amitié* (Example 4-7) "a charming little piece," his *Etude de concert*, Op. 9, and *Valse caprice*, Op. 17, "distinguished in style and of good effect."[9] Chopin's *Berceuse*, Op. 57, is certainly the model for Mason's *Lullaby* of 1857 (*MinA*, No. 126); the reference to *Three Blind Mice* is surely unconscious and unintended.

EXAMPLE 4-7. W. Mason, *Amitié pour Amitié* (2nd ed.; Boston: N. Richardson, 1854), measures 1–8.

Without question the most colorful personality, the most articulate intelligence, the most talented performer, and the most provocative composer among the mid-nineteenth-century pianists was Louis Moreau Gottschalk (1829–1869). Born in the racial and ethnic melting-pot of New Orleans, Gottschalk's lineage was itself cosmopolitan: his father was a cultivated Englishman educated in Germany; his mother was of upper-class French descent. For thirteen years, Gottschalk lived in the Vieux Carré quarter, hearing among other kinds of music that of the many Negroes and Latin Americans in the southern trade center. In 1842 he was sent to Paris to study, not returning to America until 1853 as a renowned virtuoso and keyboard composer. From then on his life was virtually one long concert tour, all over the United States, up into Canada, down to the

[9] William Mason, *Memories of a Musical Life* (New York: The Century Co., 1902), pp. 88, 294.

West Indies, Panama, Mexico, and South America, where he died at Rio de Janeiro, forty years of age.

Even as a youth in Paris, Gottschalk was praised by Chopin and Berlioz, his playing spoken of in the same breath with that of Liszt and Thalberg. He became the darling of the Paris salons not only for his virtuosity but for his early compositions, which were heard as exotic mélanges of Afro-Caribbean rhythms and Creole melodies, with a Chopinesque overlay of virtuoso passagework. According to a review by Berlioz of a concert in 1851, "everybody in Europe now knows [Gottschalk's] *Bamboula, Le Bananier, Le Mancenillier, La Savane,* and twenty other ingenious fantasies in which the non-chalant grace of tropical melody assuage so agreeably our restless and insatiable passion for novelty."[10] Back in the Americas and embarked on a career as traveling virtuoso, Gottschalk became a sort of living player-piano: "I have become stupid with it. I have the appearance of an automaton under the influence of a voltaic pile. My fingers move on the keyboard with feverish heat. . . . The sight of a piano sets my hair on end." He had just finished his last tour of 1862: "I have given eighty-five concerts in four months and a half. I have traveled fifteen thousand miles by train. At St. Louis I gave seven concerts in six days; at Chicago, five in four days. A few more weeks in this way and I would have become an idiot."[11] In an age of virtuosity, Gottschalk was the virtuoso incarnate. He has also rightfully been called "our first matinee idol": the young American music student Amy Fay lamented in Berlin upon hearing of his death, "The infatuation that I and 999,999 other American girls once felt for him, still lingers in my breast."[12]

Like Chopin and other pianist-composers of the era, Gottschalk saw in print little of his music except solo piano compositions, of which there are just over one hundred. He composed in addition some songs, a few orchestral works, and purportedly three operas. The pieces mentioned by Berlioz are among the earliest and most interesting of the piano compositions, "New Orleans" pieces

---

[10] Quoted in Behrend (ed.), *Notes of a Pianist,* p. xxii.

[11] Both quotations from *Notes of a Pianist,* p. 102. Gottschalk's journal, written between 1857 and 1868, is a fascinating, kaleidoscopic account of his travels in the West Indies, the United States, and Latin America.

[12] *Music-Study in Germany* (New York: The Macmillan Company, 1897), p. 42. It was Irving Lowens who first equated the idolatry of Gottschalk with that of later stage and screen stars; see *MMEA,* pp. 223–33.

published in France and advertised there as the work of "Gott-schalk de la Louisiane." Based mostly on Negro and Creole tunes, they tend to begin with marvelously fresh, strong ideas (see Example 4-8) which before long are overwhelmed by showers of

EXAMPLE 4-8. L. M. Gottschalk, early "New Orleans" pieces. (a) *Bamboula*, Op. 2, measures 1–7. (b) *Le Bananier*, Op. 5, measures 1–8.

scales, arpeggios, passagework of all kinds. Youthful, exuberant, and immensely promising, they are nevertheless overlong and lacking in tonal or formal interest, as the genuinely gifted fledgling composer gives way to the virtuoso prodigy. The slightly later *Le Banjo*, Op. 15 (of uncertain date, but before 1852, when *Banjo Second* was written), probably has in common with Stephen Foster's *Camptown Races* (1850; see Example 5-8) a source in American Negro song. (Gottschalk could hardly have known Foster's minstrel-show song, since he was in Paris when it was published, and composed *Le Banjo* before his return to America.) Full of ingenious strumming, *Le Banjo* (*MinA*, No. 125) is one of Gottschalk's best works, although even an enthusiast like pianist John Kirkpatrick admits to its "characteristic redundance and tonal monotony."[13]

[13] "Observations on 4 volumes and supplement of the works of Louis Moreau Gottschalk" (typescript; New York Public Library's Music Division).

Gottschalk mined other folk and popular song veins as he toured through Spain (*La jota aragonesa*, Op. 14), the West Indies (*Souvenir de Porto Rico*, Op. 31; *Souvenir de Havanne*, Op. 39), and South America (*Grande Fantaisie sur l'hymn national brésilien*, Op. 69). Only occasionally, as in *Souvenir de Porto Rico* ("Marche des Gibaros"), does formal control restrain technical exuberance; however, in that piece of 1859 based on a native Christmas song (Example 4-9), Gottschalk achieves a minor masterpiece with the arching dynamic curve, waxing and waning, of a "patrol" piece and the strong syncopations of Afro-Caribbean dance music (Example 4-10). Perhaps Gottschalk's greatest *pastiche* on folk and popular source-materials, and certainly the noisiest, was *L'Union*, Op. 48 (1862), a grand "paraphrase de concert sur les airs nationaux" (*Yankee Doodle, The Star-Spangled Banner, Hail, Columbia!* and some trumpet calls) written at the height of the Civil War and received in Philadelphia, according to the composer's journal, with "unheard-of enthusiasm . . . recalls, encores, hurrahs, etc.!"

EXAMPLE 4-9. Puerto Rican *aguinaldo*, beginning, and L. M. Gottschalk, *Souvenir de Porto Rico* (Mainz: B. Schott's Söhnen, 1859), measures 17–20.

EXAMPLE 4-10. L. M. Gottschalk, *Souvenir de Porto Rico*, climax (measures 189–193).

Another side of Gottschalk's art was that of the "purely senti-mental" piece, as he called it, the genre piece of meditative and "poetic" reflection. Among the most carefully worked of these are *Ricordati*, "méditation," Op. 26, a Chopinesque nocturne; *The Last Hope*, "méditation religieuse," Op. 16 (1854), Gottschalk's monu-ment to pious sentimentality, his most notoriously successful tear-jerker, but withal a shrewdly contrived series of daringly chromatic introductions to an indestructible arc of songful melody; *Berceuse*, Op. 47 (before 1863), based on a French folk song, *Fais dodo, mon bébé*; and *Suis-moi*, Op. 45 (1862). *The Dying Poet* (1864), one of "some contraband pieces that are to be published under the aegis of a borrowed paternity" (as Gottschalk archly described his pseudo-nym, "Seven Octaves"), and *Morte! Lamentation* (1868–69), which had, said Gottschalk, "un succès de larmes," were famous pieces in the vein of *The Last Hope*.

Gottschalk noted in his journal one night in 1865 that his had been a life of "playing the piano, of having composed two or three hundred pieces, of having given seven or eight thousand concerts, of having given to the poor one hundred or one hundred and fifty thousand dollars, [and] of having been knighted twice." The remark was one of Romantic hyperbole, but so were Gottschalk's personal-ity and his music.

Orchestras and orchestral music

The Romantics loved the orchestra. Convinced that instru-mental music in general was the purest, most sublime music, they conceived of the orchestra as a kind of super-instrument. And seek-ing an ever-broader coloristic and expressive spectrum, they en-larged it from a smallish ensemble of one or two dozen players into a giant symphonic machine of more than a hundred. If, during the era, the organ was king of instruments, the piano the queen, the orchestra was emperor.

One of the most characteristic trends in American music since the mid-nineteenth century has been the proliferation of independent symphony orchestras. Whereas in Europe such orchestras have hardly existed apart from opera houses (although a few, typically state-subsidized, are now virtually independent), here the symphony orchestra has tended to develop as an independent entity, reflecting our penchant for concerts rather than opera. The American notion of a "permanent" orchestra, and one supported by public subscriptions and box-office receipts, has been a by-product of the rise of public concerts and a mass audience that I have discussed in an earlier chapter. Two decades before the Civil War, the first "permanent" orchestra still in existence today, the New York Philharmonic, was founded. By the mid-1960's, the American Symphony Orchestra League counted some 1400 orchestras in the U.S.A. and Canada. The vast majority of these were community, college, school, or "youth" orchestras (all non-professional groups) but in the United States alone there were no less than twenty-six major, permanent, professional orchestras with annual budgets exceeding $100,000.[14]

The beginnings of this astonishing development go back to the early nineteenth century, when Gottlieb Graupner, who had been one of the musicians in Salomon's London orchestra during the famous visit of Haydn in 1791, organized a group of Boston Instrumentalists into a "Philo-Harmonic Society" to meet informally and play through symphonies of Haydn and others. Notices of rehearsals appeared regularly in the semi-weekly Boston newspapers from October 4, 1809, and the society soon began playing for the public. John Rowe Parker, editor of the first American music periodical, *The Euterpeiad, or Musical Intelligencer* (issued April, 1820–March, 1822), signalized the historic importance of Graupner's instrumental organization (and the other society Graupner helped to found) when he wrote, "Until the formation of the Philo-Harmonic for instrumental, and the institution of the Haydn and Handel Societies, for vocal performances, regular concerts have never succeeded in this metropolis" (*Euterpeiad*, April 8, 1820). They did not succeed well enough, apparently, for the Philo-Harmonic Society of Boston gave its last concert late in 1824.

Meanwhile, in Philadelphia a Musical Fund Society was organized in 1820 by Benjamin Carr and others; it was active as a choral-orchestral organization up to 1857, and more sporadically to the present. In the nearby Moravian center of Bethlehem a Philharmonic Society was founded, also in 1820, which flourished until about 1839. And in 1842 a group of musicians led by Ureli Corelli

---

[14] Ulysses Kay, in cooperation with the American Symphony Orchestra League, *1964–65 Orchestral Program Survey* (New York: Broadcast Music, Inc., 1965).

Hill (1802–1875), Henry Christian Timm (1811–1892), and William Scharfenberg (1819–1895) founded the New York Philharmonic Society. Numbering about fifty-five players, give or take the few who found it impossible to give up other jobs to play in the three concerts of the first season (four in each season thereafter through 1858), the orchestra initially had no single conductor; six of the musicians shared the duties. From the 500-seat hall of the Apollo Rooms on Broadway below Canal Street, the orchestra graduated to Niblo's Theatre (Broadway and Prince Street), then in 1856 further uptown to the elegant Academy of Music at 14th Street and Irving Place.

That our first permanent orchestra should have been established in New York City reflected an important social development: New York's skyrocket rise, stimulated especially by the opening of the Erie Canal in 1825, to supremacy as the nation's first port, largest city, and principal commercial center. As such it became also the nation's center of those performing arts which rested on a foundation of mass-audience support. New York's pre-eminence as a musical performance center already by the mid-nineteenth century is confirmed by the fact that not until 1881 would the second permanent American symphony orchestra, the Boston Symphony, be established.

Three other orchestras heard in pre-Civil War America should be cited briefly here for their catalytic influence on American music. One was the Germania Musical Society, a group of twenty-five young musicians who left Berlin in May of 1848, heading for the United States "in order to further in the hearts of this politically free people the love of the fine art of music through performance of the greatest German composers."[15] The Germanians' first concerts in New York led to others elsewhere, and the well-trained, well-balanced ensemble was heard, before its dissolution in 1854 (all its members by then American citizens), in many American and Canadian cities from Richmond to Minneapolis and from Boston to St. Louis (where one young woman, hearing Beethoven's Second Symphony for the first time, remarked, "Well, ain't that funny music!"). American attitudes as to the "standard repertory" of

15 H. L. Albrecht, *Skizzen aus dem Leben der Musik-Gesellschaft Germania* (Philadelphia, 1869), trans. H. Earle Johnson, "The Germania Musical Society," *MQ*, XXXIX (1953), p. 75.

orchestral music were strongly shaped by this group's concentration on Germanic works from Haydn to Mendelssohn.

Another, briefer symphonic visitor was the orchestra brought from London to New York for one year by the French conductor Louis Antoine Jullien (1812–1860). "A splendid, bold, and dazzlingly successful humbug," wrote the New York *Courier and Enquirer*. To his forty-piece orchestra Jullien added sixty local musicians (among them two young violinists named George Bristow and Theodore Thomas, of whom more shortly); on August 29, 1853, after a strenuous advertising campaign, he initiated a series of "Monster Concerts for the Masses" at Castle Garden. The *Courier and Enquirer* had to admit that "the discipline of his orchestra is marvelous." *The New York Clipper* was not so charitable; that lively precursor of *Variety* and *Billboard*, which proclaimed itself "A Weekly Sporting Paper, devoted to the Ring, the Turf, Yachting, Pedestrianism, Cricket, Rowing Matches, Theatricals, Music, and the various sports of the Old World and the New," took up the cudgel against "these 'highfalutin' gimcracks" in its issue of September 3:

> There were not quite 3,000 persons in the building, and perhaps not quite 2,500 who paid for their tickets [at 50¢ each]. . . . It is now more difficult to humbug us than it was a few years since. . . . With encouragement, America can produce musical wonders as well as reaping machines; an American Forrest [Edwin Forrest (1806–1872), American actor] as well as American Clippers. . . . Several European celebrities have lately returned to their homes, not at all pleased with our reception of them. Stand fast, Americans! encourage those who are with us. . . . Monster concerts for the masses, indeed!

The chauvinist tone is of interest: here spoke the vernacular tradition of American music, weary of the European monopoly over American cultivated taste. In its next issue (September 10) the *Clipper* chuckled over the "but middling success" of Jullien's nightly concerts, and on September 17, headlining "A Failure in New York" for Jullien, it urged its readers to "encourage our own musicians, and endeavor to do away with the puffing system adopted by foreign professionals." Jullien's concerts had not in fact failed, but he got the message: he began to include some works by American-born composers on his programs, among them Bristow and William Fry.

It was the first recognition that American composers of symphonic music had had.

A notable graduate of Jullien's orchestra and of nine years' playing experience with the New York Philharmonic (1854–63) was Theodore Thomas (1835–1905). His potential as a director was recognized when he was a violinist in the group organized by William Mason in 1855 for chamber music evenings: Mason conceded in his *Memories* that Thomas's "was the dominating influence, felt and acknowledged by us all." After some tentative beginnings in 1862 and 1863, Thomas initiated a long and brilliant career as conductor of his own orchestra late in 1864. An astute impresario and a canny program-builder, Thomas knew how to create and hold an audience with programs that might be called crescent-shaped, with the heaviest fare in the center; thus he might flank orchestral movements by Beethoven, Schubert, Mendelssohn, even the radical Wagner, with simpler music: the waltzes of Strauss, the Bach-Gounod *Ave Maria*, and other crowd-pleasers. It was an original format, which gave up the old reliance on maintaining interest by a potpourri of instrumental and vocal works, and one destined to become a stereotype. Characteristic is the following program[16] from one of Thomas's Summer Night Concerts in New York's Central Park Garden (August 7, 1868):

Coronation March	Johann Strauss
Overture to *Die Heimkehre aus der Fremde*	Mendelssohn
Waltz from *Masaniello*	Auber

Intermission

Overture to *Tannhäuser*	Wagner
2nd movement, Symphony No. 8	Beethoven
3rd movement (Scherzo), Symphony No. 7 (C major)	Schubert

Intermission

Grand March for the Schiller Centenary	Meyerbeer
Overture to *Mignon*	Thomas

[16] Adapted from Rose Fay Thomas, *Memoirs of Theodore Thomas* (New York: Moffett, Yard and Company, 1911), p. 49. Later programs of Thomas's Orchestra had fewer "light" works and included complete symphonies; some were one-man exhibitions of works by a single composer.

Ave Maria	Bach-Gounod
Waltz, "Die Sphärenklänge"	Johann Strauss
Turkish March [arranged from Piano Sonata, K. 311?]	Mozart

Between 1869 and 1878 the Thomas Orchestra made regular, lengthy tours through the East and the Middle West as far as Chicago, with a roster of about fifty players.[17] Both in New York and throughout the country, its influence on standards of performance and on ideas of a standard orchestral repertory was immense. The modern symphonic ideal, according to which dozens of players submit through careful rehearsal to the rigorous, not to say autocratic, direction of a conductor in the interests of polished perfection, was Thomas's ideal. His ideas on repertory were inevitably governed by an Austro-Germanic bias; nevertheless, he occasionally played music by American composers. They were very few, however; Thomas had high standards and, as he put it, "I do not believe in playing inferior works merely because they are American" (*Memoirs*, p. 67).

Thomas became conductor of the New York Philharmonic in 1877, resigned for an abortive year as first head of the Cincinnati College of Music, resumed the Philharmonic directorship in 1880, then moved permanently to Chicago in 1891 to become conductor of the newly established Chicago Symphony Orchestra. For the last half of the nineteenth century he was the acknowledged master of the symphony orchestra, the first American virtuoso conductor.

Orchestral Music

What about American orchestral music, as opposed to American orchestras, in the period up to the Civil War?

With only a few orchestras in the land, and with orchestral music, as distinct from music for solo instruments or small chamber groups, identified mainly with European composers and conductors, it is not surprising that American composers produced comparatively little symphonic music. Nevertheless, a few composers stand out as our first symphonists.

"The Beethoven of America" is what Parker's *Euterpeiad* called

---

[17] When it played the opening concert of Harvard's Sanders Theatre, November 21, 1876, the make-up of the orchestra was eight first violins, eight second violins, four violas, four 'cellos, and four basses, plus woodwinds and brasses in pairs, according to *Dwight's Journal of Music*, XXXVI (March 3, 1877), p. 398. Presumably there was a percussionist as well.

Anthony Philip Heinrich (1781–1861) in its issue of April 13, 1822. Born in Bohemia, heir to a fortune which quickly dissolved in his hands, Heinrich came to the United States perhaps as early as 1810. He was a merchant at Philadelphia for a few years, acted as volunteer director of music at the Southwark Theatre, then in the fall of 1817 traveled via Pittsburgh to the "solitary wilds and primeval forests of Kentucky," as he put it. Here he immediately organized a benefit concert for himself, playing the violin and the piano and directing the "full band" in a "Simfonia con Minuetto" by Beethoven —perhaps the First Symphony, and certainly an extraordinary work to present at Lexington, Kentucky in November, 1817.

Heinrich began composing at about that time; to a pathetic plea for funds written late in his life (1856) he added this postscript:

> P.S. The Composer did not commence writing music until verging upon the fortieth year of his age, when dwelling by chance in the then solitary wilds and primeval forests of Kentucky. It was from a mere accident that music ever became his profession. . . .[18]

Once embarked on composition, however, Heinrich poured out songs; piano works; marches and dances; choral music; and orchestral overtures, fantasies, concertos, and symphonies. His "opera prima," published at Philadelphia in 1820, was titled *The Dawning of Music in Kentucky, or The Pleasures of Harmony in the Solitudes of Nature*, a huge collection described by the composer as including "*Songs* and *Airs* for the *Voice* and *Pianoforte, Waltzes, Cotillions, Minuets, Polonaises, Marches, Variations* with some pieces of a national character adapted for the Piano Forte and also calculated for the lovers of the Violin" (preface reprinted in *ACS*, pp. 42–43). To it he added a companion collection of songs and instrumental pieces, *The Western Minstrel* (also 1820). The two anthologies contain Romantic programmatism and virtuoso technical demands of the most extravagant sort. Heinrich's was an expansive and mercurial muse: he himself characterized his music as "full of strange ideal somersets and capriccios"; the pontifical J. S. Dwight of Boston said, "bewildering . . . wild and complicated."[19]

---

[18] Heinrich, manuscript scrapbook, Library of Congress, p. 836.

[19] *The Harbinger*, July 4, 1846. Dwight's lengthy review of a 65th birthday concert for Heinrich, almost a one-man show, is reprinted in full in W. T. Upton, *Anthony Philip Heinrich* (New York: Columbia University Press, 1939), pp. 199–201.

The major part of Heinrich's orchestral music consists of descriptive symphonies in several elaborately titled movements or one-movement programmatic fantasies divided into contrasting sections. Their subjects are those of a hyper-enthusiastic, Romantic newcomer to America: Indian lore (*Pushmataha, a Venerable Chief of a Western Tribe of Indians*, 1831; *Manitou Mysteries; or, The Voice of the Great Spirit. Gran sinfonia misteriosa indiana*, before 1845); American history (*The Treaty of William Penn with the Indians. Concerto grosso. An American national dramatic divertissement, for a full orchestra, comprising successively 6 different characteristic movements, united in one* . . . , 1834, revised 1847; *Der Felsen von Plymouth; oder, Die Landung der Pilger Väter in Neu-England*); the American landscape (*The War of the Elements and the Thundering of Niagara. Capriccio grande for a full orchestra*, before 1845); hero-worship (*Schiller. Grande sinfonia dramatica*, in five movements composed at various times between 1820 and 1857; *The Tomb of Genius: To the Memory of Mendelssohn-Bartholdy. Sinfonia sacra, for grande orchestra*, after 1847 and before 1857; *To the Spirit of Beethoven*, in fourteen "tableaux," before 1845); and finally, patriotic encomiums (*The Jubilee. A Grand national song of triumph,* for orchestra and chorus, 1840).

The style of these extraordinary orchestral outbursts is indeed one of "strange somersets and capriccios," mingling simple dance tunes (especially folkish Ländler types) and elaborately chromatic melodies; crystal-clear Classic-era harmonies and wildly modulating passages; basically homophonic, diatonic textures and a profusion of decorative chromatic counterpoints (most often solo woodwind voices over a background of strings); predictable, periodic phrase forms and surprising extensions (or, instead of the latter, the opposite: unexpected grand pauses of dead silence). For a latecomer to composition, Heinrich had a remarkable ear for orchestral color and an expansive imagination that led him to write for unusual instruments as well as the conventional orchestral core. The third ("The Adagio") of the four movements of the symphonically-scaled *Manitou Mysteries* includes extensive and effective use of pizzicato. Among the instruments in the very large orchestra required for *The Indian War Council* is a "harmonicon" or "glassichord," a mechanized set of musical glasses invented by Benjamin Franklin (see *AM*, pp. 89–92). *Pushmataha* is a fourteen-minute fantasy for thirty-three different orchestral voices including piccolo, basset horn, serpent, contrabassoon, three kinds of drums, triangle, cymbals, and tambourine as well as the normal full orchestra. For reasons unclear (but possibly relating to the first public Independence Day celebration at which S. F. Smith's *America* was sung to the tune: July 4, 1831), this paean to a mighty Indian chief culminates with a majestic and characteristically chromaticized quotation of *God Save the King* (Example 4-11).

EXAMPLE 4-11. A. Heinrich, *Pushmataha* (1831), measures 460–65 (reduced from the Library of Congress copy of the orchestral score).

It might be expected that the intense musical life of the German-speaking communities in Pennsylvania would have inspired some orchestral music, but the Moravians seem for the most part to have been content with European scores, and thus far we know of no orchestral productions of the other sects. Surprisingly, one of the earliest known American orchestral works, a Symphony in D in two movements, dated 1831, by a William C. Peters, was discovered in 1960 at the Harmony Society of Ambridge, beyond Pittsburgh in western Pennsylvania, which was hardly more than a frontier settlement in 1831. For Philadelphia's Musical Fund Society and Bethlehem's Philharmonic Society a few orchestral works seem to have been written by Americans. Charles Hommann (ca. 1800–ca. 1850) contributed an orchestral overture (ca. 1840) to the former society and dedicated to the Bethlehem organization a Symphony in E-flat (ca. 1840); both are well-crafted, rather Schubertian works. Donald McCorkle has discovered another overture by Hommann at Nazareth.

George F. Bristow (1825–1898) and William H. Fry (1813–1864) were the best-known mid-century composers of orchestral music in New York. Bristow was the better trained, a professional violinist and conductor who composed six symphonies in a polished Mendelssohnian style, among them a fine Symphony in F-sharp minor, Op. 26 (performed by the New York Philharmonic under Jullien as guest conductor in 1856) and a more lengthy Symphonie for Grand Orchestra, "The Pioneer" (Arcadian), Op. 49 (1874), which includes perhaps the first use of an American Indian melody in a work of art-music. The opera *Rip Van Winkle* (1855) and cantatas *The Great Republic* (1879) and *Niagara* (1898) have strong overtures. Fry, famous as a noisy champion of American composers amidst the deluge of Europeans just before the Civil War, composed four symphonies, *Santa Claus*, *The Breaking Heart*, *Childe Harold*, and *A Day in the Country*, all performed by Jullien's orchestra in 1853–54 and all provided with interminable programs which explain, but do not make coherent, the naive tone-painting and narrative forms of the works. An *Overture to "Macbeth"* (1862) reminiscent of Auber is well-scored and never dull.

The Romantic tendency to gigantism, exemplified by Jullien's "monster concerts," is suggested also by two in which Gottschalk was involved in Cuba and Rio de Janeiro. For a concert at Havana early in 1860 Gottschalk composed three works: a cantata, *Triumphal Hymn* (the music, long thought lost, is now in the New York Public Library), and a *Grand March*. His orchestra, he reported in his journal, numbered 650, plus 87 choristers, 15 solo singers, 50 drums, and 80 trumpets—"that is to say, nearly nine hundred persons bellowing and blowing to see who could scream the loudest." And at Rio in 1869, for a concert which included the

Andante of his symphony *A Night in the Tropics,* Gottschalk dreamed of "eight hundred performers and eighty drums to lead."[20] He got about 650, made up from bands of the Brazilian National Guard, the Imperial Navy, the Army, the War Arsenal, and from three orchestras assembled for the occasion (November 11, 1869). *A Night in the Tropics,* which may or may not be complete with the Andante and Finale movements that are extant, is a colorful work in the French tradition of Berlioz; John Kirkpatrick's "Observations . . ." cite its "poetic atmosphere" and "surprising expansion" of line. The brilliant, brassy Finale, which calls for separate sections of cornets, trumpets, trombones, and euphoniums, with each section divided, is overwhelming. Another symphony, in one movement, has recently been rediscovered: the "Montevideo" Symphony (1868?), subtitled "Romantique."

Opera

Of all the kinds of art music of the American cultivated tradition between 1820 and the Civil War, the least significant, and the least widely heard, was opera. The ballad opera of the eighteenth century, or at least plays with music, continued in unbroken tradition through the period. Its function, however, changed with the introduction of other kinds of music and musical theater, which tended to keep the musical play a vernacular entertainment without any growing pretensions to becoming "fine art." By the 1860's the ballad opera as such was virtually non-existent, except in transformations like *The Black Crook* (1866) (an extravagant mixture of Frenchy ballet and Germanic melodrama, to an American variation on the plot of Weber's *Der Freischütz*) or parodies like those of the minstrel shows at Buckley's Ethiopian Opera House in New York. European operas gained a foothold in America during the period, however, and the first "grand operas" by American composers were produced.

By far the most lively operatic center was New Orleans, where a cultivated French contingent of the cosmopolitan population had maintained support for French opera from 1796, when the theater

[20] Octavia Hensel, *Life and Letters of Louis Moreau Gottschalk* (Boston: Oliver Ditson Company, 1870), p. 174.

on St. Peter Street produced Grétry's *Sylvain*. In the 1805–6 season alone, the St. Peter Theatre produced sixteen different operas by nine composers, among them Monsigny, Grétry, Dalayrac, Boieldieu, Méhul, and Paisiello, and this for a town of some twelve thousand people. With the establishment of a permanent opera company at the Orleans Theater in 1810, New Orleans was unrivalled as operatic center of America. Northern cities—Boston, Philadelphia, Baltimore —heard their first grand opera when the New Orleans company toured during the seven summers from 1827 to 1833; and New York admitted that the southern troupe was "fully equal to that we imported from foreigners," referring to Manuel García's Spanish company, which had given New York its first foreign-language opera in 1825.[21]

García's, the first of a number of traveling companies to play in New York, was to stay a year. Its repertory favored Rossini: *Il Barbiere di Siviglia* was the first production, followed by *Cenerentola, Semiramide, Tancredi, Il Turco in Italia*, and Mozart's *Don Giovanni*. Later troupes introduced other fare to those New Yorkers who went to the operas: Bellini, Donizetti, Auber, Halévy. The increasing numbers of German immigrants, especially after 1848, provided support for German opera; during the 1862–63 season, for instance, some 65 performances were heard, with the favorites being Weber's *Der Freischütz*, Beethoven's *Fidelio*, Mozart's *Magic Flute* and *The Abduction from the Seraglio*.

As with symphonies in New York, the names to reckon with in opera of the period are those of Fry and Bristow. Fry's early life was spent in Philadelphia, and it was at the Chestnut Street Theatre on June 4, 1845 that his *Leonora*, a full-scale three-act work on a libretto derived by Fry's brother from Bulwer-Lytton's *The Lady of Lyons* (1838), was first heard. Presented in what must have been an unusually lavish production for the time, at the hands of the English company of Arthur Sequin with an orchestra of sixty and a chorus of eighty, *Leonora* had a successful run of sixteen performances. Its fashionably Romantic plot and Belliniesque music must have made it seem very up-to-date (two arias in *MinA*, Nos. 128 and 129; Fry's prefatory remarks in *ACS*, pp. 46–52). Fry composed three other operas, only one of which, *Notre Dame de Paris*, was produced.

Fry was perhaps less gifted as a composer than as a journalist. As such he was a belligerent and articulate champion of the rights of American composers to be heard in America. Ironically, however, it was not Fry but his friend Bristow who turned to American subjects: his *Rip Van Winkle* (1855) was successful; his *Columbus* was never finished. The former (two arias and chorus in *MinA*, Nos. 130, 131) is less derivative from Italian opera than is Fry's *Leonora* and reveals Bristow's solid grounding in German instrumental music of his time, although the gap between his fluid, chromatic harmony and his square-cut phrase structure is seldom successfully bridged.

Bibliographical notes

Stevenson's *Protestant Church Music in America* is a well-documented basic source for the material in this chapter, as well as for Chapter 1. Arthur Rich's biography of *Lowell Mason* (Chapel Hill: University of North Carolina Press, 1946) has not yet been superseded. Mason's own *Musical Letters from Abroad* (1854) have been republished (New York: Da Capo Press, 1967); one reviewer of the reprint (in *American Quarterly*, XX, 1 (Spring 1968) has said, "No serious student of nineteenth-century American priggery can afford to ignore them."

No really adequate study of the songs of 1820–65 has been published. W. T. Upton's *Art-Song in America* (Boston: Oliver Ditson Company, 1930; supplement, 1938) may be consulted. Carol Brink's *Harps in the Wind* (New York: The Macmillan Company, 1947) and P. D. Jordan's *Singin' Yankees* (Minneapolis: University of Minnesota Press, 1946) are both on the Hutchinson family. J. T. Howard's *Stephen Foster, America's Troubadour* (New York: Thomas Y. Crowell Company, 1934; rev. eds. 1953, 1962) is the standard biography, E. F. Morneweck's two-volume *Chronicles of Stephen Foster's Family* (Pittsburgh: University of Pittsburgh Press, 1944) the basic documentary source book.

The chapters on the U.S.A. in Loesser's *Men, Women and Pianos* make fascinating reading. Both Richard Hoffman and William Mason wrote their memoirs, characteristically devoting the most space to their European years; see Hoffman, *Some Musical Recollections of Fifty Years* (New York: Charles Scribner's Sons, 1910) and Mason, *Memories of a Musical Life* (New York: The Century Co., 1902). Jeanne Behrend's edition of Gottschalk's *Notes of a Pianist* (New York: Alfred A. Knopf, Inc., 1964) is excellent, while Vernon Loggins's Gottschalk biography, *Where the Word Ends* (Baton Rouge: Louisiana State University Press,

1958), fictionalized and largely undocumented, must be read with caution.

John Mueller's *The American Symphony Orchestra* (Bloomington: Indiana University Press, 1951) is a musical sociologist's study. The basic (and only) biography of Heinrich is W. T. Upton's (New York: Columbia University Press, 1939). Upton is also the author of the biography, *William Henry Fry, American Journalist and Composer-Critic* (New York: Thomas Y. Crowell Company, 1954).

For opera in New Orleans to 1841, see H. A. Kmen's *Music in New Orleans* (Baton Rouge: Louisiana State University Press, 1966) and in New York Julius Mattfeld's *A Hundred Years of Grand Opera in New York* (New York: New York Public Library, 1927).

5

The Vernacular Tradition, 1820-1920

Having considered the development of the cultivated tradition through the Civil War, let us go back to the early nineteenth century to consider vernacular-tradition music, carrying forward the discussion to the end of World War I and treating religious music, especially that of the revivals and camp meetings; the music of the popular lyric theater, the minstrel show; dance music; marches and other band music; and ragtime, at first a music of limited use among American Southern Negroes but by the turn of the twentieth century a music of national popularity.

Religious music

We have noted in the foregoing chapter the rejection of the music of the First New England School in the very area that had spawned it. Under the influence of the composers of "scientific" church music led by Lowell Mason and Thomas Hastings, the fuging tunes, anthems, and set-pieces of the Yankee tunesmiths were gradually eliminated from the churches as well as the singing schools, not only of New England but of the Middle Atlantic States as well. The imaginative shape-note notation of Smith and Little's *Easy Instructor* and its imitators was equally rejected in the North as being no more than "dunce notes" (Hastings's epithet). By 1853, as we have seen, a Boston historian of American church music believed that shape-note tunebooks and their music, "if used at all, have been crowded to the far West, mostly out of sight and hearing."[1]

He was wrong. Shape notes and the music of the New Englanders were still within "sight and hearing" of many Americans. They had indeed been crowded out of the Northern and Eastern cities, but they were flourishing in the Upland South and the Deep South, as well as in the "far West" (by which Gould probably meant any land west of the Appalachians). Spurned by the urban arbiters of cultivated taste in music, the tunesmiths' pieces had become essentially a rural music in the sparsely settled South and toward the frontier. There they would join with several other kinds of religious song to form the basis of a vernacular music tradition that is still alive today. These other kinds of song are our immediate concern: the spiritual folk songs and the revival hymns of the camp meetings, and the gospel hymns of the "City Revival" of the 1870's and later.

The beginnings of the migration to the South of the shape-note tunebooks are reflected in several Pennsylvania publications of the first two decades of the nineteenth century. For the English-speaking population appeared such imitations of *The Easy Instructor* as the 1807 edition of *Philadelphia Harmony; Ecclesia Harmonia* (1807); and *The Musical Instructor* (1808). German-speaking Pennsylvanians first learned shape-note singing from *Der leichte Unterricht* of 1810 (its title a literal translation of *The Easy Instructor*'s) and *Die Franklin Harmonie* (1821). The latter two were published

---

[1] Gould, *History of Church Music in America*, p. 55.

by a Harrisburg printer, John Wyeth (1770–1858), who also issued English-language tunebooks, among them *Repository of Sacred Music* (1810) and *Repository of Sacred Music, Part Second* (1813). The *Repository . . . Part Second* proved to be "the first really influential anthology of what the late George Pullen Jackson dubbed spiritual folk-song."[2]

Spiritual folk songs are just what the term implies: religious songs set to folk melodies, whether secular song melodies, patriotic airs, or popular dance tunes. Three types of spiritual folk songs may be distinguished: religious ballads, folk hymns, and revival spiritual songs. Wyeth's collection of religious songs in two, three, and four voice-parts included both ballads and hymns, besides many tunes from earlier New England collections (Billings, Jenks, Law, Chapin) and thirteen by Elkanah Dare (1782–1826), who may have been Wyeth's musical adviser. (*Fairton*, Dare's setting of Watts's "God of mercy! hear my call" is in *MinA*, No. 91.) *Heavenly Union*, for example, is a ballad in some ten strophes which begins with the balladeer's typical invitation to listen to a story:

> *Come, saints and sinners, hear me tell*
> *The wonders of Emmanuel,*
> *Who saved me from a burning hell,*
> *And brought my soul with him to dwell,*
> *And gave me heav'nly union.*

The tale goes on in a characteristically folkish, colloquial way:

> *When Christ the Saviour from on high*
> *Beheld my soul in ruins lie,*
> *He look'd on me with pitying eye,*
> *And said to me as he pass'd by,*
> *"With God you have no union."*

The folk hymns are briefer, non-narrative pieces; many are new settings to anonymous tunes of old favorite texts by Watts or Wesley. *Hallelujah* is one of the three settings of the popular text of Robert Robinson, eighteenth-century English hymnodist, "Come thou fount of ev'ry blessing"; the tune, which was to be resecularized to the text "Go tell Aunt Rhody," appears in print for the first time in Wyeth's *Repository* as an anonymous and presum-

---

[2] Lowens, *MMEA*, p. 134. Lowens is referring to the pioneer studies of Jackson in a series of books from 1933 on, and specifically to his *Spiritual Folk-Songs of Early America*.

ably well-known folk tune (Example 5-1a; a later, gospel-hymn version shows how decades of popular usage reshaped the tune into the form known best today [Example 5-1b]).

EXAMPLE 5-1a. *Hallelujah, Repository of Sacred Music, Part Second* (2nd ed.; Harrisburg: J. Wyeth, 1820), p. 112.

EXAMPLE 5-1b. *Come, Thou Fount*, attributed to John Wyeth in *Gospel Hymns. Nos. 1 to 6 Complete* (New York: Biglow & Main Co., 1894), No. 633 (soprano part only).

As one can hear in *Hallelujah*, with early nineteenth-century folk hymnody we are back again in the musical world of the Yankee tunesmiths: the parallel fifths of measures 2-3 and 4; the implied modal harmony; the "gapped" melody which makes the tune seem fundamentally pentatonic; the simple, sturdy rhythm. These old style-characteristics are maintained, indeed emphasized, in Wyeth's shape-note hymn collection, which was to be the model for later tunebooks in the developing tradition of Southern spiritual folk songs.

"Spiritual folk song" suggests the better-known term "spiritual." And in fact songs like *Hallelujah* have been termed "white spirituals" by historians beginning with Jackson, who coined the term for his *White Spirituals in the Southern Uplands* (1933). The complex relationships between such white spirituals and Negro spirituals are not yet wholly clear. What is clear is that the Negro spirituals, which were hardly ever discussed in print and never transcribed before the Reconstruction period after the Civil War, had their source in the evangelical song of the great revivals in the American South and West in the period after 1800.[3] These began with the Great Revival of 1800 in Kentucky, which set off a wave of emotional religious revivalism led by the aggressive Methodists, Presbyterians, and Baptists that soon swept across Georgia, the Carolinas, Pennsylvania, Tennessee, and Ohio. The instrument of the revivals was the camp meeting of worshippers who brought tents, bedding, and food for the four- or five-day (and night) marathons of preaching, praying, and singing. Attendance could run in the thousands: at Cane Ridge, Kentucky in 1801, more than thirty ministers preached to a crowd estimated variously to be between 10,000 and 20,000. With meetings of such size, a new kind of religious song inevitably appeared—the revival hymn—simpler even than the traditional hymns and having the text repetitions or verse-and-refrain structure found in many folk cultures. This kind of song was often termed a "spiritual song," as in the title of John C. Totten's pocket-sized book of hymn texts, *A Collection of the Most Admired Hymns and Spiritual Songs, with the choruses affixed, as usually sung at camp-meetings* (New York, 1809). At least one critic of camp-meeting revivalism

---

[3] See Nettl, *Folk and Traditional Music of the Western Continents*, pp. 182–85. For a dispassionate, well-documented survey of sources in a field beclouded by prejudice of various kinds, see Dena J. Epstein, "Slave Music in the United States before 1860," *Notes*, XX (1963), 195–212, 377–90.

believed that the repetitive choral refrains of the new type of hymn derived from the Negro: John F. Watson, in a tract of 1819 bemoaning what he called *Methodist Error*, spoke of one

> . . . most exceptionable error, which has the tolerance at least of the rulers of our camp meetings. In the *blacks'* quarter [of the camp ground], the coloured people get together, and sing for hours together, short scraps of disjoined affirmations, pledges, or prayers, lengthened out with repetition choruses. These are all sung in the merry chorus-manner of the southern harvest-field, or huskingfrolic method, of the slave blacks.

Watson lamented that "the example has already visibly affected the religious manners of some whites":

> From this cause, I have known in some camp meetings, from 50 to 60 people crowd into one tent, after the public devotions had closed, and there continue the whole night, singing tune after tune . . . scarce one of which were in our hymnbooks. Some of these from their nature, (having very long repetition choruses and short scraps of [text] matter) are actually composed as sung, and are indeed almost endless.[4]

"Short scraps" of verse, interspersed with "repetition choruses," sung in a "merry chorus-manner," often "actually composed as sung" —this is as good a definition as any of the typical revival hymn. It first appeared in print in pocket songsters, without the music but often with a separate section of "choruses" that could be added to or interpolated in the song leader's chanting of the verses. Wyeth's *Repository . . . Part Second* contained no such revival hymns, but the later Southern tunebooks, which otherwise borrowed so much from Wyeth (Yankee fuging tunes and other pieces, religious ballads, and folk hymns) added revival hymns as well. The most successful such tunebooks were Ananias Davisson's *Kentucky Harmony* (1816) and its *Supplement* (1820); Allen Carden's *Missouri Harmony* (1820); the *Columbian Harmony* (1825) of William Moore from Wilson County, Tennessee; William Caldwell's *Union Harmony* (Maryville, Tennessee, 1837); John Jackson's *Knoxville Harmony* (1838). Especially notable, because so popular, are *The Southern Harmony* of William Walker and *The Sacred Harp* of B. F. White and E. J. King.

---

[4] Quoted in Don Yoder, *Pennsylvania Spirituals* (Lancaster: Pennsylvania Folklife Society, 1961), pp. 27–28.

"Singin' Billy" Walker (1809–1875) of Spartanburg, South Carolina published *The Southern Harmony* in 1835. In the preface to his *Christian Harmony* (1866; preface reprinted in *ACS*, pp. 67–69) he claimed to have sold 600,000 copies of the earlier work, and he is known to have added proudly to his signature the initials A.S.H. ("author *Southern Harmony*"). The index to the 1854 edition, the last and largest, names 334 pieces, including many new tunes "suitable for revival occasions." Walker's name is attached to forty of the compositions; in his preface to the first edition, he explains that in addition to having "composed several tunes wholly," he also "composed the [accompanying] parts to a great many good airs (which I could not find in any publication, nor in manuscript), and assigned my name as the author." Thus was a popular tune turned into a spiritual folk song. One such tune was *Auld lang syne*, which appears with the title *Plenary* as a setting for an Isaac Watts hymn (*MinA*, No. 99); another, surely an Irish reel in its first incarnation, is *The Good Old Way* (*MinA*, No. 98). Yet another, attributed in *The Southern Harmony* to a David Walker, is *The Hebrew Children*, an infectious hexatonic tune that is known also as a Negro spiritual ("Wonder where is good ole Daniel?"), an Ozark Mountains play-party song ("Where, O where is pretty little Susie?"), and, of later vintage, a college song ("Where, O where are the pea-green freshmen?").[5] The thrice-asked question of each stanza, "Where are the Hebrew children?" (". . . the twelve apostles? . . . the holy Christians? etc.), is answered by the refrain, "Safe in the promised land," in a characteristic form of the verse-with-refrain revival hymn.

Typical of the compilers of Southern folk hymn books, Walker drew tunes that pleased him from no matter what source, transforming them into the rugged, sonorous shape-note style by the addition of two or three surrounding parts. Thus, not only do we find in *The Southern Harmony* borrowings from the eighteenth-century Yankee composers, newly composed pieces by Walker and others, but even Lowell Mason's *Missionary Hymn* and the patriotic song *Hail, Columbia!* The Scottish folk song *Braes o' Balquhidder*

---

[5] Walker's *The Hebrew Children* is in *MinA*, No. 97, along with the first stanza of the Negro version, apparently taken from R. Nathaniel Dett, *Religious Folk-Songs of the Negro as Sung at Hampton Institute* (Hampton, Va.: Hampton Institute Press, 1927), p. 73. The play-party version is in Vance Randolph (ed.), *Ozark Folk Songs* (4 vols.; Columbia, Mo.: State Historical Society, 1946–50), III, 364. The college version is part of my own experience.

is made over into *Lone Pilgrim*, and both *Thorny Desert* and *Something New* sound like folk-hymn variants of Scotch-Irish reels.

Far more lastingly popular than *The Southern Harmony* was *The Sacred Harp* (1844) of Benjamin Franklin White (1800–1879) and his lesser-known co-compiler E. J. King (d. 1844?). As late as 1960, in a revision of 1911 supervised by the Alabama singing-school master S. M. Denson (1854–1936), copies of this tunebook, affirmatively retitled *Original Sacred Harp*, were still rolling off the press of the Sacred Harp Publishing Company of Cullman, Alabama. The Denson Revision consisted mainly in adding alto parts to 327 of the 609 tunes, making four-part songs out of the older three-part ones; otherwise, the twentieth-century *Sacred Harp* preserves the "dispersed harmony" (one part per staff), the four-shape notation (*fa* △, *sol* ○, *la* □, *mi* ◇), and the traditional inclusion of an introduction on "The Rudiments of Music." Even the basic "old time" style is fairly well preserved. Example 5-2 shows the beginning of the moving folk hymn *Wondrous Love* in the three-part setting common to both *The Southern Harmony* (see *MinA*, No. 101) and the first edition of *The Sacred Harp*, with Denson's alto part added in cue-sized notes. It can be heard that occasionally the "modern" full triad sound is created by Denson's adding a third to the original's open fifth.

EXAMPLE 5-2. The folk hymn *Wondrous Love*, measures 1–8. Soprano, tenor, and bass parts from W. Walker, *The Southern Harmony* (New Haven, 1835), 1854 ed., p. 252. Alto part composed by S. M. Denson for "Denson Revision" (1911) of *The Sacred Harp* (Philadelphia, 1844); *Sacred Harp* version is whole-tone lower in original.

EXAMPLE 5-2 continued.

One of the best-known American spiritual folk songs, *Wayfaring Stranger*, appeared in print for the first time in the 1844 *Sacred Harp*. Its poignant text and mournful pentatonic tune tend to disguise the revival-hymn refrain of the last two lines (Example 5-3a). More characteristic of the lusty vigor of most revival songs is *The Old Ship of Zion*, a tune known in several variants including Negro ones, that of *The Sacred Harp* identified by William Hauser in his tunebook *The Olive Leaf* (1874) as a "North Carolina Version" (Example 5-3b).

(a)

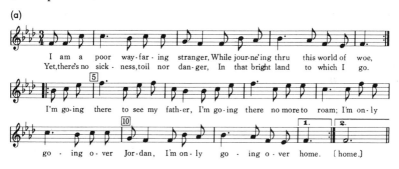

(b)

EXAMPLE 5-3. Two revival hymns from *The Sacred Harp* (1844). (a) *Wayfaring Stranger* (p. 457 of Denson Revision; tenor part only). (b) *The Old Ship of Zion* (p. 79 of Denson Revision; tenor part only).

EXAMPLE 5-3b continued.

Besides the tunebooks cited above, which used the four-shape notation of Little and Smith's *Easy Instructor* based on a *fa, sol, la, mi* solmization system, others appeared in a seven-shape notation that reflected the pressures of the "scientific" school of musical thought to adopt the European *do, re, mi, fa, sol, la, si* (or *ti*) system. The first of these was *The Christian Minstrel* (Philadelphia, 1846) compiled by Jesse Aikin, who showed his respect for Lowell Mason by including eighteen of Mason's hymns in the work. Another, destined to be almost as long-lived as *The Sacred Harp*, was the eastern Tennessee tunebook *The Harp of Columbia* (Knoxville, 1848); present-day singers from this book call themselves "Old Harp Singers" as opposed to the "Sacred Harp Singers." One of the last shape-note tunebooks in the traditional style of spiritual folk song, and one which used Aikin's seven shapes, was *The Olive Leaf* (1878), printed at Wadley, Georgia by William Hauser (1812–1880). But this book also reveals the impact of a new style in American vernacular hymnody, that of the gospel hymn.

The gospel hymn, like the earlier revival hymn, was the product of a revival movement. However, unlike the earlier nineteenth-century revival hymn, which arose mainly in the back country and on the frontier, the gospel hymn of the last half of the century was urban. Its musical background was the correct, bland style of Mason and Hastings, but its harmony tended to be more chromatically engorged, its texts more sentimentally swollen. From the earlier revival hymnodists, the gospel-hymn writers, equally intent on engaging large masses in cathartic songfests, took the idea of repeated refrain-choruses. As Stevenson puts it, in thinly disguised scorn for the genre, "the verse-and-refrain pattern of the revival song joins with Sweet Adeline harmonies to make the gospel song"; Edwin Pierce remarks perceptively on the influence of German secular

Volkslieder (as they might have become known in the American imitations of the *Männerchöre*).[6]

William B. Bradbury, whom we have met as the composer of *The Lament of the Blind Orphan Girl* (see above, p. 59), fore-shadowed the gospel song's tone in his *Woodworth* of 1849 ("Just as I am, without one plea"). However, the biggest names among gospel-hymn composers (and the Broadway connotation of that terminology is not inappropriate considering the polished publicity and commercial enterprise of the urban revivals) were those of Philip D. Bliss (1838–1876), Ira D. Sankey (1840–1908), and a some-what lesser light, Rev. Robert Lowry (1826–1899). Lowry's *Beautiful River* ("Shall we gather at the river?") appeared in *The Olive Leaf;* its skipping rhythms entranced generations of Americans and were incorporated in instrumental works by Charles Ives ("Children's Day at the Camp Meeting" violin sonata) and Virgil Thomson (*Variations and Fugues on Sunday School Tunes*). Sankey, fresh from a two-year revival tour of Great Britain (1873–75) as organist and song-leader for the spellbinding evangelist Dwight L. Moody and immersed in Moody's revival meetings at the Brooklyn Rink in New York City, for which he directed a choir of 250 in addition to playing the organ for his own singing, still found time to see into print a book of *Gospel Hymns* (New York, 1875). Bliss collaborated with him in this hymn book, and in a second enlarged edition the next year; after Bliss's death, Sankey and other collaborators continued to issue enlargements through a sixth cumulative volume, *Gospel Hymns. Nos. 1 to 6 Complete* (1894).

The gospel hymns of Bliss and Sankey are easily denigrated as a "slough of sentimental music-hall sloppiness . . . flabby and futile," as a British observer has put it. But the same historian, shifting critical gears, views them rightly if perhaps unconsciously in the context of an American urban vernacular tradition when he admits that "at its best this music is honestly flamboyant and redolent of the buoyancy of the civilization that created New York and Pittsburgh and Chicago."[7] Bliss's *Pull for the Shore* may have a

---

[6] Stevenson, *Protestant Church Music in America*, p. 90n; Edwin H. Pierce, "Gospel Hymns," *MQ*, XXVI (1940), 355–64.

[7] Erik Routley, *The Music of Christian Hymnody* (London: Independent Press, 1957), p. 166.

text as metaphorically exaggerated as a seventeenth-century Italian opera aria and as artfully homespun as the doggerel of Edgar Guest, but the tune of its chorus is an almost irresistible march, perfectly suited to its soul-stirring evangelistic purposes (Example 5-4). The

EXAMPLE 5-4. P. Bliss, *Pull for the Shore*, No. 51 of *Gospel Hymns. Nos. 1 to 6 Complete* (New York: Biglow & Main Co., 1894), soprano part of Chorus only.

universality of some gospel hymn tunes and text phrases is undeniable. The tune everyone has sung as "How dry I am!" can be found as No. 543 in the 1894 *Gospel Hymns*, beginning "O happy day that fixed my choice/On Thee, my Saviour and my God." Bliss's *Hallelujah, 'tis Done* (No. 2 of the 1883 compilation) became the irreverent parody, "Hallelujah, I'm a bum." Snatches of gospel-hymn texts have become commonplaces in the American vernacular: "Sweet by-and-by" (No. 110, 1894 collection); "Arise and shine" (No. 103); "Throw out the life-line" (No. 441); "Hold the fort" (No. 11); "The old, old story" (No. 28); "Where is my wand'ring boy tonight?" (No. 631); and many others.

I have been speaking, of course, about the major vernacular tradition in American nineteenth-century worship music. Offshoots of this (the Negro spirituals, for instance, or the Pennsylvania Dutch German-language spirituals) deserve and would repay independent attention in a more exhaustive study. So too would various other separate, minor vernacular sub-traditions, such as the music (and its unique notation) of the Shakers ("Shaking Quakers"), or of the California missions, or of other minority sects.

Blackface minstrelsy

Early in 1854, when Jullien's orchestra was in New York offering "monster concerts for the masses," when the St. Charles

Theatre in the Bowery had been presenting German opera for several months, when an Italian opera company producing Donizetti and Bellini was struggling to survive, and when Fry and Bristow were complaining of the New York Philharmonic's neglect of American composers, *Putnam's Monthly* for February called attention to another kind of musical entertainment:

> The only places of Amusement where the entertainments are indigenous are the African Opera Houses, where native American vocalists, with blackened faces, sing national songs, and utter none but native witticisms. These native theatricals . . . are among the best frequented and most profitable places of amusement in New York. While even [the] attempt to establish an Italian Opera here, though originating with the wealthiest and best educated classes, has resulted in bankruptcy, the Ethiopian Opera has flourished like a green bay tree.

This report pinpoints nicely the high point of a kind of American vernacular lyric theater, eschewed perhaps by the "wealthiest and best educated classes" but flourishing among the others. A few months earlier the *Musical World* (October 8, 1853) had noted that "Ethiopian Minstrelsy is on the increase. We now have, in New York, six companies of Minstrels in full blast." The "native theatrical" of blackface minstrelsy was in full flower.

The American minstrel show had crystallized as a form of public entertainment in the early 1840's. Like many other facets of early nineteenth-century American culture, it had British antecedents. In the 1700's it was not uncommon for British dramas to include Negro characters and so-called "Negro songs," usually of an insufferably patronizing and sentimental character. Some British comedians blackened their faces and impersonated Negroes; one of these, Charles Mathews, came to America in 1822. Unfamiliar with American Negroes, he was fascinated by them, especially their dialect and their humor. In New York, at the Negroes' own theater, he noted their performance of *Hamlet* and transcribed the song *Opossum up a Gum Tree*. In Philadelphia he heard a black revivalist preacher and tried to reproduce on paper the sermon's dialect. He collected "scraps of songs and malaprops."[8] With such first-hand experience Mathews's skits and mock-lectures, enlivened by dialect

[8] *Memoirs of Charles Mathews, Comedian, by Mrs. Mathews* (London, 1839), III, 391.

songs, tended ever so slightly toward more realistic if still stereo-typed parodies of the Negro and helped to stimulate an American style of Negro stage impersonation, which some twenty years later would be the foundation of the minstrel show.

As other Northern comedians exploited the fad for Negro sketches in the 1820's and '30's, two stereotypes tended to crystallize, perhaps first in the skits and songs created by George Washington Dixon in the late 1820's, such as *Coal Black Rose* and *My Long-Tail Blue*. Like the other two early American comic heroes, the shrewd, taciturn Yankee peddler and the lusty, bragging backwoodsman, the two Negro stereotypes were oversimplified exaggerations of real life. One was the plantation hand, a tatterdemalion of low estate but high spirits; the other was the urban dandy with affectedly modish ways and a fashionable "long-tailed blue" dress coat. Jim Crow or Gumbo Chaff, Zip Coon or Dandy Jim—these were the archetypes as sketched by early American blackface comedians like Dixon and Thomas Dartmouth ("Daddy") Rice (1808–1860), who created the internationally famous stage character of Jim Crow, legendarily based on a Negro stable groom in Louisville, where Rice was playing in 1828.

Bit by bit such comedians, with faces blackened by burnt cork, enlarged their repertory of skits, songs, and dances; gathered into small troupes; and began to develop the format for a whole pro-gram. One important milestone was the formation by four star comedians in New York of a minstrel band of instruments associ-ated with the Negro. The *New York Herald* announced their premiere, set for February 6, 1843, as one of the major attractions of the Bowery Circus:

> First Night of the novel, grotesque, original, and surprisingly melo-dious Ethiopian band, entitled the *Virginia Minstrels*, being an exclusively musical entertainment combining the banjo, violin, bone castanets, and tambourine, and entirely exempt from the vulgarities and other objectionable features which have hitherto characterized negro extravaganzas.

Successful in New York, the four Virginia Minstrels enlarged their act into a full evening's entertainment of songs, dances, and a parody "lecture on locomotives" and opened with it at the Masonic Temple in Boston on March 7; they called it an "Ethiopian Con-cert." It was the first real minstrel show.

Following the successes of the Virginia Minstrels, other troupes were formed, and the ones already in existence enlarged their shows; soon the Christy Minstrels, Bryant's Minstrels, The Sable Harmonists, The Kentucky Rattlers, The Ethiopian Serenaders, and dozens of others were traveling across the country. Dialect solo songs; satirical stump speeches and dialogues; burlesques; instrumental numbers and dances, either solo or group; and "walk-arounds" (small-scale vernacular *Gesamtkunstwerke* combining solo song, choral song, and dancing to instrumental "symphonies") became the staples of the minstrel shows as the craze for them rose to an early peak in the 1850's. Through them all, at this period, ran a strain of affectionate, good-humored caricature of the Negro, who was portrayed both as jokester and butt of jokes, as comedian and (less often) tragedian. Even if by today's standards the stereotypes and the heavy dialect of the early blackface minstrels are found offensive, they did present the Negro as a comic hero.[9] The minstrel shows had their villains, but they were of other kinds. Standing up for American popular culture, the minstrels lashed out in stinging parodies and burlesques at the arty and pretentious, the foreign and imported. In the 1850's the "Tyrolean business," mocking the vogue of singing families like the Hutchinsons and the Rainer family, was often to be heard, with such titles as "Tyrolean Solo, displaying a flexibility and volume of voice astonishing and inimitable" and "We Come from the Hills, burlesque à la Rainer family." Italian opera was a favorite target; *Lucia di Lammermoor* was burlesqued as "Lucy Did Lam a Moor." *The New York Clipper* of January 21, 1854 crowed over the Christy Minstrels' satire on Jullien's monster concerts. The virtuosity of visiting violinist Ole Bull and of the fabled Paganini was deprecated by the minstrels, who claimed that

> *Loud de banjo talked away,*
> *An' beat Ole Bull from de Norway;*
> *We'll take de shine from Paganini,*
> *We're de boys from ole Virginny.*

This was an echo of "Daddy" Rice's *Jim Crow* (*MinA*, No. 104), who had boasted about 1828 that

> *I'm a rorer on de fiddle,*
> *And down in ole Virginny*
> *Dey say I play de skientific*
> *Like massa Pagganninny.*

[9] See Constance Rourke, *American Humor* (New York: Harcourt, Brace & Co., 1931), Chapter III; also her *Roots of American Culture* (New York: Harcourt, Brace & Co., 1942), pp. 262–74.

Sometimes the minstrels portrayed the Negro as the same kind of swaggering superman as the frontiersman heroes:

> *My mama was a wolf*
> *My daddy was a tiger,*
> *I am what you call*
> *De Ole Virginny Nigger:*
> *Half fire, half smoke,*
> *A little touch of thunder,*
> *I am what you call*
> *De eighth wonder.*

And sometimes, in transparent disguise, he was shown as a clever outsmarter of authority:

> *A bullfrog dressed in soger's close*
> *Went in de field to shoot some crows,*
> *De crows smell powder an' fly away,*
> *De bullfrog mighty mad dat day.*

The music of the minstrel shows was a mélange of well-known popular songs (even some of the sentimental household type), of adaptations from other sources (even of British and Italian-opera airs), of dance tunes and dialect songs. These last two were the mainstays of the shows and had the most remarkable music.

The typical minstrel band of the 1840's was that established by the Virginia Minstrels: banjo, tambourine, bone castanets, and violin, with perhaps also an accordion, a triangle, or a second banjo. All of these except the accordion were instruments associated with the Southern Negro, particularly the banjo; it was known to be used by Jamaican slaves in the seventeenth century and described by an English observer of a "Negro Ball" in Maryland in 1774 as a "musical instrument (if it may be so called) . . . made of a Gourd something in the imitation of a Guitar, with only four strings and played in the same manner."[10] To the four-stringed banjo, which prevailed on the minstrel stage through the 1840's, was added a fifth string, the instrument then having this tuning:

5th   4th   3rd   2nd   1st string

[10] Quoted in Epstein, "Slave Music," *Notes*, XX (1963), 201.

In the minstrel shows, a singer often accompanied himself on the banjo, tapping his foot in a steady metronomic beat and varying his sung melody on the instrument. Thus *The Boatmen's Dance* (see *AM*, p. 272), claimed by Dan Emmett as his own song but known at least in part on the Ohio River in the 1820's and '30's, might have been played as shown in Example 5-5b. The variation style of short, even running notes is not new:

EXAMPLE 5-5. (a) D. Emmett, *De Boatmen's Dance* (Boston: C. H. Keith, 1843), measures 13–16 (air only); and (b) *The Boatman's Dance*, Frank B. Converse, *Frank B. Converse's Banjo Instructor* (New York, 1865), measures 1–4. After *Dan Emmett and the Rise of Early Negro Minstrelsy*, by Hans Nathan. Copyright 1962 by the University of Oklahoma Press.

we have met it in the dance music, under English influence, of the late eighteenth and early nineteenth centuries (see above, Example 2-5).

   Much more novel, indeed so fresh as to be a source for the indigenous American rhythms of ragtime and early jazz, are the banjo "jigs" of the minstrel-show dances. Hans Nathan, who first called attention to these remarkable tunes, describes them thus:

> The motion . . . is animated by many irregular stresses: hectic offbeat accentuations projected against the relentless, metrical background of the accompanying taps [of the feet], which change $\frac{2}{4}$ into $\frac{6}{8}$. A large number of accentuations result from sudden, brief rests on one of the four beats in the measure.[11]

A fine example is Emmett's *Pea-Patch Jig*, one of forty-eight banjo tunes in an early manuscript compiled by Emmett; surprisingly, it also appeared in print in *Kendall's Clarinet Instruction Book* (Boston, 1845). The combinations of triplets and duplets and of even and uneven rhythms in running passages, the repeated notes, and above all the frequent accentuated rests on strong beats contribute to the propulsive, "swinging" character of the music (Example 5-6).

---

[11] Nathan, *Dan Emmett*, p. 195.

[Sounds an octave lower]

EXAMPLE 5-6. D. Emmett, *Pea-Patch Jig*, first (= closing) strain only. From *Dan Emmett and the Rise of Early Negro Minstrelsy*, by Hans Nathan. Copyright 1962 by the University of Oklahoma Press.

Evidence suggests that although the ultimate source of this style lay in British, especially Scottish and Irish, folk-dance music, the concentration of offbeat accents and other rhythmic shifts derived from the manner in which such music was played by the American Negro, who then provided the direct models for Northern minstrel-show banjoists. As the clarinet instruction book mentioned above shows, the banjo-jig idiom was imitated on other instruments: it crops up not only in Kendall's clarinet book but in violin, fife, and flute manuals as well, and the piano music of early ragtime is clearly indebted to it.

Something of the same buoyant, swingy, chattering spirit enters the dialect songs and the music for walk-arounds of the minstrel shows. The two outstanding composers were Daniel Decatur Emmett (1815–1904) and Stephen Foster. Emmett was the more versatile: banjoist, fiddler, singer, and comedian; author of lyrics, stump speeches, plays for the minstrel stage, and instruction manuals for both fife and drum. He also composed in addition to banjo tunes many songs for the minstrel shows; about seventy were published. By far the most famous is *Dixie* (*MinA*, No. 109), originally presented by Bryant's Minstrels on April 4, 1859 and announced on the playbill as "Mr. Dan Emmett's new and original song and dance, *Dixie's Land*, introducing the whole troupe in the festival dance." Nathan's description cannot be improved upon:

> The tune is characterized by a heavy, nonchalant, inelegant strut. . . . If music, lyrics, and dance style are taken as an entity, there emerges a special kind of humor that mixes grotesqueness with lustiness and down-to-earth contentment—comparable, to overstate the case, to a blend of Brueghel and Mickey Mouse. . . . "Dixie" indeed is no polite genteel tune. It has a considerable measure of toughness. . . .[12]

[12] *Ibid.*, pp. 247–48, 250.

Like others of Emmett's walk-arounds, *Dixie* derived from various sources: its "song" and "chorus" melodies can be related to English and Scottish dance tunes as well as to *Gumbo Chaff*, a minstrel song of the 1830's; its closing instrumental "dance" was published in Emmett's *Fife Instructor* with the title "Albany Beef" and is a jig of Irish-Scottish ancestry. Nevertheless, like the best of Emmett's other songs and walk-arounds, *Dixie* integrated these raw materials in a new synthesis. Its rhythmic jolts, related to the banjo-jig syncopations, and its ridiculous homespun humor, common to the minstrel show but originating on the American frontier, make for "a very characteristically national music," as it was described in a Scottish encyclopedia of 1864 in an entry on Negro minstrelsy.

Essentially, although it appeared on the minstrel-show stages of Northern cities, the early minstrel song's earthiness, lustiness, lack of sentimentality, and sinewy vigor came from the world of the frontiersman and the boatman, in those days when the frontier was just over the next range of hills and when rivers and canals were the highways of America. This connection with "primitive" America was certainly one reason why the genteel society of the cities— "the wealthiest and best educated classes"—looked down their collective noses at the minstrel show and its music. And this is why the other outstanding composer of minstrel-show song, Stephen Foster, had to justify with a fine but defensive show of resolution his decision to move whole-heartedly into the field of minstrel-song composition. In a letter of 1852 to E. P. Christy, leader of Christy's Minstrels, Foster declared: "I have concluded . . . to pursue the Ethiopian business without fear or shame and . . . to establish my name as the best Ethiopian song-writer."[13] By 1852 Foster was a well-known songwriter, both of household songs and of minstrel-show songs. His comment to Christy shows, however, what lingering doubts he must have had about the propriety and gentility of identifying himself unreservedly with the latter. (He had an economic reason, however, for overcoming those doubts, for his biggest hit, *Old Folks at Home*, had been published under Christy's name as composer; Foster rationalized in the same letter to Christy that "I cannot write at all unless I write for public approbation and get credit for what I write.")

Foster's first songs for the minstrels, four published between

---

[13] The entire text of this interesting letter printed in *AM*, pp. 293-94, and, along with three other letters to Christy, in *ACS*, pp. 54-57.

1847 and 1848, were already in the full-fledged indigenous style of the minstrel music of the 1840's. The banjo twang on the after-beats in the accompaniment to *Lou'siana Belle* and the strumming, rattling rhythm of *Away Down South* (Example 5-7) made those songs immediate successes, like *Uncle Ned* as well. But of the four early songs it was *Oh! Susanna* that was to prove indestructibly vital.

EXAMPLE 5-7. S. Foster, early minstrel songs. (a) *Lou'siana Belle* (Louis-ville & Cincinnati: Peters, 1847), measures 9–12. (b) *Away Down South* (Louisville & Cincinnati: Peters, 1848), measures 9–16.

Oh! Susanna (*MinA*, No. 107) was probably derived in part from the earlier, anonymous *Gwine 'long Down* (1844), just as Foster's later *Nelly Bly* (1849) seems to come from *Clare de Kitchen* (late 1830's) and his *Camptown Races* (1850) from *Picayune Butler* (1847). But, like Emmett's *Dixie, Oh! Susanna* was a transcendent synthesis of varied elements, not only because of the fine swinging movement of its solo verses and the solid stomp of its five-part chorus (with a potent jolt on the last two syllables of "Oh! Su-*san-na*") but because of the deadpan nonsense humor of its text:

> *It rained all night the day I left,*
> *The weather it was dry,*
> *The sun so hot I frose to death,*
> *Susanna don't you cry.*

Between the summers of 1849 and 1850 Foster published nine songs for the minstrel shows, as compared with five for the parlor. Among them were *Nelly Bly*, with its "dulcem melody" rocking along in a heavy-footed two-step rhythm, and *Camptown Races*, with its perfect matching of text and music and its irresistible verve (Example 5-8). Its chorus bears a striking resemblance to that of *Lord, Remember Me*, first printed in the significant collection of Negro songs compiled by Allen, Ware, and Garrison: *Slave Songs of the United States* (1867). Also a product of this period was *Nelly Was a Lady,*

EXAMPLE 5-8. S. Foster, *Camptown Races* (Baltimore: Benteen, 1850), measures 8–15.

its text unusually sympathetic and sweet:

> *Nelly was a lady—*
> *Last night she died;*
> *Toll de bell for Lubly Nell,*
> *My dark Virginny bride.*

In the summer of 1851 appeared the song that would be most completely identified with Foster's name, despite its publication under Christy's: *Old Folks at Home* (*MinA*, No. 108). Wilfrid Mellers was the first to point out[14] that with this song Foster introduced into the minstrel-show context the same nostalgia that pervades his household songs:

> *All up and down the whole creation,*
> *Sadly I roam,*
> *Still longing for the old plantation,*
> *And for de old folks at home.*
>
>   .   .   .
>
> *One little hut among de bushes,*
> *One dat I love,*
> *Still sadly to my mem'ry rushes,*
> *No matter where I rove.*

The same note is heard in the other, later "best-loved" Foster songs issued as "plantation melodies": *My Old Kentucky Home, Good Night* (1853) and *Old Black Joe* (1860). Interestingly, as if conscious of having blurred the distinction between household and minstrel songs, Foster published these two without any Negro dialect spellings.

The reaction of the cultivated-tradition establishment to the fantastic popularity of *Old Folks at Home* was predictable. In its issue of October 2, 1852, *Dwight's Journal of Music* reported with perplexed incredulity on the universal appeal of the song:

> *Old Folks at Home* . . . is on everybody's tongue, and consequently in everybody's mouth. Pianos and guitars groan with it, night and day; sentimental young ladies sing it; sentimental young gentlemen warble it in midnight serenades; volatile young "bucks" hum it in the midst of their business and pleasures; boatmen roar it out . . . all the bands play it.

---

[14] *Music in a New Found Land* (New York: Alfred A. Knopf, 1965), p. 249.

More than a year later (November 19, 1853) *Dwight's* was forced to an all-out attack—the cultivated against the vernacular tradition:

> We wish to say that such tunes . . . become catching, idle habits, and are not popular in the sense of musically inspiring, but that such and such a melody *breaks out* every now and then, like a morbid irritation of the skin.

We can see now that Dwight's criticism was silly—like downgrading daisies because they are not orchids. It was also futile: Negro minstrelsy and its "morbid irritations" were on the rise in the 1850's. The genre was to continue through the 1860's as the most vital kind of "native theatrical," with some thirty established nontouring companies and many other traveling companies. From the 1870's on, however, the character of the minstrel show began to change: it tended to become more and more a variety show, foreshadowing vaudeville and burlesque; its integrity was diluted by the introduction of non-Negroid characters and sketches; its format was inflated in a trend to gigantism reflected in the names of such troupes as Haverly's Mastodons, Cleveland's Colossals, and Leavitt's Giganteans. One irony of the minstrel show's declining years was the appearance on the minstrel stage of genuine Negroes, sometimes even in blackface make-up. One such performer, and the only notable composer of the later period of minstrelsy, was James A. Bland (1854–1911), who wrote some seven hundred songs, among them *Carry Me Back to Old Virginny* (1878), *In the Evening by the Moonlight* (1880), and *Oh, dem Golden Slippers* (1879).

Bands and band music

The vernacular tradition's equivalent to the symphony orchestra was the wind band. By the early twentieth century hardly an American hamlet was without its village band; hardly a public occasion passed without the sound of the brasses, woodwinds, drums, and cymbals of a band; hardly anyone in the Western world was ignorant of at least one American band composer, John Philip Sousa.

The American band developed out of the pre-Revolution British Army regimental bands. Early American bands were often attached to units of the local militia; as well as playing for parades and drills, they sometimes gave concerts. Two early bands whose rosters were exclusively filled with militiamen were the Massachusetts Band, organized in 1783, and the United States Marine Band (1798). In 1800 the Marine Band was made up of two oboes, two clarinets, two horns, a bassoon, and a drum; thus its constitution differed from that of a chamber orchestra only in its lack of stringed instruments. With the invention in Germany about 1815 of valves for cornets, trumpets, and horns, these instruments (admirably suited to the band's outdoor requirements of portability and plenty of sound) gained a new flexibility, hence new popularity. As the bands added brasses to their complements, the woodwinds were first forced out entirely (as, for instance, from New York's City Brass Band, reorganized in 1834 by Thomas Dodworth as an exclusively brass-instrument ensemble) only to be reintroduced, about the middle of the century, in even greater numbers to balance the noisier brass.

Band concerts up to the Civil War, like other concerts, were potpourris inevitably alternating solos by "guest vocal performers" with pieces by the band. Each item was carefully numbered in the printed programs of the day, hence the colloquial use of "number" for a musical composition. The staples of the mid-century band repertory were quicksteps and other marches; dances, especially the popular waltz and polka, with usually a fast $\frac{2}{4}$ galop in conclusion; an occasional overture; and almost always a solo for keyed bugle or the novel valve cornet to amaze the audience with the newly-won agility of the brass instruments. Band music was seldom published as such; because of the lack of a standard band instrumentation each band usually made its own arrangements.

Most prominent among the many nineteenth-century American bandmasters was Patrick Sarsfield Gilmore (1829–1892), who came to the United States via Canada from his native Ireland as a boy of nineteen, already a cornet virtuoso. After leading several bands in the Boston area, in 1859 Gilmore took over the Boston Brigade Band and reorganized it as a professional concert-giving and dance-playing group of thirty-two members known as Gilmore's Grand Boston Band. During the Civil War, Gilmore was for a time in New Orleans, where he organized the first of the gargantuan concerts he became noted for. Like Berlioz, Gottschalk, Jullien, and others, Gilmore dreamed of a monster concert to end monster concerts. Back in Boston after the war, he began organizing such an affair on an unheard-of scale, a National Peace Jubilee to be held in 1869 and to surpass by far the chorus of 5000 and band of 500 (plus supplementary drum and bugle corps) he had mustered in New Orleans. Support for the idea was not easy to come by: Dwight, the Handel and Haydn Society, and other Boston nabobs were shocked at the Barnumesque plan. However, Gilmore cleverly gained the backing of first one, then both the rival directors of the newly established (1867) Boston and New England Conservatories; launched a careful publicity campaign; found building funds for a three-and-a-half-acre Coliseum to house the festival; issued periodic rehearsal orders like a battlefield general to some one hundred choral organizations totaling 10,296 singers; inveigled the great Ole Bull into being concertmaster of 525 orchestra players; commandeered a band of 486 wind and percussion players; and on June 15, 1869, as scheduled, the Jubilee was on. It lasted five days, with a grand opening concert, a second day's "symphony and oratorio" concert, a fourth's "classical" concert, and a final "Children's Day." The third day's concert was called "People's Day"; it featured three overtures, several national and religious songs, a trumpet solo, and two marches. The *pièce de résistance* was the "Anvil Chorus" from Verdi's *Il Trovatore* for the entire massed ensemble plus electrically operated city bells and a dozen cannon, with "the Anvil part performed by One Hundred Members of the Boston Fire Department."

Pleased with the popular (and financial) success of the National Peace Jubilee, Gilmore aimed to outdo it. Termination of the Franco-Prussian War gave him an excuse to try, and in 1872, in a new Coliseum holding an audience of 50,000 he staged a World's Peace Jubilee. A chorus of 20,000 (some from points as remote from Boston as Milwaukee, St. Louis, Iowa City, and San Francisco) and an instrumental assemblage of almost 2000 proved, not surprisingly, unmanageable; the second Jubilee was a monumental failure, although somehow all ten days' concerts were presented.[15] Gilmore attempted no more musical gigantism; nevertheless, having become in 1873 leader of the 22nd Regiment Band of New York, he enlarged it to sixty-six players, taking it on popular and influential tours throughout the States and, in 1878, Europe.

Gilmore died in 1892, on tour and playing at the St. Louis Exposition. His band settled on a new leader a year later, an Irish-born 'cellist and composer named Victor Herbert (1859–1924); Herbert was to remain director of the 22nd Regiment Band for seven years.

[15] A historical footnote: concluding the fifth day's program, with the audience requested to sing the last two verses, was the venerable hymn *Coronation* (1793) of the eighteenth-century singing master Oliver Holden.

Meanwhile, another bandmaster was rising to prominence: John Philip Sousa (1854–1932).

As a bandmaster, Sousa became internationally renowned. Appointed in 1880 leader of the Marine Band, he made it into a balanced ensemble which by 1891 included 49 players (26 reeds, 20 brass, 3 percussion). Sousa organized his own band in 1892 and with it toured the United States, Canada, Europe, and, in 1910–11, the world. Long-lived, he is the first musician we have encountered in this study to live into the radio-and-recordings era and to help enlarge the popular audience through the new technology of the twentieth century.

As a composer, Sousa essayed many kinds of popular music, notably songs and operettas; the well-known march *El Capitan* was fashioned from two of the songs in an operetta (1896) of that title. But it was as a composer of wind-band marches that Sousa triumphed. He lived at a time when the march was especially popular: not only was it the foundation of the repertory of military and parade bands and of the ubiquitous village bands; it also provided the music for many ballroom dances (e.g., the Two-Step of the 1890's), songs, and hymns. The marches of Sousa were so keenly attuned to his time's temper, so finely honed, such perfect exemplars that Sousa understandably came to be known as "The March King."

The typical Sousa march is a fairly brief work in, of course, duple meter—an even-pulsed $\frac{2}{4}$ or $\frac{2}{2}$ or a galloping $\frac{6}{8}$—with a number of sixteen- or thirty-two-measure strains preceded by a four- or eight-measure introduction. Within this conventional framework Sousa was able to achieve remarkable flexibility and variety, particularly in the harmony, which is by no means predictable and is often surprisingly wide-ranging, given the narrow confines of the march form. Sousa's most famous march, *The Stars and Stripes Forever* (1897), is constructed like this: introduction (4 measures); first (16) and second (16) strains, each repeated; Trio (32); "break" (24), unstable, dramatic, and suspensive, leading to a repetition of the Trio, louder and with new piccolo counter-melody; repetition of the "break," leading again to the Trio, with yet another counter-melody in trombones added (see Example 5-9). Typically, although the march begins in E♭, the Trio is in A♭ and the piece ends in the key a fifth lower than its beginning.

EXAMPLE 5-9. J. P. Sousa, *The Stars and Stripes Forever* (1897), after a photostat of the autograph manuscript, Music Division, New York Public Library. (a) Introduction and first-strain theme. (b) Second-strain theme. (c) Trio theme. (d) "Break," beginning.

Sousa composed about one hundred and forty marches, between *The Revival* of 1876 (which appropriately uses for its Trio theme the gospel hymn *In the Sweet By-and-By*) and *The Kansas Wildcats* of 1931. About half are in the skittish ⁶⁄₈ meter, including some of the best-known: *Semper Fidelis* (1888), *Washington Post* (1889), and *The Liberty Bell* (1893). *El Capitan* combines $\frac{6}{8}$ and $\frac{2}{4}$, as do several others taken from operettas. Richard Franko Goldman (b. 1910), like his father Edwin Franko Goldman (1878–1956) a prominent bandmaster, has urged more performances of "such magnificent examples as *The Fairest of the Fair* (1908), *Hands Across the Sea* (1899), *The Invincible Eagle* (1901), *The Gallant Seventh* (1922)."[16] Like the earlier favorites, these live up to Sousa's own ideal of a band march: "It must be as free from padding as a marble statue. Every line must be carved with unerring skill. Once padded, it ceases to be a march." Having thus spoken as an artist, Sousa spoke also for the free-and-easy eclecticism of the vernacular tradition:

> The composer must, to be sure, follow accepted harmonization; but that is not enough. He must be gifted with the ability to pick and choose here and there, to throw off the domination of any one tendency. If he is a so-called purist in music, that tendency will rule his marches and will limit their appeal.[17]

Sousa saw himself as a highly skilled and tasteful purveyor of entertainment: true to the vernacular tradition, he was not concerned with elevating his audience but with pleasing it. He unconsciously but sharply distinguished between the thought of the cultivated and vernacular traditions in a reflection made after spending an afternoon with Theodore Thomas:

> Thomas had a highly organized symphony orchestra . . . I a highly organized wind band. . . . Each of us was reaching an end, but through different methods. He gave Wagner, Liszt, and Tchaikowsky, in the belief that he was educating his public; I gave Wagner, Liszt, and Tchaikowsky with the hope that I was entertaining my public.[18]

Mechanical Instruments

A note on mechanical instruments is appropriate here. American technology of the nineteenth century led to a wide variety of them, the so-called nickelodeons of public places and the player-

---

[16] "John Philip Sousa," *Hi Fi/Stereo Review*, XIX, No. 1 (July 1967), 35–47.

[17] *Marching Along* (Boston: Hale, Cushman and Flint, 1928), p. 359.

[18] *Ibid.*, p. 132.

pianos of American living rooms. The former, cheaper in the long run for barrooms, poolrooms, brothels, restaurants, and ballrooms than live musicians, came in all shapes, sizes, and degrees of complexity. The Automatic Harp of the Rudolph Wurlitzer Co. was advertised as "especially desirable where a piano cannot be used, on account of its being too loud." The Violano-Virtuoso of the Mills Novelty Co. was a coin-operated, mechanically played violin with piano accompaniment. The Banjorchestra, when fed a nickel, would produce music from an automatic banjo, with support from piano, triangle, drums, tambourine, and castanets. Orchestrions, basically mechanical pipe organs with extras, ranged in size and cost up to the Wurlitzer behemoths, the Paganini Violin Orchestra and the Pian-Orchestra. The Seeburg Company's catalogue described the "KT Special" orchestrion as "piano, xylophone, mandolin attachment, bass drum, snare drums, tympani, cymbal, triangle, castanets, tambourines, Chinese block," all encased in a head-high glass-fronted cabinet of rich birdseye maple.

Mechanically operated player-pianos or "pianolas" (the name reflecting the great success of the Aeolian Company's Pianola model) were the domestic counterpart. Activated by foot pedals or electricity, bellows-operated, and fed with perforated music rolls, player-pianos were fabulously popular from the 1890's through the 1920's, when radio, phonorecordings, and ultimately the Great Depression spelled their demise. A later connoisseur and collector, Lewis Graham, claimed that "between 1895 and 1912 there were more player pianos in the United States than bathtubs,"[19] and according to U.S. Department of Commerce statistics some 205,556 of the 347,589 pianos sold in 1923 were player-pianos.

Ragtime

In 1899 the novelist and musical enthusiast Rupert Hughes (1872–1956) commented:

> . . . If Negro music has its "Go down, Moses" . . . so it had also its hilarious banjo-plucking and its characteristic dances. It is the latter mood that is having a strange renascence and is sweeping the country like a plague of clog-hopping locusts.[20]

[19] *The New York Times,* November 3, 1966.
[20] "A Eulogy of Rag-Time," *Musical Record* (Boston), No. 447 (April 1, 1899), pp. 157–59.

Hughes was speaking of the craze for ragtime, which indeed swept the country in the 1890's through the media of piano players, player-pianos, dance bands, and commercial sheet music. In the diluted form of the cakewalk march, it was played by Sousa's and other concert bands here and in Europe, where according to a publisher's blurb "the native bands have taken up this peculiar style of distinctly American music, even going so far as to play the *Marseillaise* in rag time."

Many threads of earlier American music came together to form the fabric of the ragtime of the 1890's. Earliest, perhaps, was an emphatic use of syncopation by American Negroes, partly derived from African drumming, partly from Afro-Caribbean dance rhythms. Among the few reports we have on secular slave music, several mention the practice of "patting Juba." Reading between the lines of these brief comments, one gets the impression that the practice involved intricate rhythmic patterns played off against a regular beat; syncopation, in short, but of a consistent, insistent kind. Thus, a correspondent of Edgar Allan Poe's, likening irregularities in poetic meters to "clapping Juba," described the latter for Poe in a letter of 1835:

> There is no attempt to keep time to *all* the notes, but then it comes so pat & so distinct that the cadence is never lost. . . . Such irregularities are like rests and grace notes. They must be so managed as neither to hasten or retard the beat. The time of the bar must be the same, no matter how many notes are in it.[21]

One source couples the Negro dance-name "Juba" with the English dance-name "jig" and speaks of "patting" as an intricate rhythmic accompaniment to such a "jig"; another, a Mississippi planter discussing in 1851 how to manage a plantation, tells of his slaves' Saturday night dance music: "Charley's fiddle is always accompanied with Ithurod on the triangle and Sam to 'pat.' "[22] A particular *kind* of syncopated rhythm, conceivably one essence of "patting Juba," shows up in two disparate sources of 1859. Gottschalk's *Souvenir*

---

[21] *The Complete Works of Edgar Allen Poe*, ed. James A. Harrison (New York: Thomas Y. Crowell Co., 1902), vol. 17, p. 22.

[22] Both comments quoted in Epstein, "Slave Music," *Notes*, XX (1963), 383.

de Porto Rico (see above, Example 4-10) opposes a typical $\frac{2}{4}$ *danza* bass rhythm of the Caribbean to a strongly syncopated upper part, emphasizing ♫♩ and ♪♫♫ patterns. In the same year, James Hungerford, of Maryland, published an autobiographical novel, *The Old Plantation,* and in it reproduced a "corn song" one of his slaves had sung on an outing in 1832. Prominent in an otherwise regularly accented $\frac{4}{4}$ meter are the syncopes ♫♩ and, one level higher, ♪♩ ♪. Even before the 1850's, however, such patterns were well known and were identified with the Negro: they are commonplaces in the songs of the minstrel shows of the 1840's (see above, Example 5-8; cf. the choruses of *Oh! Susanna* and *Dixie, MinA,* Nos. 107, 109), particularly the walk-arounds, the dancing for which, in later minstrelsy, was the cakewalk with its prancing kick-steps, bows back and forward, salutes to the spectators. These particular mild syncopes became in fact the hallmarks of the cakewalk Two-Steps played by the Northern bands of the 1890's. Compare, for example, the excerpts in Example 5-10 from the "corn song" transcribed in 1859 by Hungerford and from the "Cake Walk-Two Step" *Bunch o' Blackberries* of 1899, as played by Sousa's band.

(a)

Hooray, hooray, ho! Roun' de corn, Sal - ly!   Dis lub's er thing dat's sure to hab you, Roun' de corn, Sally!

(b)

EXAMPLE 5-10. Negro slave song and cakewalk rhythms. (a) *Roun' de Corn, Sally!* as transcribed in James Hungerford, *The Old Plantation, and What I Gathered There in an Autumn Month* (New York: Harper & Brothers, 1859), p. 191 (excerpts). (b) Abe Holzmann, *Bunch o' Blackberries* (New York: Feist & Frankenthaler, 1899), Trio (treble melody only), measures 1–8.

Ragtime included the simple syncopations just cited, plus others. Perhaps the earliest American music to suggest the intricate and fanciful rhythms of ragtime is that of the banjo dances of the early minstrel shows (see above, p. 107). Again, we can relate at least one aspect of these—accentuated rests—to "patting Juba." The poet and musician Sidney Lanier (1842–1881) observed that

... every one who has noticed a Southern Negro's "patting" will have been apt to hear an effect ... produced by omitting the stroke, of foot or of hand, which the hearer expects to fall on the accented note at the first of the bar, thus:

Allegro vivace

and similar forms.[23]

The minstrel-show banjo tunes were generally called "jigs." So was early ragtime: until about 1897, when the terms "rag" and "ragtime" gained currency, a pianist or a band that played in the ragtime style was called a "jig pianist" or a "jig band." (Here we see the origin of the malodorous equation of the term "jig" with "Negro.") Thus, in its rhythmic aspects, ragtime derived from the banjo dance-tune style, which may itself be related to "patting Juba."

Ragtime typically involved two layers of rhythmic activity: a regularly accented, even bass and a strongly cross-accented treble. Against the bass, which normally stomped along with a heavy two-beat (♩ ♩) or pranced in the band-like oom-pah, oom-pah rhythm of ♪ ♪ , the treble was "ragg'd" by throwing accents onto other, sub-beats. Melodic phrasing of even sixteenths could do it: or, more common, (the relationship of the first pattern to the *danza*'s is worth noting). Variants of these, throwing an accent on the fourth sixteenth (the bass would come down on the fifth), are many in the early printed rags: , , , and all begin the same way. The phrase may run along evenly but bump into an offbeat accent— , —or be drily articulated: . Accentuating the eighth sixteenth in a measure, usually by anticipating the first note of the next and holding it over the barline, is common also ( ), especially in patterns borrowing the cakewalk motif (or). In Scott Joplin's *Stoptime Rag* (1910) the old banjo-tune technique of accentuated rests is expanded: the composer instructs that ". . . the pianist should stamp the heel of one foot heavily upon the floor, wherever the word 'stomp' appears in the music," which it does on *rests* appearing on normally accented beats.

[23] *The Science of English Verse* (New York: Charles Scribner's Sons, 1880), p. 189.

This brief account of ragtime rhythms has been based only on printed rags. First-hand experience with the playing of ragtime pianists still alive—e.g., Willie ("the Lion") Smith (b. 1897)—suggests that, as with most dance music of any era, the rags in print tend to be a simplified form of the music as performed.

The formal design and the basic meter and tempo of ragtime, as it was first published in the 1890's, came from Euro-American dances (quadrilles, polkas, schottisches) and especially post-Civil War marches, with their several strains, each repeated and one or two dipping into the subdominant key, and their heavy two-beat meter. Joplin's celebrated *Maple Leaf Rag* (1899), the best-known early piano rag to be published, is in $\frac{2}{4}$ marked "Tempo di Marcia"; Joplin elsewhere used "Slow March Tempo" and even cautioned performers, "Notice! Don't play this piece fast. It is never right to play 'Ragtime' fast." *Maple Leaf Rag*, from the formal standpoint, might almost be a Sousa march: first strain (16 measures, repeated); second strain (16, repeated); first strain again; "Trio," so named and consisting of a third strain (16, repeated) in the subdominant and a fourth strain (16, repeated) back in the tonic.

The interplay of black and white derivations and the intricate racial cross-currents of the minstrel shows which in effect prepared America to go crazy over ragtime make it less surprising that the first published rag so titled, *Mississippi Rag* (January, 1897), was by a white bandmaster, William Krell, who had toured along the Mississippi, while the acknowledged "King of Ragtime" was the Negro pianist and composer Scott Joplin (1868–1917). Joplin's first published rag was *Original Rags* (March, 1899); *Maple Leaf Rag* was published at Sedalia, Missouri later the same year. All three of these early rags are piano music of considerable polish and technical requirements; obviously the earliest published piano rags were a mature kind of music which had merely lacked crystallization in print. They were also a music of metrical precision for all their cross-accents and rhythmic jolts, music for marching or dancing, music that could adequately and accurately be reproduced on the popular player-pianos of the time—which they were, and the wide dissemination of the piano-roll undoubtedly stimulated ragtime's acceptance and popularity. Ragtime on player-piano rolls is thus the very earliest American music we can actually hear in contemporaneous performances.

One such performance is Joplin's of his own *Weeping Willow*

(1903), recorded for Connorized player-piano roll No. 10277 (since re-issued on a phonorecord). Like most early rags, the form of *Weeping Willow* is built on four different strains plus introduction, played in order Intro-1-2-1-3-4; in Joplin's recorded performance the repetition of each strain finds the treble thrown up an octave to provide new color (Example 5-11). In some later rags, the harmonically adventuresome *Euphonic Sounds* (1909), for example, Joplin turned to a clear-cut rondo form, while in the darkly colored, dense-textured *Magnetic Rag* (1914) the form is a rounded Intro-1-2-3-4-1-Coda. Other ragtime composer-performers modified still other aspects. The New Orleans pianist Ferdinand ("Jelly Roll")

EXAMPLE 5-11. S. Joplin, *Weeping Willow* (St. Louis: Val A. Reis Music Co., 1903). (a) First strain, beginning. (b) Second strain, beginning. (c) Third strain, beginning. (d) Fourth strain, beginning.

Morton (1885–1941) exemplified the Crescent City's style of fairly slow rags with swingier rhythms than the St. Louis manner of Joplin, and with melodic "walking" basses, as in Morton's *King Porter Stomp* (copyrighted 1906; published 1923). The New York pianist James P. Johnson (1894–1955) marks the turn to jazz piano from ragtime: in works like *Caprice Rag* (1914), *Harlem Strut* (1917), and *Carolina Shout* (1925) his striding left hand emphasizes the off-beats and transforms the older two-beat meter into a jazzy four, while his right-hand style dissolves the classic ragtime syncopes into long-breathed runs of even eighths and triplets (Example 5-12).

EXAMPLE 5-12. James P. Johnson, *Caprice Rag* (1914), measures 5–8. © 1963 by Mills Music, Inc. Used by permission.

With this shift in style, the short, happy public career of ragtime was over, just as the era of the blues was about to begin, at least in the public consciousness of America.

Bibliographical notes

George Pullen Jackson's books on the shape-note tradition are necessarily the foundation for any further study; following the seminal *White Spirituals in the Southern Uplands* (Chapel Hill: University of North Carolina Press, 1933; reprinted New York: Dover Publications, 1965) appeared *Spiritual Folk-Songs of Early America* (1937; reprinted 1964); *Down East Spirituals and Others* (1939); *White and Negro Spirituals* (1943); *The Story of the Sacred Harp* (1944); and *Another Sheaf of White Spirituals* (1952). In addition to the important article cited in footnote 3, Harold Courlander's *Negro Folk Music U.S.A.* (New York: Columbia University Press, 1963) is a thoughtful study. One survey of revival hymnody is the Union Theological Seminary dissertation of John Norman Sims, "The Hymnody of the Camp Meeting Tradition" (1960). Facsimile reprints of Wyeth's *Repository . . . Part Second* (New York: Da Capo Press, 1964) and Walker's *Southern Harmony* (Los Angeles: Pro Musicamericana, 1966) are available, as is the Denson Revision of

Original Sacred Harp (Cullman, Ala.: Sacred Harp Publishing Co., 1960). Edwin H. Pierce has written on "Gospel Hymns," *MQ*, XXVI (1940), and Robert Stevenson on "Ira D. Sankey and Gospel Hymnody," *Religion in Life*, XX, No. 1 (Winter 1950–51).

The standard history of the minstrel shows, although virtually silent on their music, is Carl Wittke's *Tambo and Bones* (Durham: Duke University Press, 1930). Hans Nathan's sovereign study, *Dan Emmett and the Rise of Early Negro Minstrelsy* (Norman: University of Oklahoma Press, 1962), is triply valuable as a biography of Emmett, an account of the early period of minstrelsy, and an anthology of minstrel-show music. The chapter on "That Long-Tail'd Blue" in Constance Rourke's *American Humor* (New York: Harcourt, Brace & Co., 1931) is sympathetic and insightful. Four anthologies of music contain minstrel-show songs: Daily Paskman and Sigmund Spaeth, *"Gentlemen, Be Seated!"* (New York: Doubleday, Doran & Co., 1928); S. Foster Damon's facsimile series of *Old American Songs* (Providence: Brown University Library, 1936); Arthur Loesser, *Humor in American Song* (New York: Howell, Soskin, Inc., 1941); and Charles Haywood, *The James A. Bland Album of Outstanding Songs* (New York: E. B. Marks, 1946).

Richard Franko Goldman's *The Wind Band* (Boston: Allyn & Bacon, 1961) has a brief but excellent historical account of American bands and their music. No serious study has been made of Gilmore nor, surprisingly, of Sousa. Goldman's article in *Hi Fi/Stereo Review* (see footnote 16) is a good introduction. Sousa's autobiographical *Marching Along* (Boston: Hale, Cushman and Flint, 1928) and his *Through the Year with Sousa*, a journal-like collection of epigrams, poems, and anecdotes, are primary sources.

Mechanical instruments have been chronicled in Harvey N. Roehl's *Player-Piano Treasury* (Vestal, N.Y.: The Vestal Press, 1963) and Q. David Bowers's *Put Another Nickel In* (Vestal: The Vestal Press, 1966).

The most authoritative and carefully documented account of ragtime is *They All Played Ragtime* (rev. ed.; New York: Grove Press, 1959) by Rudi Blesh and Harriet Janis. Thanks to the later popular revival of the music, piano rags by Joplin, Morton, Johnson, and others are again in print, and phonorecordings, many made from early piano-rolls, are available.

6
The Cultivated Tradition, 1865-1920

American music of the cultivated tradition from the end of the Civil War to the end of World War I was largely dominated by the attitudes, the ideals, and the modes of expression of nineteenth-century Europe, particularly Austria and Germany. Our leading composers almost to a man were initiated into music by first-generation Americans emigrated from Europe, were trained professionally during sojourns in Europe, and when they came back their music was played by ensembles, choruses, and orchestras led either by Europeans or Europe-trained conductors. Some of their music was even published first in Europe, by Breitkopf & Härtel in Leipzig or by the Leipzig branch of the Boston firm of Arthur P. Schmidt

(1846–1921), who in grateful return for an American career (he was German-born) made it a point of conscience to publish American music. In Chapter 3 we examined the sources of this Germanophilia; in Chapter 4 we saw evidences of its rising tide up to the Civil War; in the present chapter we see its highwater mark. However, towards the turn of the twentieth century the work of a few composers reflected other currents: a new interest in American folklore, in developments in French and Russian music, and in topical subject-matter related to the American scene. By the end of the period one remarkable individualist, Charles Ives, had completed most of a body of work which, drawing on both the cultivated and vernacular traditions, offered the possibility of a new synthesis.

It was during the 1860–1920 period that the institutional foundations of the cultivated tradition were firmly consolidated. Music conservatories were founded, among them some still considered pre-eminent: in 1860 the Peabody Institute in Baltimore (its completion delayed by the Civil War and by other problems until 1868); in 1865 the Oberlin Conservatory in Ohio; in 1867 the New England Conservatory in Boston as well as the Cincinnati Conservatory and the Chicago Musical College; in 1904 the Institute of Musical Art in New York, to be merged in 1926 with the Juilliard Foundation; in 1916 New York's Mannes Music School; in 1917 the San Francisco Conservatory. Thanks to Lowell Mason's efforts of the 1830's, music was a part of school curricula across the land; after the Civil War it entered the colleges and universities as well. The first full professorship in music was established at Harvard in 1875, followed closely by the University of Pennsylvania, Yale University, and others. The Music Teachers National Association was founded in 1876, the Music Educators National Conference in 1907 (under the name of Music Supervisors National Conference).

With monies provided not by government but by groups of private citizens spearheaded by individual philanthropists, major concert halls were built: Philadelphia's Academy of Music (1857), Cincinnati's Music Hall (1878), the Auditorium in Chicago (1889; designed by Louis Sullivan); Carnegie Hall in New York (1891); Boston's Symphony Hall (1900). The Metropolitan Opera House in New York was inaugurated in 1883 (razed 1966).

During the entire period New York City was the performance

center of the cultivated tradition. But the ideological center was undoubtedly Boston, where John Sullivan Dwight (1813–1893) reigned through his *Journal of Music* (1852–1881) as chief spokesman for the tradition. A Harvardian who had trained for the ministry, Dwight began his career as the first really significant and influential American music critic and arbiter of taste with a series of more than one hundred articles in *The Harbinger*, journal of the Transcendentalist community at Brook Farm from 1845 to 1849. *Dwight's Journal*, which ran through 1,051 issues in its nearly thirty years of publication, was the most substantial and long-lived music periodical America had known (although by no means the first), despite a comparatively small subscription list. It included critical reviews, analyses, reports on concert life in both Europe and the United States, essays on music history and theory, and translations from German and French music treatises, biographies, and journals. Throughout its existence, it was informed with Dwight's unshakably high-minded belief in music—fine-art music, at least—as the language of feeling and of natural religion, whose purpose was "to hallow pleasure, and to naturalize religion" (as he had expressed it in an address to the Harvard Musical Association as early as 1841). In announcing his *Journal*, Dwight promised that "it will insist much on the claims of 'Classical' music . . . because the *enduring* needs always to be held up in contrast with the ephemeral."[1] The *Journal* did so insist, with Dwight of course determining what was to be considered "the enduring."

Among the contributors to *Dwight's Journal* who might appropriately be mentioned in this summary of the "institutional foundations" of the cultivated tradition were America's first musicologist and the first historian of America's music: Alexander Wheelock Thayer (1817–1897), whose *Ludwig van Beethoven's Leben* (Berlin, 1866–1879, with posthumous volumes added by Deiters and Riemann; abridged English translation published 1921) is still the best biography of the great German composer; and the Alsatian-born Frédéric Louis Ritter (1834–1891), whose *Music in America* (New York, 1883) was the first attempt at a comprehensive survey. Ritter relieved himself of any responsibility to treat the vernacular tradi-

---

[1] Quoted in George Willis Cooke, *John Sullivan Dwight* (Boston: Small, Maynard & Co., 1898), p. 147.

tion by saying flatly, as he began a last chapter on "The Cultivation of Popular Music," that "the people's song . . . is not to be found among the American people."

If Dwight and contributors to his journal like Thayer and Ritter were the literary voices of the art-music of the age, a group of New England composers was the musical voice. I shall call them the Second New England School, grouping them together by virtue of their common inheritance, attitudes, and general style much as I grouped the late eighteenth-century composers of the First New England School.

The Second New England School

Oldest of the group, and teacher of many of its younger members, was John Knowles Paine (1839–1906). His first musical studies were with Hermann Kotzschmar, who had come to America in 1848 with the Saxonia Band, an ensemble like the Germanians, and had settled in Paine's home town of Portland, Maine. Aiming to become a church organist, Paine went to Germany in 1858, to stay nearly four years, studying with the Berlin organist Karl August Haupt (as did almost forty younger Americans) and others, and acquiring some reputation as a performer. Back in America in 1861, he got a post as organist in a Boston church. The next year he was appointed instructor at Harvard, to teach a non-credit music course and serve as university organist. By the mid-1870's the university was convinced of the validity of a music curriculum, and the 1875–76 academic year began with Paine as America's first professor of music. He was to remain at Harvard for thirty years, retiring in 1905.

Paine's work as a composer ranged from abstract piano pieces and chamber music to incidental music for plays, overtures, symphonic poems, and full symphonies; from hymns and choral cantatas to an oratorio, a Mass, and a full opera. Most of it cannot be faulted in workmanship, none of it in seriousness of purpose: Paine took very seriously music's mission to "hallow pleasure," and if his music seems somewhat over-aspiring to profundity, hardly daring to relax or smile, this should be ascribed not to incompetence but to his aesthetic attitude and to the difficulty of attempting to emulate the masterworks of Europe's mature cultivated tradition from a base in a still-New World.

Stylistically, most of Paine's music falls within the orbit of the early German Romantics. Mendelssohn is the strongest influence on choral works like the *Centennial Hymn*, Op. 27 (1876; on a text by Whittier), the cantata *Realm of Fancy*, Op. 36 (1882; Keats), the Mass in D, Op. 10 (first performed at Berlin, 1867, Paine conducting), and the oratorio *St. Peter*, Op. 20 (1873), which even includes accompanied chorales in the "German Lutheran custom." Schumann's symphonies are the major models for Paine's First (1876; premiered at Boston by the Theodore Thomas Orchestra) and Second ("Im Frühling"; 1880).

Paine spoke in 1872 in favor of "adherence to the historical forms, as developed by Bach, Händel, Mozart, and Beethoven" as a "healthy reaction" to the "extremely involved and complicated technics of music, like Wagner, Liszt, and their adherents."[2] However, his own style eventually reflected the music of the latter group. An orchestral prelude, part of Paine's choral and instrumental incidental music for Sophocles's *Oedipus Tyrannus*, Op. 35 (1881), is quite Lisztian in its design and its thematic transformations (Example 6-1). And Paine admitted that in his opera *Azara* (1900; libretto by Paine on the medieval legend of Aucassin and Nicolette) he had "followed throughout the connected orchestral rhythmical flow,

EXAMPLE 6-1. Thematic transformations in J. Paine, *Oedipus Tyrannus*, Op. 35 (Boston: Arthur P. Schmidt, 1881), Prelude, measures 26–29, 54–57, 78–80.

[2] Speech at Boston University; quoted in M. A. DeWolfe Howe, "John Knowles Paine," *MQ*, XXV (1939), 257–67.

EXAMPLE 6-1 continued.

and truth of dramatiç expression characteristic of Wagner."[3] Nevertheless, Paine's basic musical attitude was conservative; on one of the
very few occasions when he permitted himself to turn to a bit of
light Americana for source material, he used it as the subject of a
fugue unbelievably dry, considering the theme ("Over the fence is
out"), given as Example 6-2.

EXAMPLE 6-2. J. Paine, "Fuga Giocosa," *3 Piano Pieces*, Op. 41 (Boston:
Arthur P. Schmidt, 1884), No. 3, measures 1–2.

After Paine as unofficial members of the Second New England
School came a group of composers about a generation younger:
Arthur Foote (1853–1937), George Chadwick (1854–1931), Arthur
Whiting (1861–1936), Horatio Parker (1863–1919), Mrs. H. H. A.
Beach (1867–1944), and Daniel Gregory Mason (1873–1953). Of
these, Chadwick and Parker emerge as the most gifted, or at least
the strongest, musical personalities.

Chadwick is notable among the group for his sympathy—
reflected unevenly in his works—for the American vernacular
tradition's music; for his achievement in approaching a natural
declamation in the setting of English texts; and for an earthy
humor (occasionally joined to a social consciousness) not common
to his rather aristocratic, more isolated peers. A prolific composer,
productive from his student days in Leipzig (*Rip Van Winkle* overture, 1879) until the 1920's, he was the most versatile of the New

[3] Letter to Henry T. Finck, May 27, 1900; quoted in Kenneth C. Roberts, Jr., "John Knowles Paine," (unpublished Master's thesis, University of
Michigan, 1962), pp. 2–3.

Englanders. His Symphony No. 2 (1886) includes melodies pro-
phetic of the "Negro" themes of Dvořák's much-discussed "New
World" Symphony, and a folk-like pentatonicism crops up here
and there in works of varied character, as in the opening measures
of a Sinfonietta in D (1904) or the "Jubilee" movement of his
best-known orchestral work, the *Symphonic Sketches* of 1907 (Example 6-3). Such "American" references are sometimes well assim-
ilated; often, however, they are lodged in a lushly harmonized and
orchestrated matrix that contradicts their very nature.[4]

EXAMPLE 6-3. Folk-like themes of Chadwick. (a) Symphony No. 2 (Boston: Arthur P. Schmidt, 1888), 2nd movement, measures 5–8 and re-
hearsal-letter "M" (accompaniment omitted from both). (b) Sinfonietta
in D (New York: G. Schirmer, Inc., 1906), 1st movement, measures 4–13
(violin part only). Quoted by permission. (c) *Symphonic Sketches*
(New York: G. Schirmer, Inc., 1907), "Jubilee," measures 58–61 (string
parts omitted). Quoted by permission.

---

[4] Some listeners describe the result as being "like movie music"—a more
damning criticism, perhaps, of the generally anachronistic nature of American
film music than of Chadwick's.

One specialist in Chadwick's music has emphasized that the later works, from about 1907 to 1920, reveal "a gradual discard of the German conservatory style . . . a more mature musical language, combining pentatonic melody, subdominant-modal harmony and syncopated rhythmic elements."[5] The "syncopation" is generally limited to the short-long pattern common to English two-syllable words (cf. "wítching" and "éxile" in Example 6-5; "slúmber" and the related "lamentátion" in Example 6-6) but, even so, Chadwick's use of such natural speech rhythms, long a commonplace in songs of the vernacular tradition, sets him apart from Paine, Parker, and others of the New England school, who tend to set English as if it were German or Latin. Chadwick transfers this rhythmic motif to instrumental music as well, as in the "Scherzino" of the Sinfonietta (Example 6-4).

EXAMPLE 6-4. G. Chadwick, Sinfonietta in D (New York: G. Schirmer, Inc., 1906), "Scherzino," measures 21–28. Quoted by permission.

A song like "Adversity," one of more than a hundred by Chadwick, is in the slow waltz tempo often heard in late nineteenth-century American ballrooms and even approaches popular song style, transcending it, however, in a sensitive darkening of the harmony at the last line (Example 6-5).

[5] Victor Yellin, "The Life and Operatic Works of George Whitefield Chadwick" (unpublished Ph.D. dissertation, Harvard University, 1957), p. 291.

EXAMPLE 6-5. G. Chadwick, "Adversity," *Six Songs for Mezzo-Soprano or Baritone* (New York: G. Schirmer, Inc., 1902), No. 3, measures 1–11, 28–38. Quoted by permission.

Chadwick's stage works, seven operas and operettas, range in mood and manner from the combination of American burlesque and light opera of *Tabasco* (1894), containing galops, marches, hymn tunes, waltzes, jigs, and a "plantation ballad," to the sobriety, drenched in a Saint-Saëns-like lyricism and laced with Wagnerian leitmotifs, of *Judith* (1901; see Example 6-6). Perhaps least deserving of its neglect is *The Padrone* (1912; refused by the Metropolitan Opera Company and not yet performed). It is a lone example of American turn-of-the-century *verismo*, its subject the exploitation of Italian immigrants in Boston by their dockside guarantors and landlords, the *padroni*.

EXAMPLE 6-6. G. Chadwick, *Judith* (New York: G. Schirmer, Inc., 1901),
Act I, scene 5 ("The Vision of Judith"), measures 54–62. Quoted by permission.

Chadwick, like Paine, became literally an academician, joining
the faculty of the New England Conservatory in 1882 and serving
as its director from 1897 until 1930. So too did Horatio Parker, who
became professor at Yale University in 1894, after a musical ap-
prenticeship under Chadwick and, from 1882 to 1885, Josef Rhein-
berger in Munich. Parker's most illustrious student said of him: "I
had and have ['great' crossed out] respect and admiration for Parker
and most of his music. It was seldom trivial." Charles Ives then went
on to pinpoint Parker's strengths and weaknesses:

> His choral works have dignity and depth that many contemporaries,
> especially in religious and choral compositions, do not have. Parker
> had ideals that carried him higher than the popular, but he was
> governed by the "German rule." . . . Parker was a bright man, a
> good technician, but perfectly willing to be limited by what Rhein-
> berger had taught him.[6]

The major part of Parker's creative output was music for
chorus, on medieval or religious subjects, all serious in tone. They
range from *a cappella* Latin motets (*Adstant Angelorum Chori*, Op.
45, 1899; on a text by Thomas à Kempis) through occasional pieces
(*Hymnos Andron*, ode on a Greek text for the bicentennial of Yale,

---

[6] Quoted in Henry Cowell and Sidney Cowell, *Charles Ives and His
Music* (New York: Oxford University Press, 1955), pp. 33–34.

Op. 53, 1901; *The Spirit of Beauty,* ode for the dedication of the Albright Art Gallery in Buffalo, Op. 61, 1905) to epitomes of the Victorian cantata (*The Dream King and His Love,* Op. 31, 1892) and oratorio for soloists, chorus(es), and orchestra (*The Legend of St. Christopher,* Op. 43 [1898] and *Hora Novissima,* Op. 30 [1892]). The last-named is accounted Parker's masterpiece: an hour-long choral cantata in eleven big movements, it is a setting of a portion (describing the glories of Heaven) of a twelfth-century Latin poem. The spacious work is all the more impressive for its disguising of the rigid tercets of the poem ("Hora novissima/tempora pessima/ sunt, vigilemus") through long, leisurely, wide-ranging harmonic sequences, extensive fugues on expansive subjects, and masterly handling of the choral-orchestral medium. In one aria (No. 3, "Spe modo vivitur") $\frac{4}{4}$ and $\frac{3}{4}$ measures in alternation—something of a novelty for the time—hide the metrical rigidity of the verses. Though its solo movements suggest Italo-French influence, the main atmosphere of *Hora Novissima,* like other choral works of Parker, is that of a German-American hymnic grandeur, rich in sound and powerfully stable in rhythm; this may be suggested by the several fugue subjects given in Example 6-7.

(a)

EXAMPLE 6-7. Fugue subjects by Horatio Parker. (a) *Hora Novissima* (London & New York: Novello, Ewer and Co., 1893): (1) No. 4, measures 27–31; (2) No. 10, measures 1–5; (3) No. 11, measures 41–44. (b) *Adstant Angelorum Chori* (New York: G. Schirmer, Inc., 1899), measures 88–92. (c) *The Legend of St. Christopher* (London & New York: Novello, Ewer and Co., 1898), p. 134 (Act III, scene 2).

(b)

Con- cors vox— est   om - ni- um,   De - um— col - lau - dan - ti - um;_____

(c)

Quo-ni-am___ Tu so-lus san-ctus,   Tu so-lus Do-mi-nus,   Tu so-lus Do-mi- nus

EXAMPLE 6-7 continued.

Edward MacDowell

The composers of the Second New England School have been called "the Boston academics" (by Rupert Hughes, writing in 1900) and "the Boston classicists" (by Benjamin Lambord in 1915; most recently by Gilbert Chase in *AM*). But not all of them were academicians nor, if the term "academic" is one of disparagement, were they all or always hidebound. And none of them was a "classicist" except in the sense that Brahms was a classicist: they belonged to that wing of Romanticism that maintained a belief in the viability of the abstract instrumental forms. Like Brahms, and like Beethoven, Schubert, Schumann, and Mendelssohn before him, they wrote symphonies, sonatas, and chamber music; like Brahms, and like Handel, Bach, Mozart, and Beethoven before him, they wrote fugues and contrapuntal choruses. To the late nineteenth century such composers as Paine, Chadwick, and Parker might have seemed "classicists"; our perspective should let us rather see them in context as a group of Romantics of a particular persuasion.

To another wing of Romanticism belonged Edward Mac-Dowell (1861–1908). Not for him the abstract traditional forms of symphony and string quartet, nor the semi-abstract forms of orchestral overture or choral cantata. In the tradition of the "New German School" of Liszt and Wagner, MacDowell saw himself as a "tone-poet," trusting in the evocative power of richly colored harmony (especially when the response was directed by a suggestive programmatic title) and narrative, ongoing forms rather than the problem-solving constructivism of imitative counterpoint or the balanced logic of sonata-form. MacDowell believed that Bach was "one of the world's mightiest tone-poets [who] accomplished his mission, not by means of the contrapuntal fashion of his age, but in spite of it," and for him Mozart's instrumental sonatas were "entirely unworthy of the author of *The Magic Flute*."[7] In a climate of aesthetic opinion like that of the later nineteenth century, these attitudes must have seemed truly progressive, truly Romantic, un-tinged by a "classicistic" bent. Not surprisingly, MacDowell was viewed, about the turn of the twentieth century, as America's fore-most modern composer by those who shared his aesthetic—which is to say, all but a few.

Of Scotch-Irish descent, MacDowell was born in New York in 1861. In 1876 he was enrolled in the Paris Conservatory but, dissatisfied, he moved to Frankfurt in 1878 for two more years of study as a pianist and composer; a powerful influence on him there was the conservatory's director, the composer Joachim Raff. Except for one trip back to America to get married, MacDowell remained in Germany teaching, composing, and playing piano concerts until 1888, some twelve years after leaving the United States. He then lived in Boston until 1896, when he accepted a newly endowed chair of music at Columbia University. In 1904, after some unfortunately public wrangling with the university administration, MacDowell resigned. Mental illness, exacerbated by a horse-cab accident, pre-vented his composing any more; he declined more or less steadily until his death.

MacDowell's works were all composed between 1880 (First Modern Suite for piano; First Piano Concerto) and 1902 (*Summer Wind* for women's chorus; *New England Idyls* for piano). They consist mainly of some sixteen collections of *Charakterstücke* for piano, plus four suggestively titled sonatas and two concertos; forty-two songs for solo voice and more than twenty for chorus; four symphonic poems; and two orchestral suites. All the favorite themes and images of Romanticism are explored: landscapes and seascapes (*Woodland Sketches; New England Idyls; Sea Pieces*); medieval romances (the symphonic poem *Lancelot and Elaine;* Piano Sonata No. 3 ["Eroica"] on the Arthurian legend); exoticism (Second ["Indian"] Suite for orchestra; *Les Orientales* for piano); remi-niscences of childhood ("From Uncle Remus," *Woodland Sketches;* "Of Br'er Rabbit," *Fireside Tales*). Shakespeare inspired the sym-

---

[7] MacDowell, *Critical and Historical Essays* (Boston: Arthur P. Schmidt, 1912), pp. 265, 194.

phonic poem in two parts, *Hamlet and Ophelia;* Romantic poets are interpreted pianistically in *Six Idyls after Goethe* and *Six Poems after Heine.* In the latter collections MacDowell printed the poems at the head of the music; in many others, he indited verses of his own to stand as the "program" of individual pieces.

Considering the brevity of the composer's creative life (comparable to Foster's or Gottschalk's), a lack of stylistic development should not surprise us. More surprising, in view of MacDowell's extraordinary reputation about 1900, is the fact that having begun boldly as a composer of piano concertos of truly Lisztian sweep and breadth, he then tended to produce ever smaller, more rarefied works. After the Second Suite (1896) he wrote no more orchestral music. He never attempted opera. Of the later works, only the Third ("Norse") and Fourth ("Keltic") piano sonatas (1900 and 1901) approach large-scale forms, described by MacDowell as " 'bardic' rhapsodies" on their subjects. MacDowell ended as a composer of concise, evocative genre pieces, surprisingly terse even when their subject-matter is grandiose ("To the Sea," "From a German Forest"); basically very economical and clean of line, even fragile sometimes ("To a Wild Rose," "To a Water Lily," both from *Woodland Sketches*); very precisely fashioned and clearly projected.

MacDowell was himself a competent concert pianist, and some of his most successful piano music demands a virtuoso technique, as in the "Scherzo" of the Second Piano Concerto and various études among the Twelve Virtuoso Studies, notably "March Wind." More of it, however, is relatively easy to play and reveals MacDowell to be a late nineteenth-century composer of "household music." He has also in common with that earlier American music a considerable nostalgia: Mellers has remarked trenchantly that MacDowell's best pieces "are a boy's view of the American past, looked back to from a premature middle age,"[8] as in the song collection *From an Old Garden;* "From an Indian Lodge" and "A Deserted Farm" in *Woodland Sketches;* "From a Log Cabin" and "From Puritan Days" in *New England Idyls.*

The composer's vocabulary, which has often been likened to that of Edvard Grieg (whom MacDowell admired and to whom he dedicated the Third and Fourth piano sonatas), shares with Grieg's

[8] *Music in a New Found Land*, p. 27.

a remarkable integrity, homogeneity, and identifiability. The most characteristic features of MacDowell's style are its Wagnerian chromatic harmony, full of enharmonic modulations, appoggiatura dissonances, and inversions of triads, seventh chords, and ninth chords; its texture, which tends to be thick and fat and, although ranging freely over the entire keyboard, seems to emphasize the lower registers; and its ebb and flow of rhythmic activity and dynamic contour, both in a state of constant flux. Example 6-8, from a piece reported by MacDowell's first biographer to be one of the composer's own favorites,[9] shows most of these hallmarks of his style. In another vein, however, are many works which derive, no

EXAMPLE 6-8. E. MacDowell, "In Mid-Ocean," *Sea Pieces*, Op. 55 (Boston, Leipzig, New York: Arthur P. Schmidt, 1899), No. 8, measures 1–8.

matter how indirectly, from dance meters, including Mendelssohnian scherzos. These are lighter in texture, "snappy" in rhythmic shape (often literally so: MacDowell's Scottish background was strong and "Scotch snap" iambs appear regularly), and less chromatic in harmony, though never wholly diatonic. The "Uncle Remus" pieces of *Woodland Sketches* and *Fireside Tales*, the fifth of the Goethe *Idyls*, the third of the Heine *Poems*, "Humoreske" and "March" in the Four Pieces, Op. 24, are of this type, as are the "Love Song" and "In War-Time" movements of the "Indian" Suite for orchestra. So too is "To a Wild Rose" (MacDowell's best-

[9] Lawrence Gilman, *Edward MacDowell, A Study* (New York: John Lane Co., 1908), pp. 70–71.

known single work), although it is often mistaken for a "poetic" and sentimental piece, played with rubato not even hinted at in the score, and at a tempo considerably slower than that indicated by the composer. Faintly reminiscent of Schumann's "Traümerei" in its design, it moves "with simple tenderness" to a single strategically placed climax and a lone, conclusive iamb (Example 6-9).

EXAMPLE 6-9. E. MacDowell, "To a Wild Rose," *Woodland Sketches* (1896), Op. 51 (Boston, Leipzig, New York: Arthur P. Schmidt, 1899), No. 1, measures 43–51 (conclusion).

Other currents

Inevitably, a reaction against the predominantly Germanic cast of post-Civil War fine-art music took place. It took two forms: some composers sought to refresh American music with an infusion of folkloristic elements; others turned enthusiastically to the new modes of expression emanating from Russia and France, or to even more exotic sources.

Folklorism was hardly unknown to the European Romantics. A fascination with "primitive" peasant culture or with traditional anonymous folk forms was one manifestation of the Romantics' infatuation with the untrammeled expression of childhood, the "folk" being viewed as national or regional or even racial children. Ultimately Americans came to share this aspect of Romantic thought. The problem for composers was: what was American musical folklore? A few men had given tentative hints of *their* answer to the question: MacDowell, Chadwick, even old Father Heinrich. Others now followed the hint: all too simplistically, they looked to the most "primitive" kinds of music in the nation, the music of the American Indian and the Negro. That there might be other "folkish" music in their past and under their very noses, that the vernacular tradition of popular music might provide a usable stock of invigorating source materials, seems not to have occurred to most of these composers. But then, did not Frédéric Ritter aver that America had no "people's song"? Had not Antonin Dvořák, in a much-discussed and very influential article in *Harper's* (February, 1895), backed up by the example of his "New World" Symphony (New York, 1893), recommended the use of Negro melodies, even claiming that "they are the folk songs of America, and your composers must turn to them"?

Besides their (perhaps unconscious) Romantic interest in "folk" materials, some American composers of the late nineteenth century saw them as a nationalistic instrument as well, as had some Europeans earlier, the "Russian Five," for example. For to the degree that a nation's composers could borrow from indigenous musical sources they were assured a certain national identity; their music would be different from that of other regions or nations. In late nineteenth-century America, and indeed through the first three decades of the twentieth, this aspect of folklorism exerted a strong pull on many composers, who yearned to free themselves from a European musical yoke, hoping to be somehow recognizably "American."

Aggressive steps in this direction were first taken by the Middle Westerner Arthur Farwell (1872–1951). His own turning to Indian music was reflected in a number of works based mainly on Omaha tribal dances and songs. Perhaps even more significant was his enthusiastic championing of new currents in American music through publication by the Wa-Wan Press which he established in 1901. Looking about him, Farwell saw a "quantity of compositions . . . and my own work, all blocked as to publication." He determined to "combine my work with that of these others—we were all in the same boat—and launch a progressive movement for American music, including a definite acceptance of Dvořák's challenge to go after our folk music."[10] When the Wa-Wan Press was sold to the

---

[10] Quoted in Edward Waters, "The Wa-Wan Press: An Adventure in Musical Idealism," *A Birthday Offering to Carl Engel*, ed. Gustave Reese (New York: G. Schirmer, Inc., 1943), pp. 214–33. "Wa-Wan" is an Omaha word identified with a ceremony of peace, fellowship, and song.

firm of G. Schirmer in 1912, it had published works by thirty-seven composers. Among them were a number with folkloristic interests, especially in Indian and Negro music. Matching Farwell's preoccupation with Indian music was the interest in Negro music of Henry F. B. Gilbert (1868–1928), composer of *Comedy Overture on Negro Themes* (1905) and *The Dance in Place Congo* (1906). Other Wa-Wan Press composers with less selfconsciously "Americanist" aims were men like Arthur Shepherd (1880–1958) and Edward Burlingame Hill (1872–1960).

Hill, who had been a pupil of both Paine and Chadwick, was one of the first Americans to feel the lure of the new French music of the 1890's, reflecting it in his own works and passing on a taste for it to such of his students at Harvard as Walter Piston and Virgil Thomson. In fact, Boston, long the ideological center of American music's Germanophilia, was at last beginning to rebel, beginning to see in the more or less individual styles of Saint-Saëns, D'Indy, Fauré, Debussy, and Ravel a refreshing change. *The Musical Record* of December 1890 quoted approvingly from the *Boston Home Journal:*

> A plea for more French music and less German is demanded. . . . We grope about in German mists . . . and say it is purer and healthier than clear air and a blue sky. We pay American money for the privilege of submitting to German dictation.

Another composer trained at Harvard, John Alden Carpenter (1876–1951), shared Hill's partiality toward French music and showed it in works like the song cycle *Gitanjali* (1913), the orchestral suite *Adventures in a Perambulator* (1915), and a Concertino for piano and orchestra (1916); the Concertino and some later works also included ideas from American popular music.

Another composer who was susceptible not only to the new French music but also Russian, particularly that of Scriabin, was Charles T. Griffes (1884–1921). After four years in Germany (1903–07), his early works were, not surprisingly, Teutonic; among them are some strong songs of 1909 to poems by Heine, Lenau, Eichendorff, and others. But Griffes must have considered these works as preliminary to his real beginnings; he later commented: "When I began to write I wrote in the vein of Debussy and Stravinsky; those particular wide-intervalled dissonances are the natural medium of the composer who writes today's music."[11] In a number of songs of 1912 to poems by Oscar Wilde, including *Symphony in Yellow* and *La Fuite de la lune*, Debussyesque harmony predominates, with however a rather firm, chiseled melodic line close to Ravel's (Example 6-10). Related in style are the *Roman Sketches* for piano (1915–16), which include the best-known of Griffes's works, *The White Peacock* (later to be orchestrated delicately by the composer).

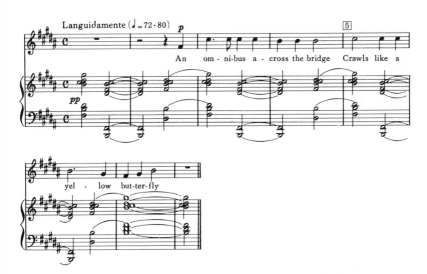

EXAMPLE 6-10. C. Griffes, *Symphony in Yellow*, Op. 3, No. 2 (New York: G. Schirmer, Inc., 1915), measures 1–8. Quoted by permission.

An interest in Oriental music shows up in *The Pleasure Dome of Kubla Khan* (piano version 1912; revised and orchestrated 1917); Oriental flavor is pervasive in a group of songs on pentatonic and hexatonic scales, *Five Poems of Ancient China and Japan;* and for a ballet titled *Sho-Jo* Griffes composed a unique score on Japanese themes, with orchestration "as Japanese as possible: thin and delicate, and the muted string *points d'orgue* serve as neutral-tinted background, like the empty spaces in a Japanese print. The whole

[11] Quoted in Edward Maisel, *Charles T. Griffes* (New York: Alfred A. Knopf, 1943), p. 112.

thematic material is given to the flute, clarinet, and oboe—akin to the Japanese reed instruments: the harp suggests the koto."[12] *Sho-Jo* was never published, nor was another unique dance-drama of the same year, *The Kairn of Koridwen* (1917), scored for an eight-piece ensemble of flute, two clarinets, two horns, harp, celesta, and piano. These works, related to Schoenberg's *Pierrot Lunaire* (1912) and Stravinsky's *L'Histoire du soldat* (1918) in their novel chamber-music instrumentation, must have been considered too exotic to be publishable.

In his last year but one, Griffes renounced the delicate shades of the French style and the Orient ("I don't want the reputation of an Orientalist and nothing more") and produced several works of power, even ferocity, that suggested he was approaching a mature synthesis of the several styles in which he had successively immersed himself. The Piano Sonata (Example 6-11), a *Notturno* for orchestra (different from the *Nocturne* transcribed from the Piano Sonata's slow section), the *Poem* for flute and orchestra, and a group of *Three Poems* to texts by Fiona MacLeod (including the shattering song "The Lament of Ian the Proud") reveal Griffes as an American composer on the brink of greatness. The promise of these works was not to be realized, however: he died early in 1921, aged thirty-five.

EXAMPLE 6-11. C. Griffes, Piano Sonata (New York: G. Schirmer, Inc., 1921), concluding measures. Quoted by permission.

[12] Quoted in Maisel, *op. cit.*, p. 206.

Bibliographical notes

One Hundred Years of Music in America, ed. Paul Henry Lang (New York: G. Schirmer, Inc., 1961) is a collection of essays some of which survey the "institutional foundations" of the cultivated tradition.

No extensive studies have been published on the Second New England School or on J. S. Dwight. Various dissertations (on Dwight, Paine, Chadwick, Foote) have been completed; others are in progress. These may be located in the various lists by Helen Hewitt of "Doctoral Dissertations in Musicology," *Journal of the American Musicological Society, passim.* Parker's daughter, Isabel Parker Semler, published "a memoir for his grandchildren": *Horatio Parker* (New York: G. P. Putnam's Sons, 1942).

MacDowell's *Critical and Historical Essays* (Boston: Arthur P. Schmidt, 1912; reprinted New York: Da Capo Press, 1968) reveal his attitudes clearly. Lawrence Gilman's study of 1908 (see footnote 9) remains the most extensive one. Irving Lowens's "Edward MacDowell," in *Hi Fi/Stereo Review*, XIX, No. 12 (December 1967), 61–72, is the most definitive biographical account; serious bibliographical and analytic investigation remains to be published.

Griffes is the subject of a somewhat gossipy biography by Edward Maisel; his music still awaits definitive cataloging and stylistc study.

7
Charles E. Ives

The most extraordinary and significant American composer of the late nineteenth and early twentieth centuries was Charles Edward Ives (1874–1954). Because of heart attacks (the first on October 1, 1918) and other serious illness, Ives composed very little after about 1921; ironically, it was only after he had stopped intensive composing and had "cleaned house," as he put it, by printing (at his own expense) the Second ("Concord") Piano Sonata (1920), some *Essays Before a Sonata* (1920), and a volume of *114 Songs* (1922) that his music began to be generally known at all. Acceptance was slow even then: not until the 1940's were many works by Ives performed. Since World War II, however, the number of performances, publications, and phonorecordings has grown steadily, as has Ives's influence on other composers' thought.

Ives grew up in Danbury, Connecticut. In later years he emphasized the importance of his father in shaping his musical thinking. George Ives was in some ways a typical late nineteenth-century provincial American musician: leader of the Connecticut Heavy Artillery First Brigade Band during the siege of Richmond, he returned after the Civil War to Danbury, where he played the piano for dances and the organ for church services, gave music lessons, organized the Danbury Band, and was in general a musical jack-of-all-trades. He knew academic music theory, was a practical music arranger, and composed a little. Where he differed from other such "town" musicians was in his passionate curiosity about sound, his experimental attitude, and his open-mindedness; all these were to be reflected concretely in his son's music and musical thought. From the age of five, Charles Ives was taught by his father: "Bach and the best of classical music, and the study of harmony and counterpoint . . . and the use of the ears and mind to think for themselves and be more independent—in other words, to be less dependent on customs and habits."[1] Ives was thus trained in music of the cultivated tradition; he was exposed, through his father's multifarious musical occupations, to both cultivated and vernacular traditions; and he was encouraged toward an open-minded independence of musical thought that could encompass both traditions.

Ives's formal music study was completed at Yale (1894–98) under Horatio Parker, for whom he had a qualified respect (see above, p. 136). Upon graduation, already aware that his music was "impractical" and sharing his father's view that "a man could keep his music interest stronger, cleaner, bigger and freer if he didn't try to make a living out of it" (Cowells, p. 37), Ives decided on a business career in life insurance. He pursued it with great success from

---

[1] Charles Ives, quoted in Henry Cowell and Sidney Cowell, *Charles Ives and His Music* (New York: Oxford University Press, 1955), p. 30. The present discussion of Ives draws, for statements by Ives himself, primarily on three sources: the Cowells' sensitive study, full of otherwise unpublished remarks by Ives; Ives, *Essays Before a Sonata and Other Writings*, ed. Howard Boatwright (New York: W. W. Norton and Company, Inc., 1962); and John Kirkpatrick, "A Temporary Mimeographed Catalogue of the Music Manuscripts and related materials of Charles Edward Ives" (New Haven: School of Music Library, Yale University, 1960). These will be referred to hereinafter simply as "Cowells," "*Essays*," and "Kirkpatrick."

1898 until his retirement in 1930. For a time (1898–1902) he was also a practicing musician as organist and choirmaster at the First Presbyterian Church in Bloomfield, New Jersey, then at Central Presbyterian Church in Manhattan; but from 1902 on he limited himself to business and to composing—furiously, at white heat— during evenings and on weekends. He never regretted his double life; in a well-known statement that reveals the New England Transcendentalist strain in his thinking, Ives said:

> . . . The fabric of existence weaves itself whole. You can not set art off in the corner and hope for it to have vitality, reality and substance. There can be nothing *"exclusive"* about a substantial art. It comes directly out of the heart of experience of life and thinking about life and living life. My work in music helped my business and my work in business helped my music.[2]

The demands on his time of business, the non-acceptance of his music, and the lack of direct involvement with the professional music world freed, or forced, Ives to develop his own aesthetic. It was a unique one, and we must understand it if we are to view his music in proper perspective.

Ives's musical thought

Ives prized what he called "substance" rather than "manner" in both music and its performance. "Manner" for Ives approached what others might call "technique," on the part of either composer or performer. "Substance . . . is practically indescribable," admitted Ives, but it "suggests the body of a conviction which has its birth in the spiritual consciousness, whose youth is nourished in the moral consciousness, and whose maturity as a result of all this growth is then represented in a mental image" (*Essays*, p. 75). Common notions of beauty have nothing to do with it; it "has something to do with character. . . . The substance of a tune comes from somewhere near the soul, and the manner comes from—God knows where" (*Essays*, p. 77). On this philosophical ground Ives based some startling concrete ideas. If substance has nothing to do with beauty or manner, then the very sound of music may be insignificant

---

[2] Quoted first in Henry Bellamann, "Charles Ives; the Man and his Music," *MQ*, XIX (1933), 45–58.

compared to the spirit in which it is produced. The roots of this idea are apparent in an anecdote about Ives's father:

> Once when Father was asked: "How can you stand it to hear old John Bell (who was the best stonemason in town) bellow off-key the way he does at camp-meetings?" his answer was: "Old John is a supreme musician. Look into his face and hear the music of the ages. Don't pay too much attention to the sounds. If you do, you may miss the music." (Cowells, p. 24)

"The music," the *real* music, resided in the humanity of its producer. This is why Ives could cry out passionately: "My God! What has sound got to do with music!" (*Essays*, p. 84) This is why, in recalling revivalist camp meetings, he could speak with affection of the aberrations in the hymn-singing, and of ". . . the great waves of sound . . . when things like *Beulah Land, Woodworth, Nearer My God to Thee, The Shining Shore, Nettleton, In the Sweet Bye-and-Bye*, and the like, were sung by thousands of 'let-out' souls. . . . If they threw the poet or composer around a bit, so much the better for the poetry and the music. There was power and exaltation in these great conclaves of sound from humanity." (Cowells, pp. 23–24) This is why he could even drive the argument to its logical conclusion and say: "That music must be heard is not essential—what it *sounds* like may not be what it *is*" (*Essays*, p. 84). And this in turn helps to explain a puzzling statement in the "Postface" to *114 Songs*: "Some of the songs in this book . . . cannot be sung,—and if they could perhaps might prefer, if they had a say, to remain as they are,—that is, 'in the leaf.' . . . A song has a few rights the same as other ordinary citizens."

Ives's music often shares the variety, the apparent disorder, the co-existence of seemingly unrelated things of life itself; characteristic is a planar, heterophonic polyphony occasionally so dense that the ear simply cannot distinguish the separate strands. Ives analogized between such co-existent but independent ideas in his music and sportsmen in a game of doubles—"Having four men playing tennis together does not always destroy personality" (Cowells, p. 32)—or the participants in the unstructured discussion and argument of a New England town meeting. In a sketch for the Second String Quartet, whose movements are titled "Discussions," "Arguments," and "The Call of the Mountains," Ives described the work as a "S[tring] Q[uartet] for 4 men—who converse, argue (in re

'Politics'), fight, shake hands[,] shut up—then walk up the mountain side to view the firmament." He seemed to view musical texture sometimes as a microcosm in which the co-existence of disparate elements does not threaten disorder any more than, say, in a forest the co-existence of different trees, rocks, mosses, flowers, animals, and insects threatens disorder; "disorder," in this instance, is an irrelevant concept, or one too narrowly conceived. Traditional devices for "ordering" musical form (repetitions, periodic phrase structure, classical tonality, and the like) although not always lacking in Ives's music are not by any means always present. Ives could scoff at such devices, questioning for instance "how far repetition is an essential part of clarity and coherence. . . . If nature is not enthusiastic about explanation, why should Tschaikowsky be?" (*Essays*, p. 99) Ives admired quite another order-principle, which he expressed most clearly in his essay on Emerson:

> His underlying plan of work seems based on the large unity of a series of particular aspects of a subject rather than on the continuity of its expression. As thoughts surge to his mind, he fills the heavens with them, crowds them in, if necessary, but seldom arranges them along the ground first. (Essays, p. 22)

This is a fair description of the tumultuous congregations of materials, and their apparent lack of continuity, in many of Ives's works.

The subject-matter of Ives's music was equally life itself, or "a series of particular aspects" of it. The pages of his manuscripts are studded with verbal comments that particularize the diary-like outpourings of his musical mind. One of the most illuminating examples is found in a manuscript copy of the first movement of the First Piano Sonata, where we read:

> What is it all about—Dan S asks. Mostly about the outdoor life in Conn[ecticut] villages in '80s & '90s
> Impressions, Remembrances, & Reflections, of Country Farmers in Conn Farmland   On pg 14 back   Fred's Daddy got so excited that he shouted when Fred hit a Home Run & the school won the baseball game   but Aunt Sarah was always humming—Where is my wandering Boy—after Fred an John left for a job in Bridgeport—there was usually a sadness—but not at the Barn Dances   with its jigs foot jumping & reels mostly on winter nights   In the Summer times, the Hymns were sung outdoors, Folks sang—as ole Black Joe—& the Bethel Band—Quickstep Street Marches, & the people

like[d to say] things as they wanted to say and to do things as they wanted to in their own way—and many old times . . . there were feelings, and of spiritual Fervency! (Kirkpatrick, p. 83)

Thus viewing some of his music as reminiscences, or re-creations in sound, of life experiences, many of which included actual music or were easily associable with specific kinds of music, Ives constantly used musical quotations in his works; they are often the very basis of the musical fabric. Traditional American hymn tunes, marches, and ragtime rhythms are the most commonly quoted, but material from other composers also appears, from Handel, Haydn, Beethoven, and Tchaikowsky to Foster, Mason, Bradbury, and Sankey. Such borrowings had nothing to do with nationalism, folklorism, or mere "local color"; they were a transcendentalist's acceptance of the validity, even divinity, of all the things under God that he had known, felt strongly, and believed to have vitality and "substance." Without naming names, but perhaps referring to Farwell, Ives wrote that the composer born in America and "so interested in 'negro melodies' that he writes a symphony over them [cannot, if he] has not been interested in the 'cause of the Freedmen'," produce something with substance, only with "color." Yet, "if a man finds that the cadences of an Apache war-dance come nearest to his soul," he can use them "fervently, transcendentally, inevitably, furiously, in his symphonies, in his operas, in his whistlings on the way to work [and] his music will be true to itself and incidentally American" (*Essays*, pp. 79–80).

Just as no kind of musical source-material was excluded from the Ives canon, no kind of performance was either. Ives found the mix-ups and mistakes, the wrong notes and off-key playing of amateur musicians just as "substantial" and thus in his view as "musical" as polished perfection, perhaps more so. Some of his music was planned to include such "mistakes": in a score-sketch for "The Fourth of July," third of his *New England Holidays*, Ives twice warned his copyist: "Mr. Price: Please don't try to make things nice! All the wrong notes are *right*. Just copy as I have—I want it that way. . . . Mr. Price: Band stuff—they didn't always play right & together & it was as good either way" (Kirkpatrick, p. 11). Ives wanted performances of his music to have a sense of involvement in action, of spontaneity and vitality. When *Three Places in New England* was first played in New York (1931) and conductor Nicolas Slonimsky apologized for a ragged performance, Ives reassured him: "Just like a town meeting—every man for himself. Wonderful how it came out!" (Cowells, p. 106) In some of his scores, Ives offers choices to the performer: a passage in the Second Sonata for violin and piano may be repeated "2 or 3 times decr[escendo] and rit[ardando] gradually," and a cadenza in the *Scherzo: Over the Pavements* is "to play or not to play! if played, to be played as not a nice one—but evenly, precise & unmusical as possible!"

"Nice" meant to Ives something weak, lily-livered, conventional, effetely genteel. Among his manuscripts is a *Take-off* on the Andante of Haydn's "Surprise" Symphony, marked "nice little easy sugar plum sounds," and under some harmonically knotty measures of his *Browning Overture* Ives wrote: "Browning was too big a man to rest in one nice little key . . . he walked on the mountains not down a nice proper little aisle." Ives felt that men's ears and minds could encompass much more than they thought possible. In terms of harmony, he equated complexity with strength; remembering Thanksgiving as a holiday celebrating the early American colonists, he noted on one of the sketches for the "Thanksgiving" movement of *New England Holidays* that "our forefathers were stronger men than can be represented by 'triads' only—these are too easy sounding" (Kirkpatrick, p. 13).

Persons of a "nice" conformist gentility were epitomized by Ives with the name "Rollo," borrowed from a mid-nineteenth-century series of children's books about a boy insufferably priggish, proper, and perfect.[3] To "Rollo," Ives addressed many sarcastic marginal comments in his manuscripts: in the Second String Quartet, "too hard to play—so it just can't be good music—Rollo"; in the *Browning Overture*, "R. B[rowning]'s mental workmanship is as sound logical & strong as easier plans [which] Rollo likes."

The other side of this ideological coin was Ives's own willingness to try anything musically, his rejection of dogmatic and exclusive musical concepts, and the embodiment of his theoretical speculations not in verbal treatises but in musical works. In an essay that comes closer to being a rounded theoretical statement than anything else he wrote—"Some 'Quarter-tone' Impressions" (1925)—Ives's open-mindedness is trenchantly expressed in two sentences: "Why

[3] I am indebted to Professor Henry Leland Clarke for clarifying this.

tonality as such should be thrown out for good, I can't see. Why it should be always present, I can't see" (*Essays*, p. 117).

In sum, Ives believed in substance over manner, in spirit over technique; he believed in music as a re-creation in sound of life itself; he felt that passionate, honest self-expression, by composer and/or performer, would create a "unity" far more significant than traditional order principles; he accepted as source material any sort of musical idea, his own or others', cultivated or vernacular; he identified difficulty with strength; he abhorred the "nice," the easy-sounding, and the genteel; and he was willing to try anything.

Ives's music

Ives was a prolific composer. Kirkpatrick's "Temporary Catalogue," the most accurate listing of Ives's works, includes five completed symphonies and two orchestral "sets" (Ives's term for a group of related tone-poems; the First Orchestral Set is better known by its subtitle as *Three Places in New England*), plus other orchestral music. Many pieces for chamber or theater orchestra are yet unpublished; among those published are *The Unanswered Question*, the *Scherzo: Over the Pavements*, *Central Park in the Dark*, and two pieces called *Tone Roads*. Ives wrote some band music and also chamber music, including two string quartets, six violin-and-piano sonatas, and pieces for various other combinations. The keyboard music includes two piano sonatas (plus a *Three-Page Sonata*), numerous separate pieces for one or two pianos, and some works for organ. Many of the organ and choral works written during Ives's years on the organ bench and left in church libraries have been lost, but a considerable number of choral works remain. Finally, there are songs, almost twice as many as the *114 Songs* published by Ives.

The extraordinary diversity of Ives's music is well seen in his songs. Some sense of the bewilderment with which other composers greeted the book of *114 Songs* when they came upon it is conveyed in Aaron Copland's breathless summary:

> Almost every kind of song imaginable can be found—delicate lyrics, dramatic poems, sentimental ballads, German, French, and Italian songs, war songs, songs of religious sentiment, street songs, humorous songs, hymn tunes, folk tunes, encore songs; songs adapted from orchestral scores, piano works, and violin sonatas; intimate songs,

cowboy songs, and mass songs. Songs of every character and description, songs bristling with dissonances, tone clusters, and "elbow
chords" next to songs of the most elementary harmonic simplicity.[4]

Clearly, one cannot hope to describe such an oeuvre easily. A close
look at one or two can, however, suggest some aspects of Ives's
music.

Two Little Flowers (1921) is superficially simple, sweet, un-
complicated. The text, written by Ives and his wife, tells of "two
little flowers" seen in the backyard on sunny days; other blossoms
may be beautiful, but "fairest, rarest of them all are Edith and
Susanna" (young Edith Ives and her playmate). The atmosphere
of both text and setting is that of the nineteenth-century sentimental household song, and the melody moves predictably along
in smooth contours of pitch and rhythm (Example 7-1a). Suddenly,
however, three tiny rhythmic jolts occur, at "one in green," "passing fair," and "ever rare"; they point up, in a subtle way, the syn-
tactical divisions of the verses, and they prepare for the wholly
original melodic climax with its downward vaulting of an octave and
a third (unless the singer can't make it; and Ives offers a simpler
alternative) and its suspensive pause on "all," gratefully low in the
singer's range (Example 7-1b). The accompaniment has its subtleties too: initially sounding like a commonplace arpeggiated vamp,
it turns out to revolve in groups of seven (not eight) eighth-notes,
and rather than outlining a conventional triadic harmony it is
quintal, spanning the interval D-E. This whole-tone interval is the
basis for the harmonic events through two-thirds of the song, as
each of these notes moves outwards in whole-tone motion: D-E,
C-F♯, A♯-G♯. Approaching the end, Ives shifts to a V-of-ii, V-of-V,
I $_4^6$ pattern, full of harmonic energy, but returns to the whole-tone
idea at the climax: superimposed on the surprising, dark chord at
the word "all" is an even more surprising C-E third high in the
piano, as if the B♭-D interval were going to move upwards to the
E-G of the next measure (through C-E and D-F♯) but couldn't
wait. The song ends with chords that sound like ii-V-I, but each
contains the critical whole-tone interval: E-D, A-B, D-E.

[4] Copland, "One Hundred and Fourteen Songs," *MM*, XI (January–
February 1934), 59–64.

EXAMPLE 7-1. C. Ives, *Two Little Flowers* (1921). Copyright 1935 Merion Music, Inc.; used by permission. (a) Measures 1–10. (b) Measures 23–27.

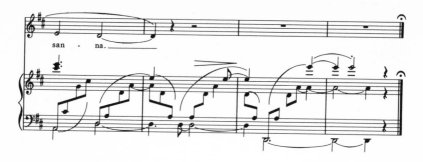

EXAMPLE 7-1 continued.

Even this brief analysis makes the music seem more complicated than it sounds: the total effect of the song is that of simplicity and "familiarity," yet the commonplace is everywhere avoided and we recognize a work in which the familiar is sublimated.

Less traditional by far in melody, harmony, and rhythm is *Cradle Song* (1919), given in its entirety as Example 7-2, although within its tiny nine-measure span it speaks just as evocatively and directly as *Two Little Flowers*. Each of the three phrases of the vocal line comes to rest on G♯, establishing that note as one tonal center, although the scale-basis of the melody might suggest F♯. The accompaniment is less certain about its tonality, finally settling on A (but G♯ appears here, too, linking voice with accompaniment). No systematic harmony is present, except an *avoidance* of simple triads; there are Debussyesque bichords (measures 1, 9), added-sixth chords

EXAMPLE 7-2. C. Ives, *Cradle Song* (1919). Copyright 1935 Merion Music, Inc.; used by permission.

We will sing— soft · est num · bers; Nought thy
Au · tumnal winds are sigh · ing; Fa ded
Peace · ful · ly flows the riv · er; So shall

sleep · ing en · cum · bers.—
leaf · lets are fly · ing.—
love— flow for ev · er. —

For 1st and 2nd Verses

For ⌢ 3rd Verse

Notes: End song on ⌢ ; This chord may be repeated very quietly at the end of verse sung last.
*It will be observed that a ♩ of the ²⁄₄ measure is a ♩ of the ⁶⁄₈ and not a ♪.

EXAMPLE 7-2 continued.

(1, 2, 9), Wagner's *"Tristan* chord" with complications (5), and other simultaneities inexplicable as single sonorities without taking into account linear aspects (e.g., the F♯ of measure 4, part of a treble line moving C♯-E-F♯-G♯). Harmonically, the song seems to "float" in a void, an effect consonant with the text. The rhythm of the piece confirms this effect, as it sways gently between ²⁄₄ and ⁶⁄₈, the ²⁄₄ ♩ = ⁶⁄₈ ♩ prescription precluding any sense of regular meter at all and allowing the rhythm to float, unmoored to a metric anchor. In measure 8, voice and accompaniment are really in different meters, the voice part ending on a disguised ²⁄₄ measure, the accompaniment continuing in its broad ⁶⁄₈.

One of the lengthiest and most powerful songs, *General William Booth Enters into Heaven* (1914), on portions of a poem by Vachel Lindsay, exemplifies Ives's use of "imitative dissonance" and of musical quotation. The hectic, militant atmosphere of the text, which celebrates the fanatic revivalism of the first commanding general of the Salvation Army, leads Ives to begin the song with a typical marching band's drum-beat: the whack of the snare drums and the thud of the bass drum, lagging a bit behind, are projected in dissonant clusters (Example 7-3a). Where Lindsay's poem quotes parenthetically (from a Salvation Army hymn, "Are you washed in the blood of the Lamb?"), so does Ives, though he uses the revival hymn tune *Cleansing Fountain* ("There is a fountain filled with blood"). His equivalent to parenthesizing it is to present it in a key far removed from the tonal sphere of the context. This melody, redolent of American gospel hymnody in general, is developed in all kinds of ways in the course of the song; other melodies quoted are the introduction to James A. Bland's minstrel-show song *Golden Slippers* (responding to the text's mention of a banjo; measures 52–55, piano part) and trumpet-calls (at the mention of trumpets, measures 69–72, and of marching, measures 103–5). One of the most moving passages of the song (Example 7-3b) finds the singer circling "round and round" on a three-note figure, the pianist's right

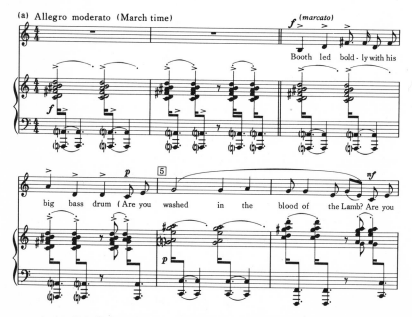

EXAMPLE 7-3. C. Ives, *General William Booth Enters into Heaven* (1914). Copyright 1935 Merion Music, Inc.; used by permission. (a) Measures 1–10. (b) Measures 82–91.

EXAMPLE 7-3 continued.

hand circling similarly but in a two-note cycle, while in the middle of the accompaniment, strangely askew, the melody of *Cleansing Fountain* winds its tranquil way. *General William Booth* ends with a haunting, parenthetically off-key statement of *Cleansing Fountain* set to hymn-book harmony, then the drum-beats, lower-pitched as if in the distance, fade—"as a band marching away," wrote Ives in the manuscript.

Other notable songs of Ives, which I can cite but briefly here, are *Charlie Rutlage* (1914 or 1915), a cowboy ballad in which Ives turns to unpitched rhythmic declamation for the climactic measures; *The Circus Band* (1894), with much prancing band music; *Serenity* (1919), to a tranquil poem by Whittier, in which a virtually monotonous chant-like vocal line is spun out against an other-worldly, "floating" harmonic oscillation; *Walking* (1902), in which the diffuse, cloudy overtones of church bells are captured subtly, and also the propulsive syncopations of ragtime. In *Majority* (originally for chorus and orchestra, 1915; arranged for voice and piano, 1921), with its perfervid Whitmanesque text, there is an equation between "the Masses" of the poem and massive chords (as many as fifteen notes) built in clusters of massed seconds; these must be played either with the forearm or a board, or with the help of a second pianist. *Soliloquy* (1907; reprinted in Cowells, p. 158) is subtitled "a study in 7ths and other things" and systematically explores non-traditional harmonies and retrograde motion.

A number of the *114 Songs* were originally choral works, but the bulk of Ives's choral music was for the church: some forty sacred choruses remain. Best-known among these is a setting of *Psalm 67* (1898), based on a bitonal plan with the men's voices in the sphere of G minor, the women's in C Major. Most awesome is an eleven-minute setting of *Psalm 90* (1898–1901?) for choir, organ, and bells, underscored throughout by a low C in the organ. Ives's wife heard him say that this was the only one among his compositions that satisfied him.[5] A number of the choral works seem to be compositional études; they reveal the speculative vein of Ives's thought, akin to Milhaud's studies in bichords and Bartók's in scales and intervals. Among these are *Psalm 24* (1897?), which is based on mirror-image counterpoint and systematic interval-expansion

[5] Reported by John Kirkpatrick in his jacket notes for *Charles Ives: Music for Chorus*, Columbia Records MS 6921.

(Example 7-4a) and the *Processional "Let There Be Light"* (1901), whose harmonies are based on consistently changing structural intervals; the chords of its core-passage are abstracted in Example 7-4b (P = perfect; A = augmented; M = major; m = minor).

EXAMPLE 7-4. "Compositional études" of Ives. (a) *Psalm 24* (1897?), measures 1–6 (after the manuscript). (b) *Processional "Let There Be Light"* (1901), harmonic plan of measures 9–18 (after the manuscript).

Among the secular choral works are *Three Harvest Home Chorales* (1898, 1902) for chorus, brass ensemble, and organ—"a kind of outdoor music," according to Ives, in which the tangled yet harmonious co-existence of "the trees, rocks, and men of the mountains in days before machinery" is expressed through radically independent counterpoint among the three sound-components.[6]

[6] The passages quoted are from an Ives letter published in Gertrude Norman and Miriam Lubell Shrifte (eds.), *Letters of Composers* (New York: Alfred A. Knopf, 1946), pp. 345–46.

Lincoln, the Great Commoner (1912), for (mostly unison) chorus, orchestra, and piano, exceeds even the *Chorales* in density of texture and heterophonic polyphony; quotations from *The Battle Hymn of the Republic, Hail! Columbia, The Red, White & Blue* ("O Columbia, the gem of the ocean"), *The Star-Spangled Banner, America,* and *The Battle Cry of Freedom* appear in almost cinematic collage, and more than once the voices split into a tumult of shouted tone-clusters, a kind of "choral noise" of overwhelming power.

The shorter instrumental works of Ives, like the songs, are remarkable for their diversity and individuality: each seems to create its own expressive world; taken together, they cover an immense range of affective ends, achieved by an equally broad spectrum of technical means.

Among the shorter piano pieces are various Studies (1907–9?), part of an incomplete series of twenty-seven (after Chopin's twenty-seven Etudes?), including *Some South-Paw Pitching,* a showpiece for the left hand under right-hand variants of Foster's *Massa's in de cold cold ground; The Anti-Abolitionist Riots;* and *22* (i.e., twenty-second in the series), in an unusually clear A-B-A-Coda form. Interesting for their relationship to Arnold Schoenberg's much later twelve-tone row technique are *Three Protests* (or *Varied Air & Variations*) of 1914 or 1916: the monophonic theme of the variations, likened by Ives to "the old stone wall around the orchard," is made up of four interlocked, row-like chromatic series—for Ives the musical embodiment of the New England stone fence where none of the stones is exactly the same size or shape. The *Three-Page Sonata* (1905), actually a substantial eight-minute work, compresses the traditional four-movement form into one, with a dramatic first section, lyric slow section, and last section alternating clangorous march motifs and jerky ragtime rhythms.

Free from the necessity to accommodate his music to conventional performance media, Ives wrote works for an astonishing variety of chamber ensembles, from two pianos tuned a quarter-tone apart (*Three Pieces,* 1923–24) to the combination of strings, brass, and four sets of bells of *From the Steeples* (1901). Many of the chamber works derived from, or were rebuilt into, other pieces. Among those originally conceived as chamber music are two well-known works of 1906 often performed separately but apparently considered by Ives as a pair—*The Unanswered Question* and *Central Park in the Dark in "The Good Old Summer Time"*; the first "A Contemplation of a Serious Matter," the second "A Contemplation of Nothing Serious." *The Unanswered Question*, for trumpet, four flutes, and offstage strings, has an elaborate metaphysical program explaining the three sound-components: the strings represent "the silence of the druids," the trumpet asks "the perennial question of existence," and the flutes—"Fighting Answerers"—attempt to find a satisfactory response. But no explanation is needed for the delicate balance in which the three components are suspended: the strings move slowly and placidly in spacious, diatonic chords from beginning to end; the trumpet occasionally sounds a disturbingly repetitive, atonal phrase from another musical world; and the flutes, increasingly raucous and agitated, provide a dynamic arc for the whole structure. As the Cowells (p. 177) write, "When the dissonant voices disappear, the faint consonant [string] chords continue to hum softly in the distance, like the eternal music of the spheres." No other work by Ives so immediately and movingly brings us in touch with his faith in the harmonious co-existence of disparate elements.[7] *Central Park in the Dark* is for a totally different ensemble (piccolo, flute, oboe, clarinet, bassoon, trumpet, trombone, percussion, two pianos, and strings) but similarly juxtaposes quiet sounds with what Ives called "off tunes & sounds."

Ives was capable of musical contemplation not only of cosmically serious matters but of earthily comic ones. *Hallowe'en*, for string quartet and piano with drum *ad libitum*, may have been composed on April 1, 1907. It is a cacophonic spoof combining the humorous surprise of April Fools Day jokes with the crude pranks of Hallowe'en. The first violin plays in the key of C, the second in B, the viola in D♭, the 'cello in D; the piano is atonal. Seldom do accents coincide. Only eighteen measures long, the piece may be repeated three or four times, omitting or altering various parts each time until the last, when, the drum adding to the general din, the tempo is to be "as fast as possible without disabling any player or instrument." The *Scherzo: Over the Pavements* (1906–13), which

---

[7] See Eric Salzman's comments on this work, accompanied by a page of the score, in *Twentieth-Century Music: An Introduction* (Englewood Cliffs: Prentice-Hall, Inc., 1967), p. 145.

includes the cadenza "to play or not to play," is for piccolo, clarinet, bassoon, trumpet, three trombones, cymbal, drum, and piano. It grew out of a work called *Rube Trying to Walk 2 to 3!!*, which suggests its emphasis on rhythmic counterpoint; this reaches a knotty climax (Example 7-5) in the second section of the A-B-C-Cadenza-B′-A′ form. Ives has the last laugh on the struggling performers in a comic ending, which sees them all together in an oom-pah, oom-pah vamp on a simple C major triad—a mocking concession to "Rollo."

Ives combined several groups of chamber pieces into "sets." One such set, a three-movement group of which the second is lost,

EXAMPLE 7-5. C. Ives, *Scherzo: Over the Pavements* (1906–13), measures 59–61. Copyright 1954 by Peer International Corporation. Used by permission.

EXAMPLE 7-5 continued.

he called *Tone Roads* (1911–15). No. 3, for woodwinds, brass, strings, piano, and chimes, is interesting for its repetitions of sections at varied tempos; its use of quarter-tone inflections; and the "tone road" of the chimes (in all but one section of the work), which approximates a twelve-tone row and is treated at the beginning like a medieval *color*, its pitch-pattern repeated in a varied rhythmic pattern (Example 7-6).

EXAMPLE 7-6. C. Ives, *Tone Roads*, No. 3 (chimes part only), measures 1–12. After a photostat of the manuscript in the Library of Congress.

In more conventional media, and somewhat more conventional forms, are the sonatas for piano and for violin and piano, and the symphonies.

Besides the *Three-Page Sonata*, Ives composed two numbered piano sonatas and began a third, now lost. The Second Sonata ("Concord, Mass., 1840–1860") is a giant four-movement cycle reflecting Ives's admiration for some of the literary participants in the "American Renaissance," as F. O. Matthieson has called it. Howard Boatwright has written, in his edition of the *Essays Before a Sonata* that Ives published in conjunction with the music:

> For some composers, one work, more than any other, may become a channel through which the streams of philosophical concept, musical technique, and style flow in singular unity. For Charles Ives, the Concord Sonata was such a work. It reflects programmatically, and also in deeper, less obvious ways, the influence of the Concord Transcendentalists; it is representative of Ives' highest achievements in richness of harmony and freedom of rhythm. (*Essays*, p. xiii)

Ives himself spoke of the work (*Essays*, p. xxv) more diffidently, saying it was "a group of four pieces, called a sonata for want of a more exact name, as the form, perhaps substance, does not justify it." He described the four movements as "impressionistic pictures of Emerson and Thoreau, a sketch of the Alcotts, and a *scherzo* supposed to reflect a lighter quality which is often found in the fantastic side of Hawthorne." Emerson, for Ives, conjures up a musical portrait of power and density; the first movement, although based on a sonata-form idea, reminds one of Ives's view of Emerson's own "plan of work" (see above, p. 152). The scherzo on Hawthorne rushes by in a blur except for one quiet, slow passage colored by two-octave-wide cluster-chords vibrating sympathetically high in the treble and another in which Simeon Marsh's hymn *Martyn* appears in a hushed, halting, hymn-book harmony. The Alcotts evoke a gentle variant of *Martyn* (which relates also to the opening motif of Beethoven's Fifth Symphony that appears throughout the "Concord" Sonata) and several of "old Scotch airs," one of *them* related (coincidentally?) to the minstrel-show song *Stop That Knocking at My Door* (1843) of A. F. Winnemore (*MinA*, No. 106). The final movement, "Thoreau," is deceptively calm in spirit; it builds to a single climax, then unwinds in a long denouement synthesizing materials from earlier movements and closing with a hauntingly tentative final gesture. Said Ives of the "Concord" Sonata: "Some of the passages now played have not been written out, and I do not know as I shall ever write them out as it may take away the daily pleasure of playing this music and seeing it grow and feeling that it is not finished and the hope that it never will be—I may always have the pleasure of not finishing it."[8]

Besides a Pre-First Violin Sonata and a Pre-pre-First Violin Sonata (lost or destroyed), Ives wrote four sonatas for violin and piano between 1903 and 1914–15. More than any other group of Ives's works, the four sonatas seem all of a piece, citizens of the same musical world. All are in three movements; all end with hymn-tune finales; all are characteristically "easy" pieces (by Ives's standards), lacking the tangled thickets of the texture of, say, the first movement of the "Concord" Sonata. Sonatas Nos. 1 and 3 are abstract; Sonata No. 2 offers portraits of "Autumn" and a square dance ("In the Barn") plus a nostalgic view of the mounting intensity of a camp meeting ("The Revival"). Sonata No. 4, entirely based on hymn tunes, is called "Children's Day at the Camp Meeting." "The Revival" movement of Sonata No. 2 is an ingeniously worked piece, a sort of freely unfolding stream of variations on the old hymn tune *Nettleton* (or *Hallelujah;* see above, p. 94). The ingenuity and freedom with which Ives "re-composed" such borrowed material can be suggested by comparing a passage from "The Revival" (Example 7-7a) with the opening of the third movement of Ives's String Quartet No. 1 (Example 7-7b). In the former, Ives sets the tune as a bitonal canon at the tritone over cloudy pedal-points on the tonic and dominant of the respective keys; in the latter, he invents a new ending and sets the tune to a cross between Schubertian and barbershop harmony.

The First String Quartet (1898?) is an assemblage from earlier organ pieces: its last three movements were originally a *Prelude,* *Offertory,* and *Postlude* composed in 1896 for use in New Haven's Center Church; the first movement derives from a fugue (on Lowell Mason's *Missionary Hymn* [see above, p. 57], soon combined with Oliver Holden's *Coronation*) that Ives had written for Horatio Parker. Ives later adapted the fugal movement for use in his Fourth

[8] Cowells, 13. Both the Cowells (pp. 190–201) and Chase (in *AM,* pp. 418–27) discuss the "Concord" Sonata at some length.

EXAMPLE 7-7. Two uses of *Nettleton* by Ives. (a) Sonata No. 2 for violin and piano (New York: G. Schirmer, Inc., 1951), 3rd movement, measures 22–23. (b) String Quartet No. 1, 3rd movement, measures 1–4. © Copyright 1961 and 1963 by Peer International Corporation. Used by permission.

Symphony. The Second Quartet (1911–13; 2nd movement 1907) I have mentioned above (pp. 151–52); it is a thoroughly mature and "tough" work, one of the most striking examples of Ives's involving the performers in "discussions" and "arguments." The third movement finds the arguments resolved and the participants "viewing the firmament," to material based on the hymn tunes *Nettleton* and *Bethany* (Mason's "Nearer, my God to thee").

As in the violin sonatas, Ives seems in his symphonies to have been mindful of traditional broad formal procedures. Following the early First Symphony (1896–98) in four movements came a Second (1897–1902) in five. Its last movement is the most "Ivesian," with its quotations (*Camptown Races*, another more lyric melody reminiscent of *Old Black Joe*, country-fiddle-style counterpoints, *The Red, White & Blue*, and *Reveille*) and with the magnificent squawk (all twelve tones) of its final chord. The earlier movements seem somewhat labored in their conventionality, particularly the self-proclaiming "developments" of material in the style of European symphonists from Beethoven to Wagner, Brahms, and Dvořák: can Ives have been spoofing? The Third Symphony (1901–12) is characterized by its subtitle, "The Camp Meeting," and is a broad, hymnic three-movement work; both first and last movements betray their origins as earlier organ pieces.

Between the Third Symphony and the completion of the Fourth, Ives wrote three other works of symphonic proportions. *A Symphony: "New England Holidays"* (1904–13) was a gathering of four earlier orchestral movements into a kind of American "Four Seasons": "Washington's Birthday," "Decoration Day," "The Fourth of July," and "Thanksgiving." The First Orchestral Set or *A New England Symphony: "Three Places in New England"* (1903–14) is a three-movement work. Its first movement, "The 'St. Gaudens' in Boston Common," is a brooding piece with some of Ives's most subtle, highly developed use of old melodies. Inspired by the monument of Augustus Saint-Gaudens to Colonel Robert Shaw and the Negro regiment he led during the Civil War, Ives based his music on Foster's *Old Black Joe*, Root's *Battle Cry of Freedom*, and Work's *Marching Through Georgia*. Example 7-8 shows one moment when Ives finds a common denominator (*a* in the example) between the phrase "I'm coming" of Foster's song and "[Hur]rah! hurrah!" in Work's; combines that material with the chorus ("The Union forever, Hurrah boys, Hurrah!") of *The Battle Cry of Freedom* (*b*); fashions an ostinato bass (*c₁*) from a pentatonic motive (*c₂*) common to the two Civil War songs; and underscores the whole with a traditional military band's drum-cadence (*d*). The second movement of *Three Places*, "Putnam's Camp," combines the gay, brassy music of a late nineteenth-century Fourth of July picnic (complete with the village brass band) with a child's vision of the Revolutionary War; the middle section finds the march beat of Example 7-8 (*d*) going along at two different speeds in the proportion ∘ = ♩ in a famous example of polytempo. The movement is full of hilarious gaiety and ends in a fine Independence Day burst of pyrotechnical pandemonium and a rather besotted blast of *The Star-Spangled Banner*. *Three Places* concludes, somewhat like the Fourth Symphony, in murmuring tranquility, with an autumnal portrait of a New England river: "The Housatonic at Stockbridge." A Second Orchestral Set (1912–15), again in three movements ("An Elegy to Our Forefathers," "The Rockstrewn Hills Join in the People's Outdoor Meeting," and "From Hanover Square North, at the End of a Tragic Day, the Voice of the People

EXAMPLE 7-8. C. Ives, *Three Places in New England,* 1st movement ("The 'St. Gaudens' in Boston Common"), measures 66–69. Quoted by permission of Mercury Music Corporation.

Again Arose"), completes the roster of Ives's major orchestral works before the Fourth Symphony. A Third Orchestral Set and a *Universe Symphony* (see Cowells, pp. 201–3) were left unfinished.

Ives labored off and on between 1909 and 1916 at his Fourth Symphony, one of the mightiest works in the history of American music. Scored for a huge orchestra and chorus plus a "distant choir" of strings and harps and a special "battery unit" of percussion, it had to wait until April 26, 1965 for its premiere performance (under Leopold Stokowski, assisted by two other conductors). Two movements had been performed in 1927, and program notes for that performance were written by Henry Bellamann, obviously from information supplied by his friend Ives:

> This symphony . . . consists of four movements,—a prelude, a majestic fugue, a third movement in comedy vein, and a finale of transcendent spiritual content. [The order of the second and third movements was later reversed.] The aesthetic program of the work is . . . the searching questions of What? and Why? which the spirit of man asks of life. This is particularly the sense of the prelude. The three succeeding movements are the diverse answers in which existence replies. . . . The fugue . . . is an expression of the reaction of life into formalism and ritualism. The succeeding move-

ment [i.e., the movement ultimately made the second] . . . is a comedy in the sense that Hawthorne's Celestial Railroad is a comedy.[9]

Ives added to Bellamann's notes a word on the last movement: ". . . an apotheosis of the preceding content, in terms that have something to do with the reality of existence and its religious experience."[10]

The four movements of the Fourth Symphony resolve into two pairs. The Prelude, with its choral inquiry ("Watchman, tell us of the night/What the signs of promise are"), leads to the "comedy" movement, in which nostalgic song-passages are constantly interrupted by strident marches, rags, square-dance tunes, and patriotic ditties not just separately but sometimes all at once. The fugue, stately, hymnic, suffused with 16- and 32-foot organ pedal color, serves as preparation to the last movement, which is even more complex in texture than the second, but a tapestry of murmurs rather than shouts. It begins mysteriously, like a distant march, with a complex percussion pattern that never ceases, is wholly independent of the rest of the movement's music, and, lingering after the orchestra (with wordless voices) dissolves, fades off in the distance as the symphony ends. For all its growing, then ebbing complexity, the movement breathes a spirit of utter tranquility. Ives wrote no more profoundly conceived and perfectly realized music than this.

Seen against the nineteenth-century background of an American musical culture sharply divided between cultivated and vernacular traditions, Ives's historical position is a unique one. Alone among his contemporaries, he embraced both traditions without reservation: his works emphatically declared that in its vernacular tradition American music had an artistically usable past; they also embodied the highest aspirations of the cultivated tradition. Moreover, Ives's open-mindedness and freshness of musical imagination were to be a continuing challenge to American composers after 1920. Ives is seen by many as the fountainhead of a new tradition in American music,

---

[9] Quoted in John Kirkpatrick's extensive preface to the published score (New York: Associated Music Publishers, 1965), p. viii. Kirkpatrick includes a detailed account of the background of the symphony and an authoritative identification of its many musical quotations.
[10] Ibid.

a basically experimental, pathfinding one. In a few sentences that are rather Ivesian in their bluntness and humor, Virgil Thomson, commenting on "the composer who lives by non-musical work," has remarked:

> [He] makes up his music out of whole cloth at home. He invents his own aesthetic. When his work turns out to be not unplayable technically, it often gives a useful kick in the pants to the professional tradition. The music of . . . Charles Ives did that very vigorously indeed.[11]

It promises to do so for some time to come.

Bibliographical notes

Besides the basic works cited in this chapter's first footnote, there is surprisingly little substantial work on Ives in print. Peter Yates writes a sympathetic "Introduction to Charles Ives" in his *Twentieth Century Music* (New York: Pantheon Books, 1967). Philip E. Newman has written a dissertation on the songs (Ph.D., University of Iowa, 1967). Elliott Carter, who knew Ives well, wrote in 1944 of "Ives Today: His Vision and Challenge," *MM*, XXI, 4 (May–June 1944), 199–202. An article notable for its excellent illustrations (photographs and facsimiles) is David Hall's in *Hi Fi/Stereo Review*, XIII, 3 (September 1964), 41–58. Kurt Stone's "Ives's Fourth Symphony: A Review," *MQ*, LII (1966), 1–16, is an enlightening example of the rather ambiguous and puzzled reaction to Ives's music that must have been common during the composer's creative life (somewhat less so today). One of the very few serious studies of Ives's musical quotation practice and of his varied use of pre-existent music is Sydney Robinson Charles, "The Use of Borrowed Material in Ives' Second Symphony," *Music Review*, XXVIII, 2 (May 1967), 102–11.

[11] *The State of Music*, 2nd rev. ed. (New York: Random House [Vintage Books], 1962), p. 85.

PART THREE

After 1920

8
The 1920's

The period surrounding World War I, roughly from about 1910 to the mid-1920's, was a critical one for Western music in general and for American music as part of the larger scene. Many young European composers felt that the main Classic-Romantic tradition had reached a crisis-point and that new means had to be found to renovate it. Various reactions to the tradition, more or less violent, became apparent during this period, which was one of the most turbulent aesthetically and stylistically in the history of Western music. Paris, especially, was a cauldron of ferment; but so was Vienna, for so long a center of the tradition. Composers of other nationalities shared the same sense of crisis as well, partly out of a nationalistic urge for musical independence from Central European domination.

In some works, barbs of satire and ridicule were aimed at the presumed hyperexpressivity and bombast of the tradition. Thus Claude Debussy slyly quoted Wagner's *Tristan* in "Gollywog's Cakewalk," the most offhand piece in his *Children's Corner* suite (1906–08), with a tongue-in-cheek instruction to the pianist to play "avec une grande émotion." Erik Satie became virtually a professional musical satirist. The young Darius Milhaud reacted against the inordinate length and grandiloquence of the post-Romantic symphony and opera forms with three-minute symphonies (1917) and *opéras minutes* (1927).

Another kind of reaction was that of an outright rejection of the tradition and an attempt to revolutionize musical expression, especially in media related to the machine age: this was the aim of the Futurist group at first centered in Italy, then in Paris, where concerts of noise instruments—hissers, exploders, cracklers, buzzers, screamers, and the like—were given.

Older, established composers like Ralph Vaughan Williams, Richard Strauss, Gabriel Fauré, and Jan Sibelius, not sharing the sense of crisis of their younger colleagues, more or less unconsciously extended the tradition. But the group of composers in Vienna around Arnold Schoenberg sought *consciously* to extend it beyond past limits, particularly its element of chromaticism. Considering Classic-Romantic tonality a Procrustean bed ill-fitted to the increasingly chromatic vocabulary of melody and harmony, they wrote an ultra-chromatic music that avoided traditional tonality and approached a free atonality. In another sort of evolutionary extension of the tradition, the Czech composer Alois Hába began working with microtones, intervals smaller than the traditional chromatic semitones of the twelve-note tempered scale.

Finally, an immense number of works of the period suggest attempts to revitalize and enlarge the tradition by exotic and atavistic borrowings from musical cultures distant in space, spirit, or time. Thus the primitivistic manner of Igor Stravinsky's *Le Sacre du printemps* (1913) and *Les Noces* (1917–23); the delving into the heart of folk music of Béla Bartók; and the popularesque manner based on urban café music of Milhaud's *Le Boeuf sur le toit* (1920), Arthur Honegger's Concertino for piano and orchestra (1925), and Francis Poulenc's Sonata for piano duet (1918). Related in impulse to these works, which looked to primitive, folk, and popular music for a fresh note, were others that looked back, beyond the Romantic era, to the Classical, Baroque, and even earlier periods in Western music for inspiration: Sergei Prokofiev's "Classical" Symphony (1916–17); Stravinsky's *Pulcinella* (1920) and Octet for wind instruments (1923); Schoenberg's chamber *Serenade*, Op. 24 (1923) and neo-classic Suite for piano, Op. 25 (1924); Maurice Ravel's *Le Tombeau de Couperin* (1914–17); Ottorino Respighi's *Antiche arie e danze* (1916–31) and *Concerto Gregoriano* (1922).

In sum, the atmosphere of European music just before and after the First World War was charged with various currents and cross-currents of progressivism: "New Music" marched under a variety of banners. This atmosphere was characteristic also of the United States, slightly later, between the end of World War I and the economic collapse of 1929. An era of unprecedented prosperity in the U.S.A., the 1920's were notable in American music as years when progressive currents could flourish, and did; years when youthful composers could afford to spurn the achievements of the generation that preceded them, and did.

The older generation, composers in their forties and fifties in the decade after World War I, continued to write in an essentially nineteenth-century manner, to get performances and continued respect. Chadwick, Frederick Converse (1871–1940), Edward Burlingame Hill (1872–1960), Rubin Goldmark (1872–1936), and Daniel Gregory Mason (1873–1953) carried forward the traditionalism, the solid craft if not notable inventiveness of the Second New England School.

Some slightly younger composers were gaining reputations as the inheritors of the American cultivated-tradition ideal of a music of serious import and large-scale edification—"Americans who work along more or less conservative lines and make no attempt to write anything departing from general types of European music."[1] Among those who were to maintain some prominence during and after the decade of the 1920's was Howard Hanson (b. 1896), a composer of

---

[1] Henry Cowell, in an introductory chapter dated January 1933 for *American Composers on American Music* (1933; 2nd ed.; New York: Frederick Ungar Publishing Co., 1962), p. 9. It is interesting to compare Cowell's "grouping of composers according to accomplishments and ideals" with that of Aaron Copland written a few years earlier: "America's Young Men of Promise," *MM*, III, 3 (March–April 1926), 13–20.

big rhetorical works like the Second ("Romantic") Symphony, the choral cantata *The Lament for Beowulf* (1925), and the opera *Merry Mount* (1933). Hanson was perhaps more lastingly significant as a teacher and as director of the Eastman School of Music (Rochester, N.Y.), where from 1925 he produced annual festivals of American music. Others in this group were Leo Sowerby (b. 1895), an organist-composer who provided much viable music for his instrument, and Randall Thompson (b. 1899), who became as strongly identified with works for chorus as Sowerby with works for organ.

A few other composers leavened their academic heritage with sprinklings of some kind of popular or folk music. John Alden Carpenter's ballet scores *Krazy Kat* (1921) and *Skyscrapers* (1926) were indebted to some rhythmic aspects of American dance music. Charles Wakefield Cadman (1881–1946) took both subject and musical inflections from American Indian music for his opera *Shanewis* (1918). John Powell (1882–1963) delved in Anglo-American folk song, Emerson Whithorne (1884–1958) and Henry Eichheim (1870–1942) in Oriental music. The strains of the jazz-once-removed of white America's ballrooms and dance halls were useful for Louis Gruenberg (1884–1964) in works like *Daniel Jazz* (1925) and *Jazzettes* (1926) and his later successful opera *The Emperor Jones* (1933).

More notable than these, however, more characteristic of the era of the "Roaring '20's," were younger composers grappling with the new ideas, the new materials, the new approaches to organizing sound that had been proposed by the European leaders of "New Music" (Stravinsky, Schoenberg, the sassy young French composers, the Futurists) and by the new American "urban folk music" of jazz. As Aaron Copland, along with George Gershwin the most prominent young composer of the decade, has written: "Contemporary music as an organized movement in the U.S.A. was born at the end of the First World War."[2]

Nadia Boulanger and Aaron Copland

Copland (b. 1900) was one of a large group of American composers to become the student, in Fontainebleau and Paris, of the

[2] *Our New Music* (New York: Whittlesey House, 1941), p. 137.

remarkable musician and teacher Nadia Boulanger (b. 1887). Mlle. Boulanger's unique combination of exacting severity and liberating encouragement (the latter given in exquisitely precise proportion to the pupil's efforts) was to be a magnet for several generations of young Americans; in the 1920's, as one of her pupils of that decade has commented, "What endeared [Boulanger] most to Americans was her conviction that American music was about to 'take off,' just as Russian music had done eighty years before."[3] She was capable of training young composers without dictating one exclusive style: the measure of her phenomenal gifts as a teacher was the variety of personal styles developed in her *atelier*. Nevertheless, the example of Stravinsky was most often set before her students, and certainly Copland's work in the 1920's reveals the impact of Stravinsky more than of any other composer. It also reveals a preoccupation with "Americanism," with a national identity. The models of Farwell and Gilbert, who had turned to Negro and Indian materials, seemed irrelevant, perhaps especially to Copland, a Brooklyn-born Jew; that of Ives was as yet unknown. Besides, as Copland recalled later:

> Our concern was not with the quotable hymn or spiritual: we wanted to find a music that would speak of universal things in a vernacular of American speech rhythms. We wanted to write music on a level that left popular music far behind—music with a largeness of utterance wholly representative of the country that Whitman had envisaged.[4]

In a few works written after his return from three years (1921–1924) in Paris under Boulanger, Copland seemed to have imagined that the jazzy rhythms and blue notes of contemporary dance music would provide sources for the music he sought to write. The first of these was *Music for the Theatre* (1925), a twenty-minute suite for small orchestra in five symmetrically ordered movements with a "motto" theme appearing in each. The scale of the work, its chamber medium, its orderly structure, and its crisp unsentimental tone all evidence the precise anti-Romanticism of Copland's French experience. Its crackling sonorities, bichordal harmonies, and jerky motoric rhythms suggest Stravinsky and the younger French composers. Its

---

[3] Virgil Thomson, *Virgil Thomson* (New York: Alfred A. Knopf, 1966), p. 54.

[4] *Music and Imagination: the Charles Eliot Norton Lectures, 1951–1952* (New York: Mentor Books, 1959), p. 111.

declamatory "motto," on the other hand, has been related to Copland's Jewishness; and the rhythmic and pitch inflections especially of the second ("Dance") and fourth ("Burlesque") movements relate to dance music of the 1920's like the Charleston (Example 8-1).

EXAMPLE 8-1. A. Copland, *Music for the Theatre* (1925). (a) "Motto," 1st movement, measures 2–5 (trumpet part only); (b) 1st movement, measures 14–17; (c) 2nd movement, measures 1–7 (bassoon part only). Copyright 1932 by Cos Cob Press Inc. Renewed 1960 by Aaron Copland. Reprinted by permission of Boosey & Hawkes, Inc. Sole licensees.

Rather similar in manner but larger in conception is a Concerto for piano and orchestra of 1927. In later works of the 1920's Copland gave up the limited expressive range of dance music and turned to a more abstract, less selfconsciously "American" manner—but one equally hard, lean, and rhythmically knotty—in a *Dance* Symphony (1929; three movements adapted from the earlier ballet *Grohg*); a trio, *Vitebsk* (1929); a *Symphonic Ode* (1930); and the *Piano Variations* (1930).

For many, the *Piano Variations* mark the summit of Copland's achievement. Based on a theme of a certain hard-edged grandeur (Example 8-2a), the work treats the instrument from the outset anti-Romantically as a basically percussive one, with hammers (which of course it is). The continuous set of twenty close-knit, largely clangorous variations culminates in an overwhelmingly resonant coda. Certain variations suggest that Copland had by this time absorbed the principle of Schoenberg's tone-row technique, perhaps unconsciously, into his own lucid, often brittle, and generally rhythm-dominated style (Example 8-2b).[5] The *Variations* seem to

EXAMPLE 8-2. A. Copland, *Piano Variations* (1930). (a) Theme, measures 1–11; (b) Variation 2, measures 21–24. Copyright 1932 by Aaron Copland, renewed 1959. Reprinted by permission of Aaron Copland, Copyright Owner, and Boosey & Hawkes, Inc., Sole Publishers and Licensees.

[5] In this connection, one might note Copland's transcription of the *Piano Variations* for orchestra in the 1960's, after he had adopted the twelve-tone technique whole-heartedly.

mark a synthesis by Copland of his American background, his French training, and a range of expression and means of tonal organization related to the Viennese School; they come very close to achieving Copland's ideal in the 1920's of a music that would "speak of universal things . . . with a largeness of utterance wholly representative of the country."

Many other young composers hied themselves off to Boulanger's studio in the 1920's: Virgil Thomson, Roy Harris, Walter Piston, Elliott Carter, Robert Russell Bennett, Marc Blitzstein, and others. These, however, did not gain the early prominence of Copland; their works belong more to the story of American music after the 1920's, and I shall refer to them in later chapters.

Edgard Varèse

The "organized movement" in contemporary music in the 1920's spoken of by Copland was reflected in the many groups founded to give concerts of new music, like the series produced between 1928 and 1931 by Copland and Roger Sessions; in the contributions of some major conductors who performed new works, notably Serge Koussevitzky (1874–1951), conductor of the Boston Symphony Orchestra from 1924, and Leopold Stokowski (b. 1882), conductor of the Philadelphia Orchestra from 1912 to 1938; and in the formation of composers' groups, especially the League of Composers (which sponsored the important journal *Modern Music*, 1924–46) and the International Composers' Guild (1921–27).

Founder of the Guild and in the vanguard of American music in the 1920's (and again in the 1950's) was the Paris-born composer Edgard Varèse (1883–1965), who came permanently to New York City late in 1915. In the 1920's Varèse founded no school of composers, but with his first American work, purposely and meaningfully titled *Amériques* (1918–22), he offered a challenge to musical tradition that was reiterated with each of his important compositions of the 1920's (*Offrandes, Hyperprism, Octandre, Intégrales, Arcana*) and the celebrated all-percussion piece *Ionisation* (1930–31). Perhaps because of the last-named work and the high proportion of percussion instruments he called for in others, Varèse's name has sometimes been linked with the Futurists and their *bruitisme*. Actually, Varèse stood alone: he was uninterested in a revolutionary "noise music" or a "machine music" as such; he believed, however, in the legitimacy of *any* sound as a vehicle for musical expression, and (as he put it in an unpublished lecture at Princeton University, September 4, 1959) he had become "a sort of diabolic Parsifal looking not for a Holy Grail but for a bomb that would blow wide open the musical world and let in sound—all sounds, [including those] at that time, and sometimes even today, called 'noise.'" As early as 1917 he was writing of a "dream of instruments obedient to my thought, and which with their contribution of a blossoming of unsuspected timbres will . . . bend to the demands of my inner rhythm."[6] That dream was to be realized, but only in the electronic era of the 1950's; in the 1920's Varèse had to content himself with conventional instruments, assembled, however, in unusual groupings and supplemented with a large number of so-called percussion instruments, some *not* so conventional. Important among the latter were sirens, whose arching curves of sound embodied and projected one of Varèse's most important concepts: that of music as a spatial art, as "moving bodies of sound in space." Not only are sirens employed in *Amériques* but in *Hyperprism* (1922) and *Ionisation* as well. Their use, and that of an inexhaustible variety of drums, cymbals, gongs, tam-tams, bells, chimes, wood-blocks and castanets, slapsticks and rattles, chains and anvils, bespoke Varèse's definition of music simply as "organized sound" limited in no way to traditional notions of "musical tone" as against "noise."

Varèse's music of the 1920's is marked especially by an emphasis on sheer sonority, often achieved by multiple repetitions of notes or aggregates of them, by writing at the extremes of an instrument's range, or by spacing of "chords" in unconventional ways and by dispersing their notes through a huge registral spectrum. Stridency of sound is characteristic: the performance-indication "hurlant" (yelling) is not uncommon. Traditional formations of harmonies do not typically appear, yet neither is the music organized by anything like Schoenberg's chromatic tone-rows. Individual sounds, pulsating with a life of varied intensities and changing timbres, are important, as at the opening of *Hyperprism*, where a C♯ introduced by a trombone is variously mutated, first by different attacks and approaches, then by coloration in horn, then by dynamic, timbral, and articulative shifts among three horns (Example 8-3a). That single

[6] My translation from *391*, No. 5 (New York, June 1917).

EXAMPLE 8-3. E. Varèse, *Hyperprism* (1922); (a) measures 1-6 (percussion parts omitted); (b) measures 11-13 (percussion parts omitted). © 1924 by Edgard Varèse & assigned to Colfranc Music Publishing Corp., New York. By permission of the publisher.

note and the D-C♯ interval formed when the bass trombone enters are examples of what Varèse called "sound-masses":

> There is an idea, the basis of an internal structure, expanded and split into different shapes or groups of sound, constantly changing in shape, direction, and speed, attracted and repulsed by various forces. The form of the work is the consequence of this interaction. (*Princeton lecture*)

Varèse likened such "an idea, the basis of an internal structure," to a crystal, which although restricted in internal form can appear in limitless external forms. In *Hyperprism* the most important such "crystal" would seem to be the major seventh interval (or its inversion, a semitone): this interval appears in innumerable aggregates. The sonority of measures 12–13, for instance, is a "splitting" of the C♯ sound (measure 11) into a four-note aggregate composed of two pairs of sevenths: flute C and clarinet D♭, and trumpet C♯ and trombone C (Example 8-3b). These sevenths relate back, of course, to the first interval heard in the work, the C♯-D of measure 5 (see Example 8-3a); and the final sound-mass of the work is a nine-note aggregate made up of the following transpositions: C-B, B♭-A, G-F♯, E♭-E, F♯-F. To be noted, especially in view of some procedures in *Intégrales,* is that the initial C♯-D pair does *not* appear at the close.

"Thematic" material in a traditional sense is not characteristic of Varèse's music: sound-masses, whether based on pitch, timbre, or rhythm, replace it. These are then varied, developed, interlocked, or superimposed somewhat the way themes might be. Ironically, in view of the furor that attended its early hearings, *Ionisation* contains a very important idea (advanced by the *tambour militaire* in measures 8–13) that approximates the periodic organization of a theme (Example 8-4). However, to follow this idea through the entire work, in which there is no melody or harmony in the traditional sense, only rhythms and an extraordinary variety of timbres produced by thirteen players on about forty instruments, is a fruitful approach to Varèse's concept of musical crystals, the variety of external forms they may take on, and their "attraction and repulsion" by various forces. Another sound-mass in *Ionisation* interesting to trace through its various manifestations is the cloudy metallic sonority of gong, high tam-tam, and low tam-tam first announced in measure 1.

EXAMPLE 8-4. E. Varèse, *Ionisation* (1930–31), measures 8–13 (*tambour militaire* part only). © 1934 by Edgard Varèse & assigned to Colfranc Music Publishing Corp., New York. By permission of the publisher.

Both *Hyperprism* and *Ionisation* lead to massive single climaxes near their conclusions, *Hyperprism* on an *hurlant* sonority at top volume (measures 72–75), *Ionisation* on an all-metal crash (measure 65). This procedure links Varèse with earlier composers, indeed with the post-Romantics, who loved the quasi-dramatic plan of a build-up to a single climax. *Intégrales,* a larger work of 1924 for woodwinds, brass, and percussion, is organized in three broad sections, each with characteristic sound-mass material; it too climaxes toward its close (measures 153–54).[7]

Henry Cowell

Another composer who embodied the progressivism of American music of the 1920's in his own music, in his support of new trends, and in his writings was Henry Cowell (1897–1965). Cowell was a Californian, a fact of significance in its suggestion of the end of the American frontier and the broadening of America's musical base to encompass the entire continent, also in its reminder that though American composers had traditionally looked eastward across the Atlantic to European cultural models, they could also look westward across the Pacific to the Orient. In a long career as aesthetic gadfly of American music, Cowell sought to find a context in *world* music for that of America, interesting himself in traditional and folk music of the entire world's peoples.

In the 1920's Cowell became notorious for novel uses of the pianoforte including "tone-clusters," for extensions of the rhythmic range of music, and for many other explorations into *New Musical Resources,* as the title of his 1919 book (published 1930) put it. His fertile musical imagination first addressed itself to the piano and its untapped reservoir of sound-possibilities: in March of 1912, at the age of fifteen, Cowell amazed a San Francisco audience with pieces like *The Tides of Manaunaun* (1911), which superimposes Mac-Dowellesque thematic material over deep oceanic roars produced by playing the lowest notes of the piano with the flat of the left hand or with the forearm. *Advertisement* (1915) finds fistfuls of tone-clusters cascading frantically from top to bottom of the keyboard, in a satiric evocation of the repetitious raucousness of advertisers. Besides his use of tone-clusters of massed seconds on the keyboard, Cowell achieved other new sonorities by playing directly on the piano strings. In *The Banshee* (1925) the lower bass strings (which are wrapped in metal coils) are stroked along their length; this

---

[7] An authoritative approach to an analysis of *Intégrales* is offered by Varèse's former pupil Chou Wen-chung in "Varèse: A Sketch of the Man and His Music," *MQ,* LII (1966), 151–70.

produces sounds four octaves above the keyboard tones, with a curious and even terrifying wailing effect. In *Sinister Resonance* (1935) Cowell applied to the piano strings techniques of stopping, muting at the bridge, and producing harmonics, theretofore used only for such stringed instruments as violins.

As early as 1914, Cowell began working with textures fashioned of melodic strands in independent rhythms: the piano piece *Fabric*, for instance, begins with a three-voice texture in which the relationship of beats between the voices in the first measure is as 8 to 6 to 5, in the second measure as 9 to 7 to 5, etc. Believing that human limitations precluded the realization of the full range of polyrhythms he envisioned, Cowell developed (in cooperation with the musical-instrument inventor Leon Theremin) the Rhythmicon, an instrument capable of producing very complex combinations of beat-patterns; it was combined with orchestra in a work of 1931 titled *Rhythmicana* and in several others.

Cowell was a fighter for others' new music as well as his own. In 1927 he founded a quarterly publication of innovative scores, *New Music*, which he was to edit until 1936 without ever including a note of his own music. Volume I, Number 1 consisted of a piece for small orchestra, *Men and Mountains*, by Carl Ruggles (b. 1876), one of a number of composers who, beside Varèse and Cowell, seemed poised on the leading edge of musical practice during the 1920's: George Antheil (1900–1959), Wallingford Riegger (1885–1961), John J. Becker (1886–1961), Adolph Weiss (b. 1891), and Ruth Crawford Seeger (1901–1953).

George Gershwin

The 1920's also saw important developments in the area of popular music. Considerably broadened, and so to speak nationalized, by the establishment of commercial radio stations and phonograph records, the sounds of Tin Pan Alley, the New York-centered business world of popular music, resounded over the continent. Popular song writers and arrangers suddenly spurted in numbers, the most successful of them in income and renown as well. Their best efforts were reserved for the American derivative of operetta—musical comedy, or just "musical"—which in the 1920's tended to be a saucy and optimistic, if often sentimental, mélange of "pop songs," "production numbers," and spoken dialogue, supported by only the thinnest-boned skeleton of a plot. Following Jerome Kern (1885–1945), whose more than sixty works for the stage culminated in *Show Boat* (1927), Irving Berlin (b. 1888), whose Ziegfield Follies were an annual event from 1918, and Cole Porter (1892–1964), a product of Yale and Harvard universities with a sophisticated wit, the most gifted songwriter of the decade was George Gershwin (1898–1937).

With his brother Ira as lyricist, Gershwin wrote some of the gayest musical comedy scores of the 1920's, especially *Lady, Be Good* (1924), *Oh, Kay!* (1926), and *Funny Face* (1927), all seeming in retrospect to be preparation for the political satire *Of Thee I Sing* (1931), the first musical to weld together so firmly plot, dialogue, and music that it received the Pulitzer Prize for drama. Gershwin's later *Porgy and Bess* (1935), which he characterized as "folk opera—opera for the [popular] theatre, with drama, humor, song, and dance," was a more pretentious but hardly more artistically successful contribution. It relied mainly on some memorable songs (*Summertime, I Got Plenty o' Nuttin', It Ain't Necessarily So*) which displayed the same special characteristics as Gershwin's earlier show songs: beguiling rhythms (*Fascinating Rhythm*, 1923); unusual form (*Embraceable You*, 1928); and harmonic materials richer than those of most American popular songs (*The Man I Love*, 1924; *Liza*, 1929; *So Are You*, 1929).

That the boundary between cultivated- and vernacular-tradition American music was becoming blurred once again is suggested by the critical success of Gershwin's musical comedy *Of Thee I Sing* and the popular success of his full-scale opera *Porgy and Bess*. Before either of these works, Gershwin had successfully introduced the idioms of Tin Pan Alley into the concert hall, first with *Rhapsody in Blue* (1924), a concerto-like work for piano and dance band (later orchestrated more fully) that achieved unparalleled popularity. Belatedly, Gershwin hastened to learn some techniques of "classical" composition—the *Rhapsody* had been scored not by the composer but by Ferde Grofé (b. 1892)—and produced several other concert works, among them a Concerto in F (1925) for piano and orchestra and *An American in Paris* (1928) for orchestra. Three Preludes for piano (1926), smaller-scaled and better-controlled than the orchestral works, are unpretentious but charming trifles, among the very best "household music" of the 1920's.

City blues and jazz

For many people, Americans and others alike, the most significant American music of the 1920's, the most indigenous and unprecedented, was jazz. Jazz had existed long before the 1920's, as had the special vocal styles and forms of blues, but only as an exclusively Negroid music unknown to the larger American community. What had been a music of and for Southern Negroes began to be diffused thanks to the earliest phonograph recordings (sporadically from 1917, then in greater numbers from 1923); the First World War (which found Negroes, jazz performers among them, spread over both North America and Europe); commercial radio stations (from 1920); and the increased mobility of Southern Negroes, particularly in the direction of Northern cities like Chicago, Detroit, and New York. The surest sign of the impact of jazz on America at large was the appearance in the popular entertainment world of pseudo-jazz, like that of Paul Whiteman (1890–1967) and innumerable other dance-band leaders, and the characterization of the entire decade as "The Jazz Age." The end of the 1920's saw jazz recognized as a national phenomenon, though centered in the Negro ghettoes of Northern cities, notably Kansas City, Chicago, Detroit, and New York (besides, of course, Southern centers like New Orleans and Memphis). It saw the faithful emulation of black jazz musicians by whites, not just the diluted strains of "symphonic jazz"; it saw a whole new sub-industry of the phonorecording business ("race records"—jazz and blues recordings initially produced for and distributed to the American Negro community); it saw the beginnings of world interest in jazz as a new music; and it saw the first major shift in jazz style itself, from the small "combo" of early jazz to the "big band."

Early jazz was a synthesis of the march/dance beat and overlaid syncopations of ragtime; other kinds of syncopated dance rhythms of Afro-Caribbean origin; a rudimentary but dynamic harmony rooted in the Euro-American traditions of dance music and revival hymnody; and the expressive, flexible vocal style of various branches of American Negro song, such as the repetitive, chant-like, and usually responsorial work-song, the solitary field holler, the religious spiritual, and, hardly different from the last-named in musical style, the secular blues.

In the formally standardized, instrumentally accompanied form of "city blues" (as opposed to the formally unstandardized and earlier "country blues"[8]) the blues was to become one of the two major foundations of 1920's jazz (the other being rags). Such city blues, as recorded by the "classic" female blues singers like Mamie Smith, Ma Rainey, Bessie Smith, and Ida Cox, tended to be strophic songs with a characteristic pattern to the text of each strophe, the succession of its accompanying harmonies, and the over-all musical form. Jazz musicians appropriated the *musical* design of such blues; from then on, "blues," whether with text or not, was to mean that design. Basically, blues design is one of a twelve-measure pattern ("12-bar blues") divided into three four-measure phrases, with the harmonic progressions indicated below:

$$\frac{4}{4} \quad \overline{\begin{array}{cccc} 1 & 2 & 3 & 4 \end{array}} \; \overline{\begin{array}{cccc} 5 & 6 & 7 & 8 \end{array}} \; \overline{\begin{array}{cccc} 9 & 10 & 11 & 12 \end{array}}$$

I————————   IV—— I——   V (IV) I——

Other lengths than twelve measures are found, and elaborations of the basic harmonies are legion; I have indicated in measure 10 one of the most common in the 1920's; after that time, the general tendency was to add more and more elaborative variants to the scheme of harmonies, preserving however the twelve-measure structure and the principal harmonic pillars.

In vocal blues, the three phrases of song per stanza are super-imposed on this basic structure. Each phrase of the singer typically lasts for only about half of the four-measure unit, leaving a "hole" until the beginning of the next unit; this hole is filled, in a respon-sorial way perhaps going back to primordial call-and-response tech-niques, by some sort of instrumental or hummed or spoken response to the singer's phrase. The whole combination, then, might be suggested this way:

Singer [response]   Singer [response]   Singer [response]

$$\overline{\begin{array}{cccc} 1 & 2 & 3 & 4 \end{array}} \; \overline{\begin{array}{cccc} 5 & 6 & 7 & 8 \end{array}} \; \overline{\begin{array}{cccc} 9 & 10 & 11 & 12 \end{array}}$$

I————————   IV————I——   V (IV) I——

---

[8] Some specific meanings for these two terms, so often used loosely, are given by Charles Keil, *Urban Blues* (Chicago: University of Chicago Press, 1966); see especially Chapter II and Appendix C.

One particularly clear example (available in both a recording and a transcription[9]) among many that might be cited is the performance by "Jelly Roll" Morton of *Mamie's Blues*. In an introduction to the music, spoken as he begins to play, Morton explains that this is "no doubt the first blues [he] ever knew," which (if we can believe his memory) would place it back around the turn of the century.

If blues contributed to jazz one of its most common formal structures, it contributed even more importantly to its instrumental style. Early blues *vocal* style was one of great variety and flexibility of intonation, mode of attack, tone color, vibrato, degree of nasality, regular rhythm or rubato. These freedoms (from the viewpoint of a singer trained in the Euro-American cultivated tradition of art-song or opera) were partly inherent in the folkish lack of "sophistication" of the country blues singers, partly the result of vestiges of the primordial African style concepts of the American Negro. Significant for jazz in the vocalism of the blues was the transfer from voice to instrument of this blues style: the jazz instrumentalist, unbound by notions of "correct" performance on a trumpet, a trombone, a banjo or guitar, used his instrument as a substitute for, or an extension of, his voice, bringing to it the same broad range of expression as that of the blues singer's voice. The various narrowly prescriptive attempts that have been made to categorize the "blue notes" of jazz (usually vastly oversimplified as the flatted third and seventh of the major scale) arise from a preconception, dominated by the cultivated tradition's ideas of the musical scale and of instrumental performance technique, as to what is and what is not "basic" or "natural" in musical structure and style.

Rags were the other major source of the repertory of jazz in the 1920's, thanks to the broad popularity of ragtime as a kind of marching and dancing music early in the century. The historic first recordings of jazz, ironically made by the all-white performers of the Original Dixieland Jass (*sic*) Band (1917), included blues and rags in about equal measure, like *Livery Stable Blues* and *That Teasin' Rag*. So did the musically more significant recordings, from the middle 1920's, of the bands of Joseph "King" Oliver (1885–1938), Louis Armstrong (b. 1900), and Morton, such as the 1923

---

[9] Commodore Records album FL 30,000 (*New Orleans Memories*); Alan Lomax, *Mister Jelly Lord* (New York: Grosset and Dunlap [The Universal Library], 1950), pp. 269–71.

recordings by Oliver's Creole Jazz Band of *Dippermouth Blues* and *Snake Rag,* the 1925–26 recordings by Armstrong's Hot Five of *Royal Garden Blues* and *Muskrat Ramble* (the latter a rag composed by trombonist Edward "Kid" Ory [b. 1886]), and the 1926 recordings by Morton's Red Hot Peppers of *Jelly Roll Blues* and *Black Bottom Stomp.*

Jazz instrumentalists brought to the performance of ragtime the same flexible, vocalistic nuances of pitch and rhythm that they brought to the blues; thus, in performance style the two types of early jazz were equivalent. Within the frameworks of blues or ragtime forms, early jazz performances were built on a principle of improvisatory variation; in terms of the broad Euro-American Western tradition, the result was close to the Baroque era's "strophic variations," a chain of varied repetitions of a basic "tune." In jazz, the "tune" was more a matter of the underlying harmonies of an original piece than its melody, and virtually any music could *become* jazz, by adoption of its "tune" as the basis for improvisatorily varied repetitions in jazz style. Most of the early jazz recordings were made by New Orleans musicians, and despite attempts to contradict the legendary primacy of the Crescent City as the sole birthplace of jazz, it remains important as the first major center. The New Orleans jazz bands were typically small groups (combos) made up mainly of clarinet, cornet, trombone, and drums, deriving from the military and civic marching bands of the post-Civil War period. They played outdoors for parades and funerals and, seated in placarded wagons, for advertising; indoors, in brothels, barrelhouses, and dance halls, with perhaps a ragtime piano and a banjo or guitar added, for dancing. The ensemble style, as heard typically in the first chorus (stanza) and the last, "ride-out" chorus(es) of a piece, was a roughly contrapuntal music with the powerful cornet projecting the main melodic voice, the clarinet weaving a treble countermelody, the trombone providing a solid but melodic bass, and the drums and other instruments supplying the basic beat against which raggy syncopations could work. Between first and last choruses, individual musicians would play one or more improvisatory solo choruses in succession.

Example 8-5 shows the improvisatory melodic style of such New Orleans jazz, taken from a later recording (1947) by Louis Armstrong; the example is chosen partly to suggest the absorption

by jazz, as the 1920's closed, of a third formal pattern in addition
to those of ragtime and blues: that of the 32-measure chorus, in
AABA design, of the popular songs of Tin Pan Alley. Example
8-5a is the original melody of the pop song *Black and Blue* (1929),
with its harmonies indicated. The transcription of Armstrong's
cornet melody (Example 8-5b) does not attempt to show the
nuances of pitch and tone-quality in his solo; it does however attempt to show rhythmic nuances, as Armstrong plays slightly earlier
(+) or later (−) the notes as indicated in the notated version.

EXAMPLE 8-5. (WHAT DID I DO TO BE SO) BLACK & BLUE by Andy Razaf,
Thomas Waller, and Harry Brooks. © 1929 by Mills Music, Inc. ©
renewed by Mills Music, Inc. Used by permission. (a) as published; (b)
as played by Louis Armstrong.

EXAMPLE 8-5 continued.

The 1920's saw the appearance of the first important non-Negro jazz musicians, beginning with the New Orleans Rhythm Kings, who went to Chicago in 1920. Later in the decade came Leon "Bix" Beiderbecke (1903–1931) and the Wolverine band, and a number of Chicago musicians who, playing together from schoolboy days, have been called the "Austin High School gang." Among them were Bud Freeman and Frank Teschemacher (1906–1932), both players of the saxophone, an instrument which although not commonly used in New Orleans jazz was to become indispensable in later jazz groups. Other instruments assuming new importance in jazz of the late 1920's were the trumpet, replacing the more mellow but less brazen cornet; the guitar, replacing the earlier banjo; and the string bass, replacing the tuba of the brass bands.

Another important development in jazz of the 1920's was the formation of "big bands" rather than small combos. Large groups necessitated some kind of musical arrangements; they could not rely on the free collective improvisation of the small ones. An early precursor of such "arranged jazz," requiring a real composer, was Jelly Roll Morton's Red Hot Peppers band, which began recording as a seven-man combo in 1926 but was eleven strong by 1929. Two other pianists, Fletcher Henderson (1898–1952) and Edward "Duke" Ellington (b. 1899), were to prove themselves even more skillfull leaders of big-band jazz. Henderson, with many ideas from saxophonist-arranger Don Redman, developed a technique of scoring for the brass, reed, and rhythm sections of a big band that gave it the feeling of freedom, mobility, and relaxation of a small combo, treating each section like a single voice and maintaining an improvisatory style even in the most carefully worked-out arrangements; individuals could still improvise over the arranged backgrounds of many choruses. Famous recorded examples were *Copenhagen* (1924) and *Sugar Foot Stomp* (1925; same "tune" as *Dippermouth Blues*); in both performances Louis Armstrong figures prominently. Ellington led his band into the most distinctive and coloristically imaginative style of the era. The Ellington band's "head arrangements," worked out empirically in rehearsals, expanded the color range of the big band by employing wordless voice as an extra instrument (*Creole Love Call*, 1927), exploiting brass mutes of various kinds (*The Mooche*, 1928), and interlocking brasses and reeds in brand-new, faintly exotic sonorities (*Black and Tan Fantasy*, 1927). Ellington was also one of the first to develop new and expanded forms for jazz; early efforts culminated in *Creole Rhapsody* (early 1931).

Bibliographical notes

A book that communicates vividly the sense of ferment in European music and the other arts in the period 1885–1918 is Roger Shattuck's *The Banquet Years* (Garden City: Doubleday Anchor Books, 1961). The most comprehensive general survey of early twentieth-century music is William Austin's *Music in the 20th Century* (New York: W. W. Norton and Company, Inc., 1966).

Arthur Berger has written a sympathetic study of Copland's music

(New York: Oxford University Press, 1953). A useful bibliography of writings by and about Copland (and many others) is *Some Twentieth Century American Composers*, compiled by John Edmunds and Gordon Boelzner (2 vols.; New York Public Library, 1959–60).

Besides the article cited in footnote 7, Chou Wen-chung has published three important articles on Varèse in *PNM*, V, 1 (Fall–Winter 1966); see also Milton Babbitt's "Edgard Varèse: A Few Observations of His Music," *PNM*, IV, 2 (Spring–Summer 1966). One of the few other attempts to discuss Varèse's music in any detail is that of Marc Wilkinson in *The Score and I.M.A. Magazine*, No. 19 (March 1957).

The best biographical account of Gershwin is Edward Jablonski and Lawrence D. Stewart, *The Gershwin Years* (Garden City: Doubleday and Company, Inc., 1958; many illustrations and facsimiles). One of the few insightful and serious attempts to discuss Gershwin's music is a little-known article by Frank C. Campbell, "The Musical Scores of George Gershwin," *Library of Congress Quarterly Journal of Current Acquisitions*, XI, 3 (May 1954), 127–39. Leonard Bernstein's "Why Don't You Run Upstairs and Write a Nice Gershwin Tune," reprinted from *The Atlantic Monthly* of April 1955 in *The Joy of Music* (New York: Simon and Schuster, 1959), is deceptively off-hand. *Musical Comedy in America* (New York: Theatre Arts Books, 1950) is an adequate historical account by Cecil Smith.

After the present book was written, there appeared the first volume of a two-volume jazz study that promises to supersede all previous writings: Gunther Schuller's *Early Jazz: Its Roots and Musical Development* (New York: Oxford University Press, 1968); the remarks on jazz in this chapter should be read in the light of Schuller's highly informed criticism and history. Still valuable, in a field marked by great unevenness of bibliography, are Marshall Stearns's *The Story of Jazz* (New York: Oxford University Press, 1956; reprinted as a Mentor paperback); Rudi Blesh's *Shining Trumpets* (2nd ed.; New York: Alfred A. Knopf, 1958); and, for its analytic approach to different jazz styles, André Hodeir's *Jazz: Its Evolution and Essence* (New York: Grove Press, 1956).

9

The 1930's
and Early 1940's

The 1930's in American music were a complete contrast to the 1920's. The optimistic, progressive, strident voices of the 1920's were muted in the decade of the Great Depression. As Virgil Thomson wrote later in his autobiography, "The time was not for novelty." Copland, in a famous statement about the trend to simplicity in his own works of the 1930's, said:

> The old "special" public of the modern music concerts had fallen away, and the conventional concert public continued apathetic or in-different to anything but the established classics. . . . I felt that it was worth the effort to see if I couldn't say what I had to say in the simplest possible terms.[1]

[1] *Our New Music* (New York: McGraw-Hill Book Company, 1941), p. 229.

A characteristic gesture of the concert-music establishment was that of the Philadelphia Orchestra's management in announcing just before the 1932 season opened that "debatable" new music would be avoided on the orchestra's programs. Even the lusty voice of jazz was stilled after the stock market crash of 1929; with a few notable exceptions, it was not heard again for about six years, and then it spoke differently from before.

With the approach and onset of World War II, the political and cultural isolationism of America faded but, in music at least, it was replaced by a no less conservative tendency to emphasize national and patriotic themes and materials. Thus "the 1930's" as an era in American musical history actually extended through the early 1940's, to the end of World War II.

Themes of the period

Even if the most characteristic atmosphere of the period was one of a broad conservatism, the music of the Depression Era revealed several new and distinctive trends. Perhaps the strongest was a historical or regional Americanism. This was certainly related to the political and social thought of the era, its populist and collectivist temperament and its tendency to an American isolationism; the latter was reflected musically in a suspicious attitude toward the "Europe-ness" of the international new-music movement of the 1920's. One might speak of an "American Wave" in music of the 1930's as the art historians do of painters like Charles Burchfield, Edward Hopper, Thomas Hart Benton, and Grant Wood.

Closely related to this trend was a new and persistent preoccupation of composers with their relationship to the broad musical community and to society at large. The century's new mass media of communication (radio, phonorecordings, sound films, and [from late in the 1930's] television) had created a vast new potential audience for music, but a different one from the concert audiences of the past; many composers saw these media as a challenge to their ability to communicate on a broad scale. At the same time, conflicting impulses of individualism and integrity beset them; the role of the composer in an industrial society, wishing both to serve and be served by it, was an issue. As one major figure of American music of the 1930's, Roy Harris, put it: "How to serve society as a composer, how to become economically and socially recognized as a worth-contributing citizen, how to establish durable human contacts with individuals or groups is a harassing problem."[2]

One common way in the 1930's to become "economically recognized" was of course through trade-union organization; and in place of the idealistic and musically-minded modern-music societies of the 1920's, composers of the 1930's banded together in hard-headed, economics-minded protective associations. In addition to the theretofore practically monopolistic American Society of Composers, Authors, and Publishers (ASCAP; organized 1914), the period saw the formation of the American Composers Alliance (ACA; organized 1937) and Broadcast Music, Inc. (BMI; organized 1939). Performers too became more solidly organized: the American Federation of Musicians (organized 1895) became ever more aggressively protective under President James C. Petrillo; the American Guild of Musical Artists (AGMA), organized in 1936, watched over the fortunes especially of singers, both soloists and choristers. Some aid to both composers and performers, during the depths of the Depression, was forthcoming from the government via the Federal Music Project of the Works Progress Administration. Created in 1935, by 1938 the Project was providing work for about 10,000 persons "to avoid the necessity for specially trained musicians taking manual assignments for which they were unfitted." Project-supported concerts, music lending libraries, and music education programs in rural and congested urban areas helped to broaden the American audience; programs of collecting folk and ethnic music stimulated interest in these fields. Composers were not, however, subsidized for free musical composition (as were painters under the Federal Art Project of the W.P.A.); they were assigned musical tasks of various sorts, with a few asked to supply music for documentary films.

The major works written during this 1930–1945 period by Aaron Copland reflect the themes I have cited: a conservative trend, a historical or regional Americanism, and a search to reach a broader public. Abstract music with the ferocity and astringency of the *Piano Variations* or *Vitebsk*, from the late '20's, was replaced

2 "Problems of American Composers," in Henry Cowell (ed.), *American Composers on American Music* (1933; 2nd ed. New York: Frederick Ungar Publishing Co., 1962), p. 164; the entire essay reprinted in *ACS*, pp. 147–60.

with gentler, smoother, and generally more accessible works, virtually all of them on regional or topical themes.[3] The orchestral
tone-poem *El Salón México* (1936) was based on popular-song
material from south of the border. The ballet scores for *Billy the
Kid* (1938) and *Rodeo* (1942) evoked the spirit of the Far West
and included some skillfully re-composed cowboy tunes, while
Appalachian Spring (1944) dealt with early nineteenth-century
Pennsylvania rural life, expressed in country-fiddle-style tunes and
hymn-like cantilenas and climaxing with some lucid variations on the
Shaker-sect song *Simple Gifts*. In a cheerfully utilitarian spirit,
Copland wrote works for amateur and school ensembles, like the
high school play-opera *The Second Hurricane* (1937) and *An Outdoor Overture* (1938) for orchestra. For the new mass media he
composed works like *Music for Radio* (1937; subtitled *A Saga of
the Prairie*) and film scores for *The City* (1939), *Of Mice and Men*
(1939), *Our Town* (1940), and *The Red Pony* (1948). The entry
of the United States into World War II evoked several frankly
patriotic works from him, among them *Lincoln Portrait* (1942),
which mingled Stephen Foster song-fragments and folk songs
(notably *On Springfield Mountain*) with narrated excerpts from
speeches of the Civil War president, and *Fanfare for the Common
Man* (1942). The latter's wide-intervalled, jagged diatonic theme
typified Copland's new melodic manner, one that somehow was
inevitably associated with the broad plains and rugged mountains
of the country, though it came from the pen of an urbane New York
composer (Example 9-1).

Most of these works were not only aimed at the broad new
American audience; they drew from a wide spectrum of the
American experience for subject matter and from the American
past for musical materials. Indeed, the American musical past was
generally viewed with new interest and re-evaluation during the
period. In 1931 appeared the first really comprehensive history of
American cultivated-tradition music, *Our American Music*, by John
Tasker Howard (1890–1964). By 1946, so much new research had
been done that Howard had to revise the book completely. Especially notable was the rediscovery of the music of Charles Ives—

---

[3] The exceptions that proved the rule were two abstract sonatas, for piano
(1939–41) and for violin and piano (1943), and *Statements* (1933–35) for orchestra, in which something of the acid bite of the *Piano Variations* is to be
heard.

EXAMPLE 9-1. A. Copland, *Fanfare for the Common Man* (1942), measures 1–16 (percussion omitted). Copyright 1943 by Aaron Copland. Reprinted by permission of Aaron Copland, Copyright Owner, and Boosey & Hawkes, Inc., Sole Publishers and Licensees.

pianist John Kirkpatrick's 1939 performance of the "Concord" Sonata was a landmark—and of earlier American music, especially the eighteenth-century New England singing-school music and American folk music in general. These rediscoveries were reflected in the form of innumerable "Hoedowns," "Hayrides," "Square Dances," and the like, in a variety of media. Ross Lee Finney (b. 1906), a Middle Westerner trained under Nadia Boulanger and Alban Berg in Europe, found inspiration in Colonial music for his choral work *Pilgrim Psalms* (1945), which drew on melodies from Ainsworth's psalter, and in Federal-era music for his orchestral *Hymn, Fuguing and Holiday* (1943), which went back to the Yankee tunesmiths. Henry Cowell began a series of works titled *Hymn and Fuguing Tune* (1943–47). William Schuman (b. 1910) made use of an ubiquitous American children's call (phoneticized by him as "wee-awk-eee") in *American Festival Overture* (1939); his *William Billings Overture* (1943) drew from three singing-school pieces of the early Boston composer.

Thomson, Harris, and Blitzstein

Three composers who shared a common background of study in the 1920's with Boulanger and who participated in the musical "American Wave" were Virgil Thomson, Roy Harris, and Marc

Blitzstein. The first two were interested in America's musical past, Blitzstein in certain aspects of the present. Between Harris and Thomson, both Middle Westerners, Harris was the more aggressively "Americanist," but Thomson's music suggested an equally profound immersion in, and sympathy for, the American musical heritage; and his uses of it, which went back to the late 1920's, antedated other composers'.

Thomson once wrote a quotably succinct autobiographical note:

> I was born November 25, 1896 in Kansas City, Missouri, grew up there and went to war from there. That was the other war. Then I was educated some more in Boston and Paris. In composition I was a pupil of Nadia Boulanger. While I was still young I taught music at Harvard and played the organ at King's Chapel, Boston. Then I returned to Paris and lived there for many years, till the Germans came, in fact. Now I live in New York, where I am Music Critic of the *Herald Tribune* [from which he resigned in 1954].[4]

Thomson has called his *Sonata da Chiesa* (1926) for clarinet, trumpet, viola, horn, and trombone in three dissonant, neo-Baroque movements (Chorale, Tango, Fugue) a "bang-up graduation piece" from Boulanger's studio, but the inclusion of the popular dance rhythms of a tango suggests the impact of Satie and the younger French composers, as had *Two Sentimental Tangos* (1923) and *Synthetic Waltzes* (1925). As early as 1926, however, Thomson, a Protestant and an organist, began to turn to American hymnody. One important result was a *Symphony on a Hymn Tune* (two movements sketched 1926; completed 1928). At about the same time he composed some pointedly irreverent and very funny *Variations and Fugues on Sunday School Tunes* (1927) for organ, and settings of several texts by Gertrude Stein, who had accepted Thomson as an artistically fastidious, amusing, and courageous fellow-expatriate in Paris (*Susie Asado*, 1926; *Capital, Capitals*, 1927). Thomson's Francophilia, his sophisticated, pseudo-innocent way with American hymn-book harmony, his respect for language, his wit, and his close relation with Stein were to result in one of the most extraordinary works of American music: the opera *Four*

---

[4] Quoted in Peggy Glanville-Hicks, "Virgil Thomson," *MQ*, XXXV (1949), 210.

Saints in Three Acts, first produced by the Friends and Enemies of Modern Music of Hartford, Connecticut in 1934. Stein's own account of the genesis of the work runs like this:

> Virgil Thomson had asked Gertrude Stein to write an opera for him. Among the saints there were two saints whom she had always liked better than any others, Saint Theresa of Avila and Ignatius Loyola, and she said she would write him an opera about these two saints. She began this and worked very hard at it all that spring [1927] and finally finished Four Saints and gave it to Virgil Thomson to put to music. He did. And it is a completely interesting opera both as to words and music.[5]

Four Saints is a work of fantasy, liveliness, and inexplicable charm. Impossible to interpret literally, equally impossible to dismiss as meaningless, it offers a child-like, surrealistic procession of tableaux about saints (many more than four) doing what we suppose saints do: receiving visitors, posing for earthly reproductions, discussing human problems and saintly ones too, loving Christ, rejoicing. Thomson's setting is similarly child-like: "With meanings already abstracted, or absent, or so multiplied that choice among them was impossible . . . you could make a setting for sound and syntax only, then add, if needed, an accompaniment equally functional," he said;[6] and he composed deceptively simple music which both supports discreetly and projects impeccably the verses of Stein. The original chamber orchestration of nineteen players is dominated by the sound of an accordion, which gives a pungent reediness to the successions of plain chords that characterize the harmony. The very beginning of the Prologue establishes the tone of affected yet effective simplicity, with a waltz vamp underlying a metrically variable exhortation by the chorus, in crystal-clear octaves, to "prepare for [four?] saints" (Example 9-2). Saint Theresa is introduced with affectionate malice as one who pontificates repetitiously about the obvious ("There are a great many persons and places near together"); Thomson's music leads to a neo-Handelian climax marked "Grandioso (liberamente)." A celebrated Vision of the Holy Ghost ("Pigeons on the grass alas") begets strangely

[5] *The Autobiography of Alice B. Toklas* (New York: Harcourt, Brace & Co., 1933), p. 281.
[6] Thomson, *Virgil Thomson* (New York: Alfred A. Knopf, 1966), p. 90.

EXAMPLE 9-2. V. Thomson, *Four Saints in Three Acts* (1934), measures 1–8. Quoted by permission of Beekman Music, Inc.

moving music. A Saints' Procession finds Thomson retiring almost completely into the background, allowing Stein's leaden processional ("In wed in dead/in dead wed led/in led wed dead") to plod solemnly across the stage, over sustained chords. Ultimately the work defies description and perhaps analysis; as John Cage has sensitively written: "To enjoy it, one must leap into that irrational world from which it sprang, the world in which the matter-of-fact and the irrational are one, where mirth and metaphysics marry to beget comedy."[7]

Historically, *Four Saints* more than any other single work offered a model for the new simplicity in American music of the 1930's and suggested how the triadic harmony of the American past could be used with fresh incisiveness: as Thomson commented in his saucy survey of *The State of Music* in 1939, it had music that was "simple, melodic, and harmonious . . . after twenty years of everybody's trying to make music just a little bit louder and more unmitigated and more complex than anybody else's." A similar artful simplicity pervades the later Stein-Thomson collaboration, *The*

<hr/>

[7] Kathleen Hoover and John Cage, *Virgil Thomson: His Life and Music* (New York: T. Yoseloff, 1959), p. 157.

Mother of Us All (1947), although that opera is "fatter" than *Four Saints* in almost every respect.

Thomson was the first major American composer of concert music to write for films. But he did not enter the highly specialized and, for a concert-music composer, infinitely frustrating musical wing of the Hollywood industry; he wrote instead scores for several government-sponsored documentary films: two produced by Pare Lorentz, *The Plow that Broke the Plains* (1936) and *The River* (1937), and a wartime propaganda film for the Office of War Information, *Tuesday in November* (1945). His best-known film score, for Robert Flaherty's *Louisiana Story* (1948), was similarly composed for a documentary, produced by the Standard Oil Company. In all these, Thomson's sympathy for American folk and vernacular-tradition music was apparent: *The Plow* draws on cowboy songs; *The River* on white spirituals from *Southern Harmony* and *The Sacred Harp; Tuesday in November* on waltzes, hymns, and *Yankee Doodle; Louisiana Story* on the Acadian ("Cajun") songs and dances of the bayou country.

Roy Harris (b. 1898) was another of the early pupils of Boulanger (1926–29). A prolific composer, by the early 1940's he had produced a vast number of works in almost all media except opera. (Even as recently as 1968, the Eleventh and Twelfth Symphonies were given premieres within a single month.) From his Op. 1, a Piano Sonata (1928–29), Harris's style seemed firmly and idiosyncratically established: it was marked by expansive, rolling melodies, often modal but equally often chromatic; bichordal harmony of an immediately recognizable sort; contrapuntal textures and devices of all kinds; and a sense of form that avoided the neo-Classic types popular in the 1930's with many composers, but did include neo-Baroque principles like fugue, ostinato, and passacaglia. Harris displayed his Americanist interests in works like the *Folksong Symphony*, No. 4 (1940); the orchestral overture *When Johnny Comes Marching Home* (1934), based on a Civil War song and divided precisely in two four-minute halves to fit the sides of a 78-revolutions-per-minute phonorecord; *Gettysburg Address Symphony*, No. 6 (1944); *Railroad Man's Ballad* (1941) for chorus and orchestra; and *American Ballads* (1942) for piano. Many works, however, were musically abstract, like the two which some still consider, three decades later, to be his most masterly: the Quintet for Piano and Strings (1936) and the Third Symphony in One Movement (1938). Characteristic of the long-breathed melodic line of Harris is the theme of the second ("lyric") section of the symphony: very chromatic, uncertainly focused on any single tonic note; fluid in tempo, phrase-length, meter, and dynamics but even-paced in rhythm, it seems boundless, a grand rhetorical prose-like utterance (Example 9-3a). In sharp contrast is the terse, motive-filled, energetic yet asymmetrical subject of the fugal section of the symphony; not identifiably related to anyone else's music, its internal cross-rhythms and ambiguous meter nevertheless stamp it as "Made in U.S.A." (Example 9-3b). The "pastoral" section of the

EXAMPLE 9-3. R. Harris, *Third Symphony in One Movement* (New York: G. Schirmer, Inc., 1939). Quoted by permission. (a) "Lyric" theme (measures 60–97). (b) "Fugue" subject (measures 416–21).

Third Symphony is justly famous for its "seemingly endless succession of spun-out melodies" (the phrase is Copland's); few seem to have noticed its basis in a bellows-like ostinato figure, expanding and contracting in the bass, or its carefully planned polychordal harmony, gradually increasing in density, resonance, and tension until it bursts into the resolute fugue. The Piano Quintet is less originally shaped; it represents the more retrospective, contrapuntal turn of Harris's mind with its three movements, Passacaglia, Cadenza, and (triple) Fugue.

If works like Thomson's *Hymn Tune Symphony* and Harris's *Folksong Symphony* posited a new rapprochement between concert music and the music of America's older vernacular and folk traditions, several works for the lyric theater by Marc Blitzstein (1905–1964) did the same for contemporaneous popular music. Especially in *The Cradle Will Rock* (1937) and *No For an Answer* (1941), Blitzstein, taking a cue from the musico-dramatic style of works by Berthold Brecht and Kurt Weill, particularly *Die Dreigroschenoper* (which Blitzstein later translated), raised the Broadway musical to an exquisitely calculated level of harsh refinement. Both works were morality plays written from the Leftist, trade-unionist viewpoint; both might be seen as modern ballad operas based on the style of the American pop song and the speech of the American streets; both were deceptively "easy" works; and neither could have been composed by anybody without the thorough training (both with Schoenberg in Berlin and Boulanger in Paris) and high intelligence of Blitzstein. Preferring to call these works "plays with music," Blitzstein cunningly built up substantial scenes with a unique combination of spoken dialogue, precisely rhythmic speech (notated in score), and song; take any of these elements away, and much of the peculiar power of their blend is lost. "Penny Candy," from *No For an Answer*, is a murderous satire on a do-gooder's morbid curiosity about addiction; without its preliminary monologue, spoken over a sparse, dry accompaniment, the song itself seems only silly. Yet even the briefest excerpt of "Honolulu," from *The Cradle Will Rock*, can suggest Blitzstein's subtle transformation of popular song style: the clichés of the vocal line are cancelled out by the freshness of the accompaniment, with its irregular texture underlying the first four phrases; its hint of Hawaiian steel guitars under "-lulu" and "banned"; its offbeat accentuation of the bass under the raucous refrain; and its acrid inversion of a dominant ninth under "isle" (Example 9-4).

EXAMPLE 9-4. M. Blitzstein, "Honolulu," *The Cradle Will Rock* (1937), measures 1–13. Quoted by permission of the Estate of Marc Blitzstein.

Blitzstein was committed to an ideal of moral persuasion in his art. One of the songs in *The Cradle Will Rock* summarizes his scorn for other ideals:

> *Art for Art's sake,*
> *It's smart, for Art's sake,*
> *To part, for Art's sake,*
> *With your mind, for Art's sake,*
> *Be blind, for Art's sake,*
> *And deaf, for Art's sake,*
> *And dumb, for Art's sake,*
> *Until, for Art's sake,*
> *They kill, for Art's sake,*
> *All the Art for Art's sake.*[8]

This was a point of view common enough among socially conscious, Leftist artists of the 1930's. But periodic revivals of *The Cradle Will Rock* as well as the success of his later (and more elaborate) opera *Regina* (1949) and his powerful translation and adaptation of the Brecht-Weill *Three Penny Opera* (1952) suggest that it was not so much the message as the music that was significant in Blitzstein's art.

[8] Quoted by permission of the Estate of Marc Blitzstein.

The composer-professors

Reflecting the conservative atmosphere of the 1930's, and also a new approach to the education of musicians, many of the most highly esteemed composers of the period occupied professorial chairs in American universities. Roger Sessions (b. 1896) was at Princeton and then at the University of California at Berkeley (later to return to Princeton). His early studies at Harvard and Yale linked him with the academic tradition of the Second New England School, but more significant in his development were two years (1919–21) with the Swiss-American composer Ernest Bloch (1880–1959). In the 1930–1945 period, Sessions's style was moving from the diatonic neo-Classicism of his First Symphony (1927) and First Piano Sonata (1930), through the more chromatic and expressionistic manner of a Violin Concerto (1935) and a First String Quartet (1936), to the highly chromatic, long-lined, dense-textured, and almost serialized Second Piano Sonata (1946) and Second Symphony (1946). Walter Piston (b. 1894) was at Harvard (from which he retired in 1960), writing an elegant if icy neo-Classic music mostly in abstract, traditional instrumental forms. A sometime pupil of Boulanger (1924–26), he reinterpreted her French scholastic pedagogy in several influential textbooks: *Principles of Harmonic Analysis* (1933), *Harmony* (1941), *Counterpoint* (1947), and *Orchestration* (1955). Roy Harris moved from institution to institution. Quincy Porter (1897–1966) taught at Vassar and the New England Conservatory, then (1946) returned to Yale, where he had begun as a pupil of Horatio Parker. He was emphatically a composer of chamber music, e.g., ten string quartets, in an international style. Douglas Moore (b. 1893) was at Columbia and well into a career emphasizing operas on American subjects: *The Headless Horseman* (1936) and *The Devil and Daniel Webster* (1939) were to be followed after World War II by the highly successful, musically nostalgic opera *The Ballad of Baby Doe* (1956) and another, *Carry Nation* (1966). William Schuman was at Sarah Lawrence College, Ross Finney at Smith College.

The presence on college and university campuses of these and other eminent composers reflected the fact that, especially in institutions beyond the eastern seaboard, the professional training of young musicians, formerly limited typically, as in Europe, to the conservatories, was being taken up by academic institutions. The major conservatories in the U.S.A., such as the Juilliard School in New York, Peabody Conservatory in Baltimore, the Curtis Institute in Philadelphia, and the New England Conservatory in Boston, still offered the most thorough professional training. But more and more the colleges and universities, better endowed than the small conservatories, assumed the function of training ground for musicians. This was to have broad ramifications in the post-World War II years in the development of college instrumental ensembles and opera workshops of remarkably high calibre, and the establishment of professional performing groups, soloists, and composers "in residence." But before the war, the picture was dominated by the composer-professors, attempting to maintain their integrity as composers while employed as full-time professors.[9]

To many colleges and universities in the 1930's, furthermore, came refugees from Europe during the Nazi and Fascist regimes. The 1940's opened with such composers in America as Stravinsky, Schoenberg, Hindemith, Bartók, Weill, Krenek, Martinu, Wolpe, and Milhaud, most of whom were soon attached to college music departments. Their very presence contributed to a breakdown of the American tendency of the period to a musical isolationism and ultimately to a new role for the United States after World War II as international leader of progressive trends in Western music. Among other side-effects of the emigration of European musicians to America was the stimulus it provided for the establishment of musicology as an accepted discipline in American universities: although a chair of musicology had been created in 1930 for Otto Kinkeldey (1878–1966) at Cornell, it was really the impact of such newly-arrived European musicologists of the stature of Alfred Einstein, Curt Sachs, Hans David, Karl Geiringer, Leo Schrade, and others that led to a rapid development of musicological curricula in American universities and to the consolidation of the American Musicological Society (established 1934) and the Music Library Association (1931).

---

[9] Sessions has offered some sober speculations on the composer as professor in a "Conversation with Roger Sessions," *PNM*, IV, 2 (Spring–Summer 1966), 29–46.

Younger composers

If the composer-professors typified the basic conservatism of the 1930–1945 period, so did the rise to prominence of fundamentally conservative young composers as opposed to vanguardists. The acknowledged young leaders were probably Samuel Barber, Gian-Carlo Menotti, William Schuman, and an "Eastman School group."

Barber (b. 1910) demonstrated a conservative lyricism in his earliest works: songs and choral pieces, and an impassioned setting for voice and string quartet of Matthew Arnold's *Dover Beach* (1933). He adapted an easy, cantabile vocal line to instrumental works like the Sonata for Violoncello and Piano (1932) and to two orchestral pieces that achieved a *succès d'estime* when, alone among American compositions, they were performed by Arturo Toscanini and the NBC Symphony Orchestra: *Essay for Orchestra*, No. 1, and *Adagio for Strings* (both 1938; the *Adagio* arranged from an earlier string quartet). Despite some absorption of Stravinskyan textures in a work like *Capricorn Concerto* (1944) and of Schoenbergian chromaticism in a Piano Sonata (1949), Barber's style continued along a neo-Romantic, "expressive" path. One of the most poignant exemplars of that style, partly because of the warm nostalgia of its text by James Agee, is *Knoxville: Summer of 1915* (1948) for voice and orchestra, in a characteristically accessible rondo-like form.

A close associate of Barber's from their days together as students at the Curtis Institute was Gian-Carlo Menotti (he was to be the librettist for Barber's elaborately Victorian opera *Vanessa* [1958] and the chamber opera *A Hand of Bridge* [1959]). By the mid-1940's Menotti (b. 1911 in Italy; to America 1927) had successfully bridged the gap between the opera house and Broadway: after modest successes with *Amelia al Ballo* (produced in 1937 in English translation) and *The Old Maid and the Thief* (1939), his intense and spooky short opera *The Medium* (1946), preceded by a curtain-raising skit, *The Telephone*, began in 1947 a durable career as competitor to the spoken dramas of the Broadway playhouses. Menotti combined the theatrical sense of a popular playwright and a Pucciniesque musical vocabulary with an Italianate love of liquid language and a humane interest in characters as real human beings;

the result was opera more accessible than anyone else's at the time. Writing his own librettos, Menotti had a knack for choosing timeless themes of human conflict in topical settings: two later operas, both cannily full of *coups de théâtre*, *The Consul* (1950) based on the frustrations of life under a bureaucracy, and a Christmastide fantasy, *Amahl and the Night Visitors* (1951; commissioned for television performance), were to become even greater popular successes than *The Medium*.

William Schuman was mentioned earlier (p. 201) as a participant in the "American Wave" of the 1930's. *American Festival Overture* was followed by other works on American themes, such as the baseball opera *The Mighty Casey* (1953) and the cantata after Walt Whitman, *A Free Song* (1943). Schuman also wrote several big works for wind band, among them *Newsreel (in Five Shots)* (1941) and *George Washington Bridge* (1950). These were a response to the immense proliferation of bands in schools and colleges across the land. The marching band, most often in evidence between the halves of intercollegiate football games, had once again become a major voice of American vernacular-tradition music. This revival of the band's popularity was accompanied, however, by cultivated-tradition ideals of polished performance. An old problem of bands, their uncertain instrumentation, was disappearing as a more or less standardized instrumentation emerged. After the football season the marching bands, often retitled "symphonic wind ensembles," became concert-giving organizations. Good contemporary music was needed for them. Schuman was not alone in helping to fill the demand: among others, Thomson contributed *A Solemn Music* and *At the Beach* (both 1949); Harris the overture *Cimarron* (1941), *Take the Sun and Keep the Stars* (1944), and *Fruit of Gold* (1949); Barber a *Commando March* (1943).

More important in Schuman's output were orchestral symphonies, string quartets, and choral works. A pupil of Harris, Schuman shared with him a fondness for either rhapsodic or ostinato forms, long chromatic slow themes, and polychordal harmony. Schuman's rhythms, however, tended to be more nervously athletic than Harris's, more clearly related to pop-music origins, and his orchestration brighter, more sharp-edged with brass and metal-percussion instruments. Two excerpts from his *Symphony for Strings* (1943), the first also a part of his *Three-Score Set* for piano (1943), can suggest respectively Schuman's resonant bichordal harmony and his energetic, stuttering fast-movement rhythms (Example 9-5).

EXAMPLE 9-5. W. Schuman, *Symphony for Strings* (New York: G. Schirmer, Inc., 1943). Quoted by permission. (a) 2nd movement, measures 1–4. (b) 3rd movement, measures 1–11 (1st violin part only).

Several other younger composers of promise in the late 1930's and early '40's were graduates of the Eastman School of Music at the University of Rochester, under Howard Hanson's direction; they had studied either with Hanson or with Bernard Rogers (1893–1968). This "Eastman Group" included David Diamond (b. 1915), Robert Palmer (b. 1915), Robert Ward (b. 1917), William Bergsma (b. 1921), and Peter Mennin (b. 1923). All shared the relatively conservative, evolutionary attitudes of their mentors; all seemed to share an aim to write the Great American Symphony by way of the Depression-era Overture, a one-movement piece ten minutes in length or less, usually titled something like *Jubilation* (Ward; 1946), *Poem* (Palmer; 1938), *Psalm* or *Elegy* (Diamond; 1936 and 1938 respectively), with at least one section of broadly arching, wide-intervalled, mostly diatonic melody supported by slow-moving, rich harmony. The latter, although functional and directive, avoided structures like dominant sevenths or ninths and diminished-seventh chords; non-tertial sonorities replaced them, as did sometimes triads or added-tone chords derived from diatonic (but not major) modes. Related to these Eastman School composers in his general style, but possessing the lyric gifts of a Barber as well, was Norman Dello Joio (b. 1913), a prolific composer on whose works was stamped the impress of his Italianate background and of his training under Paul Hindemith.

The only strong avant-garde impulse during the period was felt on the West Coast: there, carrying on where Henry Cowell had begun, younger composers like John Cage and Lou Harrison (b. 1917) interested themselves in percussion music, non-Western scales, and new means of formal organization; an older one, Harry Partch (b. 1901), pursued a lonely path to a whole new theory of music based on division of the octave into forty-three tones. Partch codified his theory in detail in the book *Genesis of a New Music* (1949).

Cage (b. 1912) studied with both Cowell and Schoenberg. In a foreword to a catalogue of his works, he summarized "the various paths my musical thought has taken"; those of the period before World War II were:

> . . . chromatic composition dealing with the problem of keeping repetitions of individual tones as far apart as possible (1933–34); composition with fixed rhythmic patterns or tone-row fragments (1935–38); composition for the dance, film and theatre (1935–   ); composition within rhythmic structures (the whole having as many parts as each unit has small parts, and these, large and small, in the same proportion) (1939–56); intentionally expressive composition (1938–51). . . .[10]

Few people in the period were aware of Cage as an early exponent of Schoenberg's tone-row technique, or as a composer who applied rather similar principles to the organization of rhythm. Hardly anyone, however, was unaware of Cage's "prepared piano." "Preparation" was the alteration of the instrument's tonal quality by inserting between the strings various bits of material; the preparation varied depending on the expressive aim. The sonorous result was not unlike an Indonesian orchestra of gongs and delicate percussion. "The need to change the sound of the instrument arose through the desire to make an accompaniment, without employing percussion instruments, suitable for the dance . . . for which it was to be composed,"[11] is Cage's comment on the first prepared-piano piece, *Bacchanale* (1938). Cage's most extended work for prepared piano, the seventy-minute *Sonatas and Interludes* (1946–48), aims

[10] *John Cage* (New York: Henmar Press Inc., 1962), p. 5.
[11] *Ibid.*, p. 15.

to express the various "permanent emotions" of (East) Indian tradition; his interest in the Orient, later to be decisive in his musical thought, was already apparent. Two movements for prepared piano flank two all-percussion trios in *Amores* (1943), and Cage's interest in what Varèse had called "sound—any sound" led him to write a number of all-percussion pieces, adding to the more or less conventional instruments such new sound-sources as recordings of constant and variable pitch-frequency, sound-generator whines, and other mechanical and electronic devices (*Imaginary Landscape No. 1*, 1939).

Jazz: swing and bop

Jazz of the 1930's underwent a major change in style from that of the 1920's. For most of the pre-World War II period, in fact, the very term "jazz" implied the earlier style, the "hot jazz" of the '20's. The newer style was called "swing," borrowing the word from a 1932 recording of Duke Ellington's band with singer Ivy Anderson: *It Don't Mean a Thing if It Ain't Got That Swing*. The swing style was materializing in the late 1920's and early '30's, but most Americans did not hear it until about 1935. In the intervening years, between the financial crash and the mid-1930's, the strident, earthy music of New Orleans jazz was out of fashion: America in crisis seemed to want rather to be lulled by the soothing sounds of crooners, like Rudy Vallee and Bing Crosby, and of non-jazz dance bands like Guy Lombardo's and Wayne King's. Some bands, however, found a way to compromise between the large, euphonious, popular dance band and the improvisatory, "swinging" manner of jazz: thus did the new jazz reach the ears of the public (partly through several popular late-evening radio programs, like "Let's Dance" and "The Camel Caravan," the former sponsored by a cracker-manufacturing corporation, the latter by a cigarette company).

Swing was essentially jazz for a big band. As Benny Goodman (b. 1909), the clarinetist whose band more than any other helped to popularize swing, explains in his autobiography:

> It was about this time [1934], or maybe just a little earlier, that large bands became standardized with five brass, four saxes, and four

rhythm. . . . Ten men . . . used to be considered the limit of even a large dance orchestra.[12]

In the new big-band style, the individual voices of earlier jazz combos were replaced by three "sections," one of brass instruments (trumpets and trombones), one of reeds (saxes, doubling occasionally on clarinets), and one of rhythm instruments (typically guitar, double bass, piano, and drums). Too unwieldy to permit either the casual approach to form or the collective improvisation of early jazz, the big swing band of the 1930's relied on written arrangements. Increasingly, jazz improvisation became a matter of solos set off against an arranged background music. Models for such arrangements were found in the earlier work of Fletcher Henderson and Duke Ellington, and in the arrangements for Jimmy Lunceford's band made by Sy Oliver between 1933 and 1939. These men could simulate an improvisatory style in their written-out, repetitive "riffs" for full band. Moreover, the sections did not play the notes exactly as written; through many rehearsals they shaped the written arrangements into an even more improvisatory, swinging style.[13] Partly because of the new necessity to be able to read music, partly because of the richly harmonized ensemble arrangements, and partly because the swing band had to play not only the older jazz "standards" but also the harmonically more sophisticated up-to-the-minute popular songs, the chordal vocabulary of jazz musicians expanded. This was reflected in more adventurously chromatic solo improvisations.

The rhythmic basis of swing was a strong, even $\frac{4}{4}$ ("solid" was a favorite adjective of the period) as opposed to the tendency of earlier jazz to march along in $\frac{2}{2}$. Swing drummers typically overlaid the regular thumping four-beats-to-the-measure of the bass drum with a slight emphasis on beats 2 and 4 through a conventional pattern (♩ ♫♩ ♫ | ♩) played with drumstick or wire brush on a high-hat cymbal, with totally different effect from the accents on beats 1 and 3 of early jazz. One of the first drummers to establish this convention was Chick Webb (1902–1939), but it was more

---

[12] *The Kingdom of Swing* (Harrisburg: Stackpole Sons, 1939), p. 138.

[13] The use of "square" as a term of opprobrium came into existence during the era as a precise description of the way swing was *not* to be played. To the degree that soloists and even whole sections did not round off notated rhythms and pitches in an improvisatory, feelingful way, they were "square."

closely identified with the "Kansas City style" of jazz as played by the bands of pianists Bennie Moten (1894–1935) and his successor, William "Count" Basie (b. 1904). Basie's band, along with Ellington's, was probably the most influential of all in establishing the swing style, but nationally the style was diffused by the bands of white leaders like Goodman, Tommy Dorsey (1905–1956), Artie Shaw (b. 1910), and Glenn Miller (1904–1944), perhaps mainly because discriminatory practices made it difficult for the Negro bands to get the same degree of exposure to the mass audience.

The swing style bred virtuosos, stars who improvised brilliantly over the background riffs of the big bands' "sidemen." Some of the misplaced values of any star system were evident in the development of swing, as the star players seemed to be trying to play faster or higher, or both, than anybody else. The so-called "screech trumpet" of a Maynard Ferguson, star soloist with the huge, colorful band of Stan Kenton (b. 1912), was symptomatic, as was the dazzling piano virtuosity of Art Tatum (1910–1956). Typical of a trend to choose ever faster tempos for fast pieces, Benny Goodman's trio (which included Negro pianist Teddy Wilson [b. 1912] and thus helped initiate a breakdown of "segregated" jazz) recorded *After You've Gone* in 1944 at ♩=165 , thereby shortening the first chorus by ten seconds compared to their 1935 recording of the same piece at ♩=120 . With such virtuosity, and with a transcontinental popularity bred in radio stations, recording studios, and on the stages of movie houses (where swing bands appeared increasingly "in person"), jazz began to be more than just a functional music to dance to or to drink to: it became a concert music as well. In 1938, Goodman's band appeared in concert at New York's Carnegie Hall; since that time, jazz as concert music has become commonplace and the balance between its use as utilitarian music and as a new kind of art-music has swung increasingly toward the latter.

In the early 1940's, several further developments took place. All can be viewed as reactions to certain aspects of jazz in the '30's, especially the very "bigness" of the big swing bands and the pressures on such bands to cater to public and commercial taste. The development of a concert culture for jazz meant a broadening of its base of patronage; but, just as in the development of a concert culture in art-music a century or more earlier, one result was a growing lag between the musical thought of the advanced performer and of his public. After-hours "jam sessions," in which jazz musicians played for each other rather than for the public, became important proving grounds for new jazz expression. The style of "bebop" (or simply "bop"), which emerged in New York early in the 1940's with such musicians as trumpeter John "Dizzy" Gillespie (b. 1917), saxophonist Charles "Bird" Parker (1920–1955), and drummer Kenny Clarke (b. 1914), owed its origin to such exclusive and self-consciously progressive music-making. Melodically, the bop style was asymmetrically phrased, chromatic, and built up by mannered combinations of the briefest ejaculatory motifs and very long, very fast, looping lines. Bop drummers like Clarke and Max Roach (b. 1925) gave up the incessant four-beat thudding bass drum of the swing style, reserving the instrument for occasional "bombs" dropped irregularly into a new, top-cymbal-dominated, shimmering background beat. One of the most common conceits of bop musicians was to base a piece on the harmonies of a well-known song, but to substitute for its original melody a new one in bop style and then to retitle the work. Thus, only the really knowledgeable would recognize Gillespie and Parker's *Anthropology* as a reworking of Gershwin's *I Got Rhythm*, or Gillespie's *Groovin' High* as the old popular song *Whispering* (1920) without the original melody. Example 9-6 shows the beginning of *Whispering* and of

EXAMPLE 9-6. A bop-style melody and its source-tune. (a) John Schonberger, Richard Coburn, and Vincent Rose, *Whispering*. Copyright 1920 MILLER MUSIC CORPORATION, New York, N.Y. Copyright renewal 1948 MILLER MUSIC CORPORATION and Fred Fisher Music Co., Inc. for the United States and Canada. Rest of the World owned exclusively by MILLER MUSIC CORPORATION. Used by Permission. (b) Dizzy Gillespie, *Groovin' High*. After a transcription of Rondolette recording A-11 by Frank Tirro.

Note: In Gillespie's performance, ♩♩ = approximately ♪♪, more precisely ♪♪

EXAMPLE 9-6 continued.

its bop derivative, *Groovin' High,* transcribed from the 1945 recording of Gillespie and Parker. The curt two-note figure that opens
Groovin' High is a characteristic bop motif; some say that the term
"bebop" originated as an imitation of such figures.

Also in the 1940's occurred a revival of the Dixieland style
of early jazz. This was first noticeable on the West Coast, where
the Yerba Buena band of Lu Watters (b. 1911) made some recordings in faithful imitation of the early discs of Louis Armstrong.
Actually, the New Orleans jazz revival was but one of many signs
of a growing American nostalgia for the 1920's: before long,
Americans were once again dancing the Charleston and getting their
parents' raccoon coats out of mothballs, aggressively acting out their
rosy imaginings of life in the prosperous, "secure" 1920's.

Musical comedy

The American musical of the 1930's seemed unable to match
the inspiration of Kern's *Show Boat* of 1927 or the wit of Gershwin's *Of Thee I Sing* of 1931. Nor did it strike out on any new
paths, although some of the social preoccupations of other American
music were visible, as in Harold Rome's *Pins and Needles* (1937),
the opening number of which ("Sing Me a Song of Social Significance") ushered onstage a cast drawn entirely from theater classes
of the International Ladies' Garment Workers Union. Richard
Rodgers (b. 1902) and writer Lorenz Hart were the leading team
of musical comedy writers, with *On Your Toes* (1936), *I Married*

an Angel (1938), and especially *Pal Joey* (1940) as their major works. Kurt Weill (1900–1950), who had come to the United States as a refugee in the mid-1930's, put his experience in German musical theater to good use in several Broadway musicals, most notably *Lady in the Dark* (1941) and the virtually operatic *Street Scene* (1947).

Between these years a musical was produced on Broadway that set a new standard for the genre: *Oklahoma!* This 1943 collaboration between Rodgers and Oscar Hammerstein 2nd had excitingly original choreography by Agnes de Mille that synthesized ballet movement and square-dance figures, and the artfully folkish work brought plot, music, and dance into such a tightly-knit whole that some believed themselves witnessing a new form of American vernacular opera.

Bibliographical notes

Eric Salzman's "*Modern Music* in Retrospect," *PNM*, II, 2 (Spring–Summer 1964), 14–20, analyzes the American musical mood of 1924–46 as revealed in the pages of *Modern Music*. Copland's *Our New Music* (1941; 2nd ed. titled *The New Music*, New York: W. W. Norton and Company, Inc., 1968) remains valuable as a view of things looking back from 1941; Cowell (ed.), *American Composers on American Music* (see footnote 2) as a view looking forward from 1933. Thomson's *The State of Music* (1939; 2nd ed. New York: Vintage Books, 1962) is concerned with both the aesthetic and economic ways and means of the American composer.

Thomson's *Virgil Thomson* (see footnote 6) is a deliciously written autobiography which supersedes the biographical half of Kathleen Hoover and John Cage's *Virgil Thomson* (see footnote 7); in the latter, Cage's incisive analysis of the music is masterly.

Mellers's *Music in a New Found Land*, Chapter X, is sympathetic to both the art and ideology of Blitzstein; since both are revealing of a major theme of the 1930's, Mellers's discussion is especially valuable.

Nathan Broder's *Samuel Barber* and F. R. Schreiber and Vincent Persichetti's *William Schuman* (both New York: G. Schirmer, Inc., 1954) include analyses but should be read with caution as a publisher's self-serving products.

Various jazz anthologies edited by Martin Williams contain valuable essays on jazz from 1935 to 1945. Perhaps the first anthology of competent jazz criticism, published in 1947, is Ralph de Toledano (ed.), *Frontiers of Jazz* (2nd ed.; New York: Frederick Ungar Publishing Co., 1962).

IO

After World War II

The period after World War II, like that after World War I, was one of marked progressivism and rapid development in American music, due partly to a rising prosperity which increased the sources of patronage and the audience for music. With the introduction in 1948 of the long-playing microgroove phonorecording, the cost of records diminished, sales boomed; the phonorecord became almost as important a medium for new music as the concert (more, for some). Giant industrial and philanthropic foundations, most notably the Ford and Rockefeller Foundations, as well as state, county, municipal, and (by 1965) federal organizations in support of the arts provided new money for composers' commissions and performance organizations. The audience grew spectacularly: a favorite statistic of the 1950's was one demonstrating that more Americans went to concerts than to baseball games. By the early 1960's, arts centers were being constructed in city after city, the most extensive being Lincoln Center for the Performing Arts in New York, a giant complex of buildings housing a major concert hall and several smaller ones; two theaters for drama, ballet, musical comedy, and even opera; a library-museum; and a huge opera house. Despite the advent of television, radio continued to appeal to a large audience, and a 1965 survey revealed that about 1,000 radio stations broadcast a weekly total of 13,795 hours of "concert music" (i.e., neither jazz nor pop music), an average of about fourteen hours per week per station. The number of composers increased dramatically. So did the number of performance organizations: one survey[1] reported that whereas in 1939 there had been about 600 symphony orchestras in the U.S.A., by 1967 there were 1,436, more than half of the world's 2,000 such orchestras; there were 918 opera-producing groups; there were, in American schools, some 68,000 instrumental music organizations (of which 50,000 were wind bands).

This lively, developing scene in the musical culture at large was reflected in musical composition as well. The post-war period saw various trends of widely diverging character, in rapid evolution.

Twelve-tone composition and related methods

One striking development was the triumph of the twelve-tone technique of composition. Viewed before the war as the more or less private method of composers associated directly at one time or another with Schoenberg, the technique of organizing music on the basis of a row or series of the twelve chromatic tones was now being used by a majority of younger American composers (like their European contemporaries). Some older ones as well, composers who before the war had not practiced row-technique at all, began to do so in the late 1940's.

Reflecting this trend was the belated recognition of a com-

[1] *Concert Music USA, 1968* (New York: Broadcast Music, Inc., 1968).

poser like Wallingford Riegger (1885–1961), who had long utilized
serial technique but had to wait until its general adoption before gaining the esteem of the musical community, as embodied in
the New York Music Critics Circle prize awarded his Third Symphony (1948). As was typical of the Americans who had grown
into twelve-tone technique from other directions than tutelage by
Schoenberg, Riegger's application of it, from his earliest example
(*Dichotomy*, 1932), was anything but doctrinaire. In the Third
Symphony, a twelve-tone row is the main source of the first movement's thematic material (Example 10-1), but the development section of the quasi-sonata-form structure abandons the row, reverting
to chromatic clusters of a sort found in many of Riegger's other
works, e.g. his *Music for Brass Choir* (1948–49). The second movement of the Third Symphony is not row-based at all, and the last
movement's passacaglia and fugue subjects are both seven-tone
themes (albeit ultra-chromatic).

EXAMPLE 10-1. W. Riegger, Symphony No. 3, first-movement row-based
themes. Copyright 1949 Associated Music Publishers, Inc. Used by permission. (a) "Motto," measures 1–4. (b) First-group theme, first statement, measures 4–6. (c) First-group theme, climax, measures 64–68.
(d) Recapitulation, "Quasi fugato," measures 213–16.

Two older European-born composers with twelve-tone experience also rose to prominence shortly after World War II: Ernest
Krenek (b. 1900) and Stefan Wolpe (b. 1902). Though a prolific
composer, Krenek's impact on American music was felt more
through his teaching and his didactic works, especially the books
Music Here and Now (originally *Über neue Musik;* English translation published 1939) and *Studies in Counterpoint Based on the
Twelve-Tone Technique* (1940). Wolpe, in America from 1938,
was rather to influence a number of young Americans through his
music per se, which proposed many new extensions of the tone-row
technique. His music, like that of Webern (with whom he had
worked briefly in 1933), invited a whole new method of listening
based on the perception of intervals rather than melodic "themes"
or harmonic "chords," let alone larger-dimension relationships between chords.

Among the mature Americans who gradually came to incor-
porate dodecaphonic principles in their music were Sessions,
Copland, Finney, a whole "Stravinsky school," and Hugo Weisgall.

Sessions's increasingly chromatic style of the 1930's and '40's
had led him to the brink of row usage. In the most natural way, he
began viewing his ideas as susceptible to tone-row abstraction: "As
a result of the fact that the opening theme [of the Sonata for Violin
Solo, 1953] contained twelve different tones, and seemed to go
naturally on that basis, I caught myself using the twelve-tone
system."[2] Thus Sessions's twelve-tone music *sounded* hardly different from his pre-twelve-tone music. It retained the dense texture, the
proliferation of contrapuntal filigree-work, the lengthy, non-repeti-
tive and usually non-sequential melodic line, and the Classic-
Romantic traditional expressive gestures of his earlier music.

Copland first essayed serial technique, tentatively and not without
a certain stiffness of effect, in his Piano Quartet (1950), more
masterfully in his Piano Fantasy (1955–57). In the Fantasy a ten-note
row is the basis; the other two chromatic notes (E, G♯) are reserved
for special use as a kind of cadence-interval. In fact, the work may
be heard tonally as being in or about E major. Neither the Fantasy
nor the Quartet, nor the later *Connotations* for orchestra (1962),
make use of folk or popular materials; even so, they are trans-

[2] Cone, "Conversation with Roger Sessions," *PNM*, IV, 2 (Spring–Summer
1966), 40.

parently the work of the composer of *Appalachian Spring* and *Rodeo*. In this connection, Copland had some sensible things to say about the impact (or lack of it) of twelve-tone usage on a composer's style and the expressive content of his music: "To describe a composer as a twelve-toner these days is much too vague. . . . Twelve-tonism is nothing more than an angle of vision. Like fugal treatment, it is a stimulus that enlivens musical thinking. . . . It is a method, not a style."[3]

Finney had been a student not only of Nadia Boulanger (1927–28) but of Alban Berg (1931–32); not until about 1950, however, did he interest himself in serial technique. I have mentioned above (see p. 201) his interest in the American musical past; this was expressed through a forceful, masculine style in a music distinctly tonal, rhythmically energetic, and neo-Classic in formal principles. With his String Quartet No. 6 (1950) Finney began to work with tone-rows, but with the explicit aim of reconciling them with larger plans of tonal organization, such as architectonic design of tonal centers and aspects of functional, directive harmony. Another of his concerns in the 1950's was with arch forms and other symmetrical or circular plans, as in the Sixth and Seventh Quartets. The latter (1955) he thought of as resembling a figure-eight:

> Like a skater, the first movement starts at the mid-point, then circles out, returning to the beginning, using the pitches in reverse order but making different music with them. The second [final] movement accomplishes figuratively the opposite sweep, and the quartet ends in the center with the theme.[4]

Such "spatial" visions of music, deriving from the various reversible and invertible, horizontal (linear) and vertical (harmonic) points of view in twelve-tone method, were becoming increasingly common during the 1950's.

Among other mature composers who, after many years of lack of interest in Schoenberg's method, adopted it suddenly and absorbed it into their individual styles were some identified as a "Stravinsky school." These were mainly former pupils of Boulanger

---

[3] Copland, "Fantasy for Piano," *New York Times*, October 20, 1957.

[4] The description is by Leslie Bassett (b. 1923), a former pupil and present colleague of Finney's and a Pulitzer Prize-winning composer in his own right, writing in the program booklet for The University of Michigan School of Music's 1966 Festival of Contemporary Music.

and included Louise Talma (b. 1906), Arthur Berger (b. 1912), Ingolf Dahl (b. 1912), and Irving Fine (1914–1962). At the same time that Stravinsky approached row-composition (via Renaissance counterpoint) in his *Cantata* (1952) and turned definitively to dodecaphony in the mid-1950's, these composers began to espouse the twelve-tone idea. As with Sessions and Copland, its use by them hardly affected their personal idioms although it distinctly reduced their tendency to neo-Classic formal structures.

Twelve-tone procedures and a style akin to the Viennese expressionists were heard in several operas of the 1950's and '60's by Hugo Weisgall (b. 1912), a former pupil of Sessions. A cultivated litterateur, Weisgall found libretto material in plays by Wedekind (*The Tenor*, 1950), Strindberg (*The Stronger*, 1952), Pirandello (*Six Characters in Search of an Author*, 1956), Yeats (*Purgatory*, 1959), and Racine (*Athaliah*, 1964). All are intense, densely packed works musically; *Six Characters*, leavened by wit and melodrama, has the most subtle and penetrating characterization, sensitive balancing of voices and orchestra, and theatrical presence.

Related to the intense, near-expressionist atmosphere of Weisgall's operas is the music of three other composers, all of whom felt the impact of Schoenberg's ideas or his music in significant ways. Leon Kirchner (b. 1919) actually studied with both Schoenberg and Sessions and, although he did not adopt the twelve-tone method of organization, his music carries on their highly expressive, ultra-chromatic manner. George Rochberg (b. 1918) has tended to move with the vanguard stylistically: after works of the 1940's in various neo-tonal manners, the *Twelve Bagatelles* were Rochberg's first twelve-tone pieces; dedicated to the Italian composer Luigi Dallapiccola, they reflect his lyrical and finely-ordered style. Ben Weber (b. 1916) also writes a music of lyric grace; characteristic is his Symphony in Four Movements, for baritone and orchestra (1954), on poems of William Blake. The work of all three composers suggests that for them the anti-Romantic struggle is over, its issues dead. As Rochberg put it in 1963: "Now that the question arises on all sides: after abstractionism, what next? the answer rings out clearly: the 'new romanticism.' "[5]

By about 1960, the composer whose music, though not twelve-tone, seemed most sovereignly to embody these attitudes of an

[5] Quoted in Alexander Ringer, "The Music of George Rochberg," *MQ*, LII (1966), 414.

urgent expressivity, also of high seriousness and even "monu-
mentality," was Elliott Carter (b. 1908). Carter was a "second
generation" pupil of Boulanger (1932–1935) after working under
Piston at Harvard. More important ultimately in his development
were his close association with Ives and Ives's music and his un-
shaken belief in the musical work as *communication* between composer and listener. Writing slowly and fastidiously, Carter first
achieved in his Piano Sonata (1945–46) that sense of a work's
being *sui generis* that has been typical of every later composition.
The sonata is in every way a work for pianoforte; no transcription
is imaginable, nor is any aspect of the piece derived from other instrumental idioms. Even the harmonic materials grow from the
piano's special qualities of resonance and its sostenuto-pedal effects.
Rhythmic complexities abound; at the time of the sonata's composition, Carter believed these realizable only in a soloist's work, but
later he was to find the means to make them playable by ensembles. In two big, subdivided movements, the Piano Sonata is
cyclic but ever-developmental; various ideas announced in the introduction (Example 10-2)—the conflict between B and A♯, the
material in thirds, the rising arpeggio figure—are re-presented, but in
constant flux. The scope of the work sonorously, developmentally,
and formally is very grand, and no other American piano sonata
succeeds as well in realizing to the fullest the ideas it proposes.

With each of his later major works Carter's musical conception

EXAMPLE 10-2. E. Carter, Piano Sonata (New York: Mercury Music Corporation, 1948), measures 1–7. Quoted by permission.

has seemed to grow larger, his mode of expression more commanding. The Sonata for Violoncello and Piano (1948), two string
quartets (1951, 1959), a Sonata for Flute, Oboe, 'Cello and Harpsichord (1952), the Variations for Orchestra (1955–56), and a Double
Concerto for piano and harpsichord (1961) are all "masterworks"
in terms both of their exalted aims and their realization. Notable in
Carter's development have been an increasing floridity of materials
and richness of texture; an increasing "personalization" of instrumental voices, in line with the composer's view of his scores as
"scenarios, auditory scenarios, for performers to act out with their
instruments"; and a meticulous notation of the most complex
rhythms in fluctuating meters and tempos. The latter involves what
has been called metric modulation, "a means of going smoothly,
but with complete accuracy, from one absolute metronomic speed
to another, by lengthening or shortening the value of the basic note
unit."[6] In works like the Second String Quartet, where each of the
instruments plays a kind of dramatic role, and the Double Concerto,
where each soloist is leader of a separate antiphonal chamber group,
the technique ensures the most precise temporal controls while per-
mitting the greatest degree of contrapuntal independence. Example
10-3, from the sixth variation of the Variations for Orchestra, shows
a related technique. Each six-measure period accelerates gradually
from ♩=80 to ♩=240 : as the 'cello breaks into triplet eighths at
measure 301, the viola begins the theme again in quarters, at the
initial ♩=80 tempo. The undulating, fluid effect of wavelike over-
lappings of voices at different tempos is unique; it suggests Carter's
extraordinary rhythmic imagination, apparent in every work. Example 10-3 can also suggest the thoroughgoing chromaticism, not

EXAMPLE 10-3. E. Carter, Variations for Orchestra, measures 295–307.
Copyright 1957 Associated Music Publishers, Inc. Used by permission.

[6] Richard Franko Goldman, "The Music of Elliott Carter," *MQ*, XLIII
(1957), 161.

<small>EXAMPLE</small> 10-3 continued.

quite twelve-tone in organization, of Carter's mature style, and its energetic, strongly directional melodic motion, which contributes to the sense of dynamism and "expressivity" in his work.

Systematic serial composition: Milton Babbitt

Schoenberg's "method of composing with twelve tones which are related only with one another," as he called it, was initially a substitute for the comprehensive principles of pitch organization of Classic-Romantic tonality, in which the twelve tones were related to *one*, the tonic. The twelve-tone method sought to come to terms with the chromatic vocabulary of music and to ensure a continuing and total chromaticism in the realm of pitch organization. However, just as tonality had affected aspects of music other than pitch, so too did the new "atonal" method. More consciously than Schoenberg, Webern explored these implications of serial technique. In a work like Webern's Symphony, Op. 21 (1928), the structure of the pitch row affects aspects of rhythm, dynamics, phrase-structure, counterpoint, orchestration, and over-all form; in the second movement, even the choice of row-transpositions used in each variation derives from the shape of the pitch row itself. It was this logical extension of the serial principle that made Webern, not Schoenberg, the hero of a whole generation of composers after World War II, the "post-Webernites" of the 1950's headed by the French composers Olivier Messiaen and Pierre Boulez and the German Karlheinz Stockhausen. However, even before these Europeans began working out the implications of Webern's later works the American Milton Babbitt (b. 1916) was moving in a similar direction, suggested to him perhaps more by Schoenberg than by Webern, however.

A trained mathematician, Babbitt saw not just a "method" in twelve-tone music but a real *system* (a concept denied by Schoenberg) and in the pitch row not just a "series" but an ordered *set*, in the definitive mathematical sense. As early as the mid-1940's Babbitt was using the serial principle to structure durational and other non-pitch components of his music. He was also addressing himself to control of the two dimensions of pitch, horizontal-linear and vertical-harmonic, in such a way that every note—or, to use a newer and more precise terminology, every pitch-class (C, E♭, etc., the register not specified)—was not only a member of an unfolding linear set but of another, related set, governing and in fact creating the vertical dimension. This kind of thinking led him to study of the structure of twelve-tone sets themselves, and to an extension of a principle advanced first by Schoenberg: that of "combinatoriality" (as Babbitt termed it), the combining of various forms of a set without note-duplication between simultaneous hexachords (half-rows), or, in short, the production of twelve-tone *aggregates*.

Babbitt developed further Schoenberg's discovery, formulating methods for constructing pitch sets that would be "semi-combinatorial" or "all-combinatorial." A semi-combinatorial set is so constructed that one of its transformations (besides its retrograde) can be transposed so that the first hexachord includes the same notes as the last hexachord of the original set; it can then be combined with

that transposed version without destroying the ideal of total chromaticism. The all-combinatorial set is so constructed that *all* of its
transformations and one or more of its transpositions achieve the
same end. These sorts of sets open up vast possibilities for contrapuntal techniques that still maintain total chromaticism.

The earliest works to be based on these ideas were *Three Compositions for Piano* (1947–48), *Composition for Four Instruments*
(1947–48), and *Composition for Twelve Instruments* (1948). In
the first of the *Three Compositions*, the pitch set is an all-combinatorial set. Four forms only (and their retrogrades) are used; as
Example 10-4 shows, various pairs of these may be combined without duplicating the pitch-content of corresponding hexachords
(compare "A" and "B" in the example). Constant rotation of the

EXAMPLE 10-4. Pitch-set forms used in M. Babbitt, *Three Compositions
for Piano*, No. 1.

chromatic total in the music is ensured not only by consistent
aggregate-formations but also, in single voices, by following one set
linearly with another whose first hexachord is the "opposite" of the
one just completed: in the lower voice of measures 1–8, for example,
the prime form of the set at the "zero" level (P-O; A-B hexachord
order), then the retrograde inversion at the first transposition, up a
semitone (RI-1; A-B order), the inversion at the seventh transposition (I-7; A-B order), and the retrograde at the sixth transposition (R-6; A-B order) appear successively (see Example 10-5);
the order of successive set-forms is constantly varied as the composition proceeds. In addition to pitch, Babbitt serializes other components in this movement: aspects of duration, of dynamics, and
of the formation of the three-note simultaneities characteristic of
this piece.

The numerical series 5 1 4 2 (= 12, or the number of sixteenth-
notes in a measure of $\frac{3}{4}$, which is the meter of the piece) is chosen

EXAMPLE 10-5. M. Babbitt, *Three Compositions for Piano* (Hillsdale, N.Y.: Boelke-Bomart, Inc., 1957), No. 1, measures 1–8. Quoted by permission.

as the prime form of a "durational set"; 2 4 1 5 is its retrograde, 1 5 2 4 its inversion, and 4 2 5 1 its retrograde inversion. The form of the movement, in six sections, is determined by the various uses of this set: in measures 1–8, it controls the grouping of even attacks (Example 10-6a); in measures 9–18, the articulations between groups of even sixteenths (Example 10-6b); in measures 20–28, accents and repeated notes (Example 10-6c); in measures 29–48, temporal durations between attack points (Example 10-6d). In measures 49–56 an effect of recapitulation is achieved by a return to the manner of measures 1–8. It will be noticed that the "durational set" forms parallel those of the pitch set: when for example an RI form of the pitch set appears, it is associated with the 4 2 5 1 (RI) form of the "durational set" (see Example 10-6c).

EXAMPLE 10-6. Uses of the "durational set" in M. Babbitt, *Three Compositions for Piano*, No. 1.

Dynamics are also determined to reflect and confirm the serial ordering of pitch materials in the piece. The *mezzo piano* of measure 1 is associated with the prime form of the pitch set; *mezzo forte* with the retrograde; *forte* with the inversion; and *piano* with the retrograde inversion. This holds true up to the "recapitulation" of measures 49–56, when the "dynamics set" is "transposed."

Finally, the three-note groups that appear frequently in the composition reveal a serial approach: the register chosen for the notes of each is determined by the following scheme:

$$P = \begin{array}{cccc} \uparrow 2 & 3 & \uparrow 8 & 9 \\ 1 & 4 & 7 & 10 \\ 0 & \downarrow 5 & 6 & \downarrow 11 \end{array} \qquad R = \begin{array}{cccc} \uparrow 9 & \uparrow 6 & 5 & 2 \\ 10 & 7 & 4 & 1 \\ 11 & 8 & \downarrow 3 & \downarrow 0 \end{array}$$

$$I = \begin{array}{cccc} 0 & \uparrow 5 & 6 & \uparrow 11 \\ 1 & 4 & 7 & 10 \\ 2 & 3 & \downarrow 8 & 9 \end{array} \qquad RI = \begin{array}{cccc} 11 & 8 & \uparrow 3 & \uparrow 0 \\ 10 & 7 & 4 & 1 \\ \downarrow 9 & \downarrow 6 & 5 & 2 \end{array}$$

Thus, in measure 11 (Example 10-7) the upper part is an expression of the pitch set I-1 and the particular registration of the notes of each three-note group follows the I version of the "registral set" scheme given above; the lower part, built from the pitch set RI-1, forms its simultaneities according to the RI version of that scheme.

EXAMPLE 10-7. Serial approach to three-note simultaneities in M. Babbitt, *Three Compositions for Piano*, No. 1, measure 11.

In his *Composition for Twelve Instruments* (1948; revised 1954) Babbitt went further to integrate the pitch and durational components of his music by deriving a durational set from the pitch set and composing not only in terms of a twelve-tone system but of a twelve-*duration* system as well. Example 10-8 shows (a) the prime pitch set, with each note defined by its *order* number and its *pitch* number (the latter measured in semitones from the first note); (b) the pitch set transposed up two semitones, thus altering the pitch numbers of the tones; and (c) the durational set, based on a sixteenth-note unit, that corresponds to pitch-set P-2.

EXAMPLE 10-8. Pitch and duration sets in M. Babbitt, *Composition for Twelve Instruments* (1948).

The musical expression in *Composition for Twelve Instruments* is one emphasizing single-impulse events; the pointillistic texture has been likened to a bank of different colored lights, of varied wattage, flashing on and off at different rates. Later works by Babbitt have demonstrated that other textures, other expressive qualities are perfectly possible. *All Set*, for instance, written in 1957 for a Brandeis University arts festival, is scored for a seven-piece jazz ensemble and is based metrically, rhythmically, melodically, and even at some points harmonically on the style of the "progressive jazz" of the 1940's. Several works have included voice, with a frankly *espressivo* line. Such are the song cycle *DU* (1951), the *Composition for Tenor and Six Instruments* (1960), and *Two Sonnets* for baritone, clarinet, viola, and 'cello (1955). In these, duration is not serially organized, Babbitt believing that correct prosody should be the primary rhythmic determinant. Nevertheless, various linked chains of pitch relationships exist in them, as can be heard in the opening measures of *DU* (Example 10-10), which also can exemplify Babbitt's expressive, sensitively rhythmed and contoured vocal line, reminiscent of the lyric art of Webern.

The voice exposes the prime set in four phrases of three notes each. This set is all-combinatorial and is furthermore an "all-interval" set; that is, it can be presented in such a way that every possible interval within an octave occurs once, and only once (Example 10-9). Such a set ensures a variety of interval-structures in the music

EXAMPLE 10-9. The all-interval set of M. Babbitt's *DU*.

EXAMPLE 10-9 continued.

and allows a linear deployment free from built-in symmetries and other form-dictating repetitions. Each vocal phrase of three notes is accompanied by piano music with the nine other chromatic notes; vertical dotted lines in Example 10-10 show the four chromatic aggregates thus created. Within each twelve-tone aggregate, three-note interval-structures are formed by voice and piano (circled in Example 10-10); they are the *same* structures within each aggre-

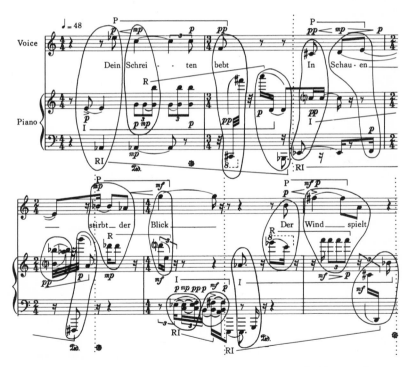

EXAMPLE 10-10. M. Babbitt, *DU* (Hillsdale, N.Y.: Boelke-Bomart, Inc., 1957), measures 1–5. Quoted by permission.

gate; in the first aggregate, for example, the four interval-structures ("molecules" might be an apposite word for them) are all based on the intervals of a major third (or its inversion, a minor sixth), a minor second (or major seventh), and a perfect fifth (or perfect fourth). Finally, the nature of the accompaniment is such that we hear it as having three "voices": a high treble voice beginning B-F♯-A, a middle-register voice (E-G-D), and a bass voice (A♭-C♯-B♭). Tracing each of these voices through the excerpt, we discover that each is itself a twelve-tone set, related directly to the prime set of the singer. Moreover, within each of the four chromatic aggregates, each of the accompanying voices is a different form of the singer's three-note phrase: the piano's treble "voice" is an intervallic retrograde, the middle-register line an inversion, and the bass a retrograde inversion. These linear relationships have been bracketed in Example 10-10.

Through such extensions of the serial principle, not only to both the horizontal and vertical dimensions of pitch but to other realms as well, Babbitt has created music with a staggeringly complex network of inter-relationships. Not only are these relationships complex: they *are* the music; the interlocked components are inseparable; it is no longer meaningful to speak of one, or to hear one, separate from the others; the music, approaching "total organization," demands total hearing.[7]

Babbitt has been second only to Schoenberg himself as formulator and codifier of serial concepts. He has also been an influential teacher of younger composers, from a base at Princeton. Among those who, taught by both Sessions and Babbitt, constitute what has been called a "Princeton school," are Peter Westergaard (b. 1931), Henry Weinberg (b. 1931), Donald Martino (b. 1931), Eric Salzman (b. 1933), Benjamin Boretz (b. 1934), and James K. Randall (b. 1929).

---

[7] Some critics would add ". . . or none at all," claiming that *analyzing* totally organized music is a more meaningful exercise than experiencing it aurally. Babbitt has countered this view in the article "Who Cares if You Listen?" *High Fidelity Magazine*, VIII, 2 (February 1958); reprinted in *ACS*, pp. 235–44. The question of "the perception and cognition of complex music" is thoroughly and provocatively discussed in chapter 11 of Leonard B. Meyer's *Music, the Arts, and Ideas* (Chicago: The University of Chicago Press, 1967).

Electronic music

Babbitt's interest in "total control" over musical materials led him inevitably to the medium of electronic music, and in the late 1950's he became one of the directors of the first major American electronic studio, co-sponsored by Princeton and Columbia and an outgrowth of the studio established at Columbia somewhat earlier.

Electronic music and tape-recorder music had begun in Europe. Pioneers in *musique concrète* (composition from pre-taped and stored sound materials, electronically manipulated and reassembled) were some French composers, notably Pierre Henry, working at the Paris studio of La Radiodiffusion Française in the late 1940's; and in *elektronische Musik* (composition directly onto magnetic tape of electronically generated sound materials) some Germans, notably Herbert Eimert and Karlheinz Stockhausen, working at the Cologne studio of the Westdeutscher Rundfunk in the early 1950's. John Cage was the first American actually to prepare a "score for making a recording on tape" (*Imaginary Landscape No. 5*, 1951–52), but two other composers began about the same time to work systematically in tape-music composition: Otto Luening (b. 1900) and Vladimir Ussachevsky (b. 1911), both professors at Columbia. Working singly and together, Luening and Ussachevsky had produced enough compositions by the fall of 1952 to present the first American tape-music concert (at The Museum of Modern Art, New York). Luening's first tape pieces were *musique concrète* based on solo flute sounds: *Fantasy in Space, Low Speed*, and *Invention* (all 1952). Ussachevsky's early work culminated in *A Piece for Tape Recorder* (1956), which combined electronically generated sounds with pre-recorded sounds on file in a library of sound-on-tape maintained at the Columbia studio; some of the latter had been used for his earlier pieces *Sonic Contours* and *Underwater Waltz*. The two composers collaborated in 1954 in two "concertos" for tape-recorded sounds and orchestra, *Rhapsodic Variations* and *A Poem in Cycles and Bells*.

The basic equipment for these composers of early electronic/tape music consisted of two or more tape recorders; an electronic generator of periodic sound signals, whether sine-wave (a fundamental pitch with no overtones), square-wave (fundamental with odd-numbered upper partial tones), or sawtooth-wave (fundamental with all upper partials); a generator of noise, whether the hissing steam-like sound of "white noise" (an infinite number of signals within the audible sound spectrum) or the cloud-like band-of-sound of "colored noise" (an infinite number of signals within a limited range of frequencies); various sound-filtering and reverberating devices; scissors, razor blade, splicing block, and a supply of magnetic tape. With such equipment the composer was for the first time in the same position as the painter or sculptor: able to create directly and concretely in his medium, not subject to re-interpretation by a performer.

Understandably, Edgard Varèse, who more than thirty years earlier had dreamed of "instruments obedient to my thought" and of music invigorated by science, turned enthusiastically to tape music, creating three major works in the new medium before his death. One was *Déserts* (1950–54), for a group of wind and percussion instruments alternating with "organized sound" material on tape, in a big A B A C A B A form, "A" standing for the sections played by instruments, "B" for tape music based on raw sounds collected by Varèse in a foundry, a sawmill, and several factories, and "C" for tape music based on percussion-instrument sounds. The work seems wholly integrated; the electronic interpolations simply broaden the expressive range of Varèse's "sound-mass" techniques of the 1920's, and the music has a power of almost terrifying dimension. In 1958, working together with the architect Le Corbusier for the Brussels World's Fair pavilion of the Philips Corporation, a Dutch radio and electronic firm, Varèse composed *Poème électronique*. Here finally all his ideas of music as spatial, of sound as "living matter," could be realized. The music was planned for tape-recorded performance through some 425 loudspeakers arranged in fifteen "tracks" and embedded in the looping curves of the ceiling and walls of Le Corbusier's building; the sound could actually sweep in great circles around and overhead, at different speeds and along various tracks simultaneously. Varèse composed the piece in a great variety of sounds, including a mysterious frictional sound originating in a tape-recording of his rubbing his palms together and also including the human voice, which lends an awesome presence to the work. In *Poème électronique* even more than in *Déserts*, Varèse approached the realization of his vision for a work never finished (*Espace*) of an apocalyptic sound montage in space: "voices in the sky, filling all space, crisscrossing, overlapping, penetrating each other, splitting up, superimposing, repulsing each other, colliding, crashing together."[8]

At the Columbia studio, as elsewhere in the 1950's, electronic music composition was a tedious task involving recording and re-recording on magnetic tape, then manually splicing together bits of tape to really "compose" a work. A great step in reducing such laborious techniques was taken with the development by the Radio Corporation of America of an electronic music Synthesizer, an advanced model of which was installed in the Columbia studio in July 1959, under the direction of Luening and Ussachevsky, Babbitt and Sessions. The Synthesizer allowed Babbitt especially to pursue his ideal of a totally organized music, for it made possible the most precise control not only of the pitch components but also the rhythmic, dynamic, and timbral. "Control," however, was of no importance to Babbitt without perception, and his work in the 1960's was strongly conditioned by a typically thoroughgoing investigation of the fundamental human capabilities of perception and relation, within the extraordinarily wide boundaries of the Synthesizer's productive capacity. The result, in works like *Composition for Synthesizer* (1961) and *Ensembles for Synthesizer* (1962–64), was a music of great lucidity sonorously and architectonically, in striking contrast to both the music of Luening and Ussachevsky, which seldom loses sight of its non-electronic musical sources, and the music of Varèse, with its cosmic stridency and gestural dynamism. Other works by Babbitt combine synthesized sound with live performance: *Vision and Prayer* (1961), *Philomel* (1964), and *Correspondences* (1966–68). In these a new vitality appears. In *Vision and Prayer*, Dylan Thomas's poem is set against a wholly synthesized accompaniment; the voice moves from recitation through speech-song and back again. *Philomel*, a wondrously musical poem by John Hollander on the transformation into a nightingale of the ravished and speechless Philomela, is set by Babbitt for live voice, taped and

---

[8] Quoted in Chou Wen-chung, "Varèse: A Sketch of the Man and His Music," *MQ*, LII (1966), 166. Varèse's third electronic work, little-known, was composed for a brief portion of Thomas Bouchard's film, *Around and About Joan Miró* (1956).

electronically altered voice, and synthesized sound. Composed for the remarkable soprano Bethany Beardslee, Babbitt's music for *Philomel* is as precisely ordered and as full of structural subtleties as any of his music; at another level it is a profoundly moving, "expressive" work. One critic has remarked that Philomela's "final triumphant phrase [Example 10-11], her ultimate recognition of her vocal powers, celebrates Mr. Babbitt's new-found voice as well."[9]

EXAMPLE 10-11. M. Babbitt, *Philomel,* conclusion (live voice part only). Copyright Associated Music Publishers, Inc. Used by permission.

Related to tape-recorder and electronic music is computer music, which may be defined as the programming of an electronic computer to generate music or, in the early stages (from which we have hardly emerged), to generate material that can be transcribed into musical notation. The first serious experiments in computer composition were carried out in 1955–1956 by the composer-mathematician team of Lejaren Hiller (b. 1924) and Leonard Isaacson, working with the Illiac automatic high-speed digital computer at the University of Illinois. Their first product was a four-movement *Illiac Suite* (1956) for string quartet, each movement titled "Experiment," intended to show the compositional possibilities of one or another aspect of computer programming. Anything but radical in sound and structure, the *Illiac Suite* was more a technological breakthrough than anything else. Hiller later produced a *Computer Cantata* (1963), much more sophisticated musically, in conjunction with Robert Baker and a more advanced (IBM 7090) computer. At the present writing (1968) various composers, mathematicians, and engineers are progressing rapidly toward a combina-

[9] Richard F. French, in "Current Chronicle," *MQ*, L (1964), 382–88.

. . . composition using charts and moves thereon (1951); composition using templates made or found (1952–   ); composition using observation of imperfections in the paper upon which it is written (1952–   ); composition without a fixed relation of parts to score (1954–   ); composition indeterminate of its performance (1958–   ).

Underlying all these means for reducing his dominance over the musical experience and letting the music "happen"[12] was Cage's discovery in 1951 that there is no silence. Previously, he had organized his music on the assumptions that the opposite of sound was silence; that duration was the only characteristic of sound measurable in terms of silence; that therefore any valid musical structure (a work of sounds and silences) must be based not on frequency, as traditionally it had been, but on duration. Then in 1951 Cage entered an anechoic chamber, as silent as technologically possible. He heard two sounds, one high, one low; the engineer in charge explained that the high sound was his nervous system in operation, the low sound his blood circulating. Cage's reactions:

> The situation one is clearly in is not objective (sound-silence), but rather subjective (sounds only), those intended and those others (so-called silence) not intended. If, at this point, one says, "Yes! I do not discriminate between intention and non-intention," the splits, subject-object, art-life, etc., disappear, an identification has been made with the material, and actions are then those relevant to its nature, i.e.:
> *A sound does not view itself as thought, as ought, as needing another sound for its elucidation, as etc. . . .*
> *A sound accomplishes nothing; without it life would not last out the instant.*
> *Relevant action is theatrical (music [imaginary separation of hearing from the other senses] does not exist), inclusive and intentionally purposeless. . . .*[13]

The most dramatic, certainly the most famous, application by Cage of these ideas is the work *4'33"* (1952), a three-part piece for

[12] Cage's influence on the mixed-media, unmatrixed, often improvisational form of theater called Happenings has been very strong, since his organization at Black Mountain College in 1952 of an event involving painting, dance, piano-playing, poetry, films, slides, phonorecordings, radios, and a lecture by himself. See Michael Kirby, *Happenings* (New York: E. P. Dutton & Co., 1965).

[13] From an article of 1955, reprinted as "Experimental Music: Doctrine" in *Silence*, pp. 13–17. The bracketed phrase is Cage's.

tion of sound-synthesizer and computer to provide a studi
composer "controlled from a central console that will be
instrument with which the composer will come into con
All that will be necessary, after composing the piece, is to
button."[10]

Experimental music

At precisely the same time that composers like Babb
chevsky, and Hiller were working to increase the compo
sonal control over musical materials and their realization i
an apparently opposite impulse was leading other compo
different direction. In their music the will and determinati
composer were *reduced:* either he found ways of prod
music by chance or random methods (thus minimizing h
the choice of the notes to be played or sung) or he prod
the actual note-symbols in ordered relationships but just mu
material, to be ordered by the performer; for some works,
the raw material was provided, only suggestions about the
activity to initiate it, or about the environment in which
take place.

Several adjectives have been used to define this musi
tory," "indeterminate," "chance," "random," "improvisat
some of them. The different connotations of each of these
sumed, however, under the more general term *experiment*
precise meaning defined by John Cage when he writes: "A
mental action is one the outcome of which is unforeseen
"action" here is that of musical composition; the "outcom
musical performance. It is in this sense that the music t
cussed in this section is "experimental."

Undisputed leader of such experimental music from
1950's was Cage himself. In the summary of his comp
methods partially quoted above (p. 214), Cage lists the
"paths my musical thought has taken" as these:

---

[10] Joel Chadabe, "New Approaches to Analog-Studio Desig
VI, 1 (Fall–Winter 1967), 107–13.

[11] "Composition as Process," three lectures given at Darmstadt i
ber 1958; reprinted in Cage, *Silence* (Middletown: Wesleyan Univer
1961), pp. 18–55.

to follow. Vaguely reminiscent of a composition by Mondrian, *December 1952* has been exhibited as a work of graphic art and has historical significance as the first wholly graphic music (at least since the staffless neumes of the earlier Middle Ages).

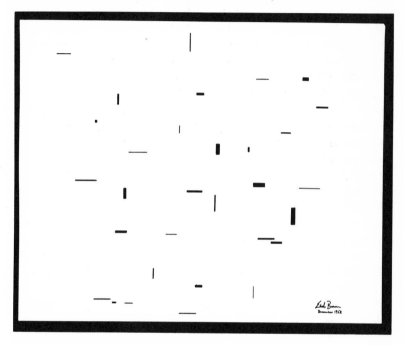

EXAMPLE 10-12. Earle Brown, *December 1952*. Reproduced by permission of Associated Music Publishers, Inc.

Utilizing various idioms of experimental and non-experimental music and various methods of notation, Brown developed further his mobile, open-form ideas in such works as *Available Forms I* for chamber ensemble (1961) and *Available Forms II* (1962) "for large orchestra four hands," i.e. with two conductors. In each of these works, Brown composed a number of brief musical events, sharply differentiated in character. These may be sounded in any order, repeated, combined, cut off in the middle, taken at different tempos, all at the discretion of the conductor, who thereby realizes one version of the work from the "available forms." Maximum possibilities of transformation and mobility (cf. Calder) exist in these works, which are formed spontaneously in performance (cf. Pollock).

Other groups of composers in the late 1950's and '60's developed Cage's idea that "relevant action is theatrical (music [imaginary separation of hearing from the other senses] does not exist), inclusive and intentionally purposeless." Viewing the way of the future as leading to a sort of *Gesamtkunstwerk*-like Happening, radically anti-Establishment, reminiscent in their mockery and humor of the Dada artists earlier in the century, these composers joined other artists in sound-and-environment events so wildly diverse as to preclude any sort of categorization here. Although New York City has been a major center, with an American wing of an international group called Fluxus particularly active, similar groups exist in Ann Arbor, Michigan (the ONCE group), Seattle ("Dimensions of New Music"), and elsewhere in the country. The subtitle of *An Anthology* (1963) edited by composer La Monte Young (b. 1935) suggests the "theatrical . . . inclusive and intentionally purposeless" diversity of this art-as-process movement:

> Chance operations / Concept art / Meaningless work / Natural disasters / Indeterminacy / Anti-art / Plans of action / Improvisation / Stories / Diagrams / Poetry / Essays / Dance constructions / Compositions / Mathematics / Music

Among the contributors, who included Cage, Brown, and Wolff, were Joseph Byrd, Toshi Ichiyanagi, Richard Maxfield, Nam June Paik, and James Waring. Young himself included a number of his compositions of 1960. *Composition 1960 #10* is reproduced below, in its entirety:

Draw a straight line and follow it.

October 1960

Composition 1960 #7—" to be held for a long time"—was

performed in New York in 1961 by a string trio; its duration was forty-five minutes, evoking a large number of ancillary sounds, mostly audience noises, but also revealing to those who continued to listen a whole inner world of fluctuating overtones in the open fifth as sustained by the players.

Among the ONCE group composers, Robert Ashley (b. 1930)

and Gordon Mumma (b. 1935) are the leaders. A typical piece of Ashley's is *Public Opinion Descends Upon the Demonstrators* (1961), for a single operator of complex electronic playback equipment with a large variety of pre-recorded sounds, and an audience. The audience is seated unconventionally so that its members can observe each other and so that the operator can observe their reactions. The operator determines the sounds of the piece according to audience activity: there are specific sound-complexes for him to produce when each of the following actions is "performed" by a member of the audience: (1) leave the auditorium; (2) walk around in the auditorium; (3) speak aloud or laugh; (4) whisper (audibly or noticeably); (5) make any kind of exaggerated gesture; (6) make any kind of secretive gesture; (7) glance "meaningfully" at another member of the audience; (8) seek a remote visual diversion (through the windows, about the ceiling, etc.); (9) look toward a loudspeaker; (10) make an involuntary physical gesture (yawn, scratch, adjust clothing, etc.); (11) show an enforced physical rigidity (waiting it out). Things get lively as soon as the audience begins to understand that in some mysterious way *it* is creating the piece: exhibitionists, angry resenters, and shrinking violets all contribute to a lively interaction between "audience" and "performer" in which traditional roles are thoroughly confused and in which no one is really certain who the "composer" is. Like Ashley, Mumma has been concerned with activating the musical experience: *Meanwhile, A Twopiece* (1961) for grand piano, percussion, pre-recorded electronic sounds, and "another instrument on which one of the performers is proficient" is written in a notation that indicates only the physical gestures to be made by the two players, with cues for them to move from instrument to instrument at certain points. In speaking of the ideology of such a piece, Mumma has said that its physicality, free choice of sounds, and interaction between performers respond partly to the fact that "with the widespread use of 'canned' music (radio, phonograph, and tape playback in serious music, commercial popular music, jazz, and electronic music) the visual or theatrical aspect of the performance of music has lost much of its significance."[19] In *Meanwhile* and in a work like *Gestures II* for two pianos (1962), Mumma strikes back, as do Ashley and other composers of "action and gesture" music.

[19] Private communication, February 23, 1962.

Bibliographical notes

For a brief survey of American music since World War II in the broader context of Western music in general, see Part V of Eric Salzman's *Twentieth-Century Music: An Introduction. The Modern Composer and His World*, ed. John Beckwith and Udo Kasemets (Toronto: University of Toronto Press, 1961), is an interesting transcript of papers and discussions of an International Conference of Composers of 1960. The book by Leonard Meyer cited in footnote 7 is an important critical-aesthetic contribution.

Elliott Carter has written some revealing self-examinations in "Shop Talk by an American Composer," *MQ*, XLVI (1960), 189–201.

Milton Babbitt's theoretical writings, for many readers almost impenetrably detailed and complex, have appeared in various journals: *Journal of the American Musicological Society*, III (1950); *The Score and I.M.A. Magazine*, June 1955; *MQ*, XLVI (1960); *Journal of Music Theory*, V (1961); *PNM*, I (1962); of these, the last cited has been perhaps the most influential among other composers. He has written a lucid account of the Synthesizer's contribution in "The Revolution in Sound: Electronic Music," *University, A Princeton Magazine*, IV (April 22, 1960), 8–16. A good discussion of Babbitt's 36-measure *Semi-Simple Variations* for piano (1957) is Elaine Barkin's "A simple approach to Milton Babbitt's semi-simple Variations," *Music Review*, 28, No. 4 (November 1967), 316–22.

Otto Luening pinpoints the chronology of electronic-music development in "Some Random Remarks about Electronic Music," *Journal of Music Theory*, VIII, 1 (Spring 1964), 89–98. The full text by John Hollander for Babbitt's *Philomel*, together with the poet's "Notes on the Text of *Philomel*," is printed in *PNM*, VI, 1 (Fall–Winter 1967), 134–41.

Hiller and Isaacson's *Experimental Music* (New York: McGraw-Hill Book Company, 1959) relates in detail the problems and progress of early computer composition and includes the score of the *Illiac Suite*. Hiller and Baker's "*Computer Cantata:* A Study in Compositional Method," *PNM*, III, 1 (Fall–Winter 1964), 62–90, summarizes later work.

Cage's essays and lectures are unparalleled sources for his ideas on the experimental music of chance and indeterminacy; they have been collected in two books, *Silence* (Middletown: Wesleyan University Press, 1961) and *A Year from Monday* (same publisher, 1968). Calvin Tomkins's *The Bride and Her Bachelors* (New York: Viking Press, 1965) is a collection of four essays (originally *New Yorker* magazine "profiles") on Cage and the related artists Rauschenberg, Duchamp, and Tinguely. One of the most refreshingly ardent partisans of what he calls the "American experimental tradition" is Peter Yates; see his criticism in *Arts and Architecture, passim*, and the relevant chapters of his book, *Twentieth Century Music* (New York: Pantheon Books, 1967).

II

Intersections, Interactions, Projections

Each of the words in the title of this last chapter might be found as heading for a musical work of the mid-1960's. The post-World War II period saw extraordinary activity in American music along apparently widely diverging lines; by the 1960's, however, it was possible to perceive some new syntheses or, if that term suggests too strongly an ultimate merger wholly completed, at least "intersections" and "interactions" among different impulses. And perhaps these projected some syntheses lying ahead. As one composer-critic of the period has put it: "For the younger composers, and many of the older ones, the barriers are down, the categories destroyed. . . . Any kind of statement is possible."[1] In all the

---

[1] Salzman, *Twentieth-Century Music*, p. 186.

areas of American music—jazz, the musical and other popular music, concert music—one of the most striking trends of the 1950's and '60's was the intermingling of musical techniques, languages, and even worlds that had seemed separate before.

Jazz, pop music, and the Third Stream

In the jazz field, three principal post-war types—cool jazz, hard bop or funky jazz, and "the new thing"—arose from interactions of attitude and intersections of style. Cool jazz may be dated from a famous series of recordings made early in 1949 by a nine-man group led by trumpeter Miles Davis (b. 1926), later gathered together in an album titled *Birth of the Cool* (Capitol Records album T-762). Based on sophisticated arrangements by Gil Evans (b. 1912) for an unusual ensemble of solo instruments including French horn and tuba, this was a chamber jazz of great musical elegance, if also of great restraint expressively compared to the contemporaneous bop style. The ruminative, often gutturally soliloquizing trumpet of Davis and the thin, pale tone of alto saxophonist Lee Konitz (b. 1927) were characteristic. Pianist in the performances of *Venus de Milo* by Gerry Mulligan (b. 1927) and in his own *Rouge* was John Lewis (b. 1920). In 1952, Lewis founded the Modern Jazz Quartet; its light sound (piano, vibraphone, bass, and drums), and a style often including contrapuntal devices like canon and fugue and based on such non-traditional source materials as Elizabethan virginal music (*The Queen's Fancy*), Bach (*Vendôme*), and an old Christmas carol (*God Rest Ye Merry, Gentlemen*), made it the epitome of cool jazz. Related in its breadth of style-sources was the music of a quartet organized by pianist Dave Brubeck (b. 1920), who had studied with both Milhaud and Schoenberg. Typical was a version of *Perdido*, recorded at a 1953 Oberlin College concert, in which the Brubeck group included witty improvisatory quotations from Gershwin's show tune *Crazy Rhythm*, a popular song of the 1930's ("The Music Goes 'Round and 'Round"), and Stravinsky's *Petrouchka*, plus a fugal exposition in the manner of Baroque-era music. Brubeck later broke out of the traditional $\frac{4}{4}$ meter of jazz with a number of works in $\frac{5}{4}$ and $\frac{7}{4}$, issued in a record album titled *Time Out*. Even more eclectic, sophisticated, and intellectualized was the piano jazz of Lennie

Tristano (b. 1919), noted as a teacher of vanguard jazz style in the 1950's.

Perhaps in reaction to such a cultivated chamber jazz, there emerged in the mid-1950's a hard, harsh, leather-lunged style sometimes called "hard bop" or "funky" jazz. The latter term, an old colloquialism for "smelly" with sexual implications like the original ones of "jazz" itself, suggested the back-to-the-roots aim of the style. As expressed first by Horace Silver (b. 1928), pianist and musical director of the Jazz Messengers of drummer Art Blakey (b. 1919); by another pianist, Thelonious Monk (b. 1918); and by bassist Charlie Mingus (b. 1922), hard bop combined the chromaticism, the asymmetrical phrases, and the sharp punctuation of the bop style with the old earthiness of New Orleans jazz. The result was a tough, angular, honking music as complex harmonically as bop and cool jazz but also as expressionistically fervent and powerfully communicative as the early jazz of the 1920's.

With the appearance in the late 1950's of saxophonists John Coltrane (1926–1967) and Ornette Coleman (b. 1930), some jazz approached the ultra-chromatic, even atonal style of certain non-jazz. This "new thing" ("free-form jazz," "atonal jazz," "the new wave" were other attempts to name it) gave up the traditional basis of jazz in a pre-existent "tune" and a steady, even beat and turned to an almost wholly spontaneous, rhapsodic, and passionately expressive style in which the players relied on virtually extra-sensory perception to follow each other's ideas. Men like saxophonists Albert Ayler (b. 1936) and Archie Shepp (b. 1937) identified the searing expressionism of the "new thing" with the struggles of the American Negro and with the militant Black Nationalism of the 1960's. Ayler commented, "It's not about notes anymore. It's about feelings!" Negro poet and playwright Le Roi Jones said: "You hear . . . poets of the Black Nation."[2] One of Shepp's early pieces had the title *Rufus;* this was an abbreviation for *Rufus Swung His Face at Last to the Wind, Then His Neck Snapped,* and the idea behind the piece was a lynching.

The back-to-the-roots impulses of hard bop and the shouting, wailing manner of the "new thing" were related to a new sense of militant selfhood in the American Negro and to the impact, perhaps

[2] Both quotations from the jacket notes of *The New Wave in Jazz,* Impulse Records album A-90.

unconsciously felt, of Negro and other "folkish" minorities on the American public's taste. This was reflected in the even broader musical world of popular music in general, which in the 1950's and 1960's underwent a major upheaval in style. American interest in its folk music, especially that of the Negro and the "hill-billy" up-lands whites of the Southern Appalachians, had been growing since the Depression. The new popular music of the 1950's, christened "rock-and-roll" and first experienced on a national scale through the singing, guitar-playing, and pelvis-centered gyrating of Elvis Presley (b. 1935), combined elements of hill-billy music ("blue-grass," "country-and-western") with the pounding beat and shout-ing song of the Negroid "rhythm-and-blues." The latter was itself a synthesis of blues vocalization, jazz improvisation, and gospel hymnody—if indeed there had ever been a stylistic separation of those musics within the Negro community. Nationally, America ex-perienced this style in the voices of gospel singer Mahalia Jackson (b. 1911) and blues singer Ray Charles (b. 1930). By the mid-1960's the intersections of these several folkish styles had trans-formed American popular music completely: pop music of the '60's was "rock," an electrified and amplified, ear-splitting, un-sentimental, "hip" style of big-beat music, visceral and glandular in appeal, "often used as a psychedelic experience . . . a 'happening,' a numbing bombardment of the auditory nerves"[3] as played and sung by rock groups like The Supremes, Jefferson Airplane, The Doors, and Vanilla Fudge. The most fantastically successful group of all, The Beatles, was a British quartet that maintained its pop-ularity by a studied eclecticism always one step ahead of the ex-panding style-basis of the international pop-music movement. Almost as ubiquitous as rock in the 1960's was the quasi-folk music of singers like Joan Baez, Bob Dylan, and Simon and Garfunkel, who capitalized on the back-to-the-roots atmosphere of the time by creating and singing folkish songs often of deadly serious im-port and sophisticated literary quality. Perhaps the most universally well-known song of the middle 1960's was an old hymn with words adjusted by folk singer Pete Seeger and others to relate it to the major socio-political drives of the time for Negro civil rights and world peace: *We Shall Overcome* (Example 11-1).

[3] H. F. Mooney, "Popular Music Since the 1920s: The Significance of Shifting Taste," *American Quarterly*, XX, 1 (Spring 1968), 67–85.

EXAMPLE 11-1. *We Shall Overcome.* New Words and Music Arrangement by Zilphia Horton, Frank Hamilton, Guy Carawan & Pete Seeger. TRO © Copyright 1960 and 1963, LUDLOW MUSIC, INC., New York, N.Y. USED BY PERMISSION. Royalties derived from this composition are being contributed to The Freedom Movement under the trusteeship of the writers.

In both kinds of the new popular music, "folk" and rock, the central instrument, for a long time basic to jazz but for even longer to American folk music, was the guitar; its popularity reached into the American home as well, making it the mid-twentieth-century equivalent to the parlor piano of the nineteenth, at least among the young. Both "folk" and rock reflected also a decentralization of the geographical sources of popular music: no longer was New York the sole center; Nashville, Detroit, and San Francisco were as important breeding-grounds as Broadway and Tin Pan Alley.

The American musical comedy, on the other hand, still dominated by New York's tendency to a sophisticated insularity, was slow to change its style and method. At least one brilliant new composer appeared, however: Leonard Bernstein (b. 1918). A pupil of Piston's at Harvard with prodigious gifts as pianist, conductor, and composer, Bernstein moved easily from one to another of America's worlds of music, "classical" and popular. His Second Symphony, "The Age of Anxiety" (1949), includes a lengthy jazz-piano solo; his ballet score *Fancy Free* was amplified into a musical, *On the Town* (both 1944). With a style that might be described as out of Stravinsky by Copland, and with complete fluency in the pre-rock popular-music idiom, Bernstein created in *West Side Story* (1957) the freshest musical of the post-war period. A recasting of the Romeo and Juliet story in terms of the ethnic melting-pot of Manhattan's upper west side, *West Side Story* was an evocative portrait of post-war urban America; its finely-balanced interaction between ballet and drama owed much to choreographer Jerome

Robbins, who had also conceived the dances of *Fancy Free*. The only other post-war musical to rival (and even out-do) the success of *West Side Story* was *My Fair Lady* (1956), composed by Frederick Loewe (b. 1904) to Alan Jay Lerner's book after Shaw's *Pygmalion*. Perhaps the American audience that responded by the millions to this near-operetta was identifying with the guttersnipe-turned-lady of the heroine; musically speaking it had little to identify with, for like all the other musicals of the late 1950's and most of the '60's *My Fair Lady* shared in no way the popular-music revolution. Only in 1967, in *Hair* (music composed by Galt MacDermot) and *Your Own Thing* (Danny Apolinar), did the popular lyric theater begin to catch up with the new American musical vernacular: both were at least perceptibly related to rock.

Several composers of the period moved freely from jazz to non-jazz or the reverse. Gunther Schuller (b. 1925) saw in the intersection of these two mainstreams of American music possibilities for a "Third Stream," as he termed it in 1957. His *Transformation* (1957) for an eleven-piece jazz-like ensemble was conceived as "a kind of musical reflection (in general terms) of the issue . . . namely, the continuing process of amalgamation of jazz and contemporary 'classical' music."[4] *Conversations* and *Concertino* (both 1959) set a jazz quartet (with the make-up of the Modern Jazz Quartet) against, respectively, string quartet and symphony orchestra. In these works "amalgamation" is a misnomer: the two styles are kept discrete; they intersect but are not synthesized. In later works like *Seven Studies on Themes of Paul Klee* (1959) and his First Symphony (1965), Schuller moved closer to a real synthesis. A substantial number of other composers also utilized jazz elements. Their incentive seemed to spring not at all from an "Americanist" ideal, nor perhaps even the Third Stream envisioned by Schuller, but from an interest in the vitalizing possibilities of improvisation in general, without, however, Cage's aesthetic of an "experimental" indeterminacy. Among these composers are Larry Austin (b. 1930), Meyer Kupferman (b. 1926), Michael Colgrass (b. 1932), and Peter Phillips (b. 1930). Another, whose tendency to witty, deceptively offhand use of jazz-derived elements is suggested in titles like *Play! No. 1* (1965), *Mandolin* (1963), and several chamber *Sere-*

---

[4] Schuller, jacket notes for *Modern Jazz Concert: Six Compositions Commissioned by the 1957 Brandeis University Festival of the Arts*, Columbia recording WL-127.

nades, is Morton Subotnick (b. 1933). One of the founders of the San Francisco Tape Center, Subotnick became interested not only in electronic music (*Silver Apples of the Moon*, 1967; commissioned to fit the two sides of a long-playing phonorecord) but in "intermedia" works combining various new arts in a semi-theatrical mélange. In *Mandolin*, for viola, tape music, and film projections, "the viola plays the role of a kind of musical narrator to a larger musical drama. The whole work is a kind of 19th century theatre piece . . . with a piano piece of Franz Liszt emerging in the middle." In one of the most unusual demonstrations of interactions and intersections of the decade, Subotnick organized *An Electric Christmas* (1967; Carnegie Hall), mingling in one long event the medieval music of the New York Pro Musica ensemble, a rock group called Circus Maximus, his own electronic music (partially taped and composed on the spot), film projections, and a "psychedelic light show"; the event culminated in an intermixed, semi-improvisatory version for all participants of the fourteenth-century love song *Douce dame jolie* by Guillaume de Machaut.

Although not ordinarily a composer of jazz-related music, Salvatore Martirano (b. 1927) has exploited, in *Ballad* for amplified singer and chamber ensemble (1966), the extraordinary vocal agility, range, and varied tonal nuance of the young rock-and-roll singers in a work combining lacerating intensity and good humor. Similar elements of virtuosity and expressivity are demanded in Martirano's *O, O, O, O, that Shakespeherian Rag* (1958), the title from T. S. Eliot, the texts from Shakespeare, and the music, for chorus and instrumental ensemble, a "so elegant, so intelligent" commentary on the verses.

Other new music

Some other new music of the 1960's revealed an interest in the interaction of chance and improvisational elements with precisely notated and controlled composition. Lukas Foss (b. 1922) organized in 1957 an Improvisation Chamber Ensemble, hoping to develop principles of non-jazz improvisation. This had a marked effect on his own music. *Time Cycle* (1959–60), four songs on texts having to do with time, clocks, or bells, appeared in two different versions ("the occasion, the size of the hall," said Foss, "will call for one or the other"), one for soprano and orchestra with improvisatory interludes between the songs. *Echoi* (1961–63), for piano, percussion, clarinet, and 'cello, in four movements, includes not only conventionally "precise" notation but also (1) "proportional" notation which, barless and beatless, requires the performers to view the entire score and to follow each others' playing; (2) passages of "no coordination" and free re-ordering of given pitches; (3) passages with random, aperiodic assortments of dynamics, articulations, pitches, or all three; (4) percussion passages written as stems without note-heads, inviting performance on any of the drums at hand, in any order. Toward the end of *Echoi IV*, two pre-recorded but uncoordinated tape tracks, one of clarinet music, the other of 'cello, are turned on; the live performers are to echo in a free manner the taped sounds of their own instruments. There are other aspects of choice and chance in *Echoi* (no two performances will ever be the same) but the composer's ideas dominate throughout. Example 11-2 can at least suggest some of the aspects I have mentioned: the notation is proportional; large notes stand for longer time, small notes for shorter; dotted lines show the moments of coordination among performers; "c. 1s." represents a rest of "about one second"; noteless stems on the vibraphone staff indicate general melodic contour but no specific pitches.

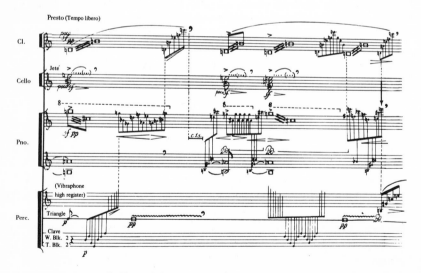

EXAMPLE 11-2. L. Foss, *Echoi*, first movement excerpt. © Copyright 1964 by Carl Fischer, Inc., New York. Reproduced by permission.

Much of the new music has put unprecedented demands on performers' abilities; it has almost seemed to create a "new virtuosity," displayed dazzlingly by such singers as Bethany Beardslee and Cathy Berberian, such pianists as David Tudor, Paul Jacobs, and Robert Miller, and such others as violinist Matthew Raimondi, percussionists Max Neuhaus and Raymond Desroches, flutist Harvey Sollberger. And these in turn have extended the range of performance possibilities envisioned by composers. This is suggested in the work of one fluent young composer, himself a brilliant performer of new piano music: Charles Wuorinen (b. 1938). In pieces like *Piano Variations* (1964), *Orchestral and Electronic Exchanges* (1965), and several chamber concertos with different solo instruments ('cello, flute, oboe), Wuorinen has written a music of ferocious intensity and furious activity, both responding to and demanding more of the new virtuosity, and approaching the outer limits of perception and comprehension.

Other new music finds sound spatialized as well as temporalized. That is, the musical discourse, no longer shaped according to principles of harmonic continuity or of underlying omnipresent "beat," is essentially one of discrete sounds or blocks of them, shaping time rather than being shaped by it. The result is an effect of sound in space more than in time, for the whole perception of time's passing is altered and attenuated by the discreteness of the sonorous events. Most composers no longer even speak of "sonorities" (let alone "chords" or "harmonies") but of "densities," "sound structures," or "sound objects." Formal principles often rest on the intersection and interaction of such sound structures, or on the equally spatial images of textures thick or thin, fluctuating or constant, combined or opposed. High-low contrasts are heard in spatial terms, as are timbral shifts. In some music, physical space itself has become crucial: symptomatically, an older composer like Henry Brant (b. 1913) who has been interested for a long time in varied placement of instrumentalists and singers in halls, auditoriums, and even the out-of-doors—e.g., *Millenium 1* (1950), *The Grand Universal Circus* (1956), *Fire in Cities* (1961), and *Voyage Four* (1964)—has achieved new recognition. Ralph Shapey (b. 1921) similarly divides performers into sub-groups disposed in different, spatially separated positions. Thus his *Ontogeny* (1958) for orchestra calls for a division of the symphonic ensemble into seven sub-orchestras, re-positioned onstage. Another orchestral work, *Rituals* (1958), is similarly conceived. In speaking of his *Incantations* (1961) for soprano and ten instruments, Shapey articulated this new spatial concept of music:

> music as an object in Time and Space
>
> aggregate sounds structured into concrete sculptured forms
>
> images existing as a totality from their inception, each a self-involved unit of individual proportions
>
> related, inter-related, and unrelated images organized into an organic whole
>
> permutations occurring only within each self-contained unit . . .[5]

In several imaginative works by Roger Reynolds (b. 1934) including *The Emperor of Ice Cream* (1963) and *Blind Men* (1966), not only is the spatial distribution of the performers specified but the scores show their movement from one area of the stage to another.

One of the most powerful, if paradoxical, effects of the new ideas of time and space in music, of "concrete sculptured forms," of the new virtuosity, and also of the music involving chance and performer-choice in a context of composer-controlled image of sound, is of a new expressionism. Unlike the post-Romantic expressionism of a Strauss or a Schoenberg, it is not the composer's feelings but those of the performers or, even more potently, of the sounds themselves that seem to be loosed. Not only do the performers seem more alive, flexible, responsive to each other, but in a peculiarly palpable way the music itself takes on an unprecedented sentience, personalization, willfulness. Hear Lukas Foss, speaking of the second movement of *Echoi:*

> . . . vibraphone shadowing clarinet (close canon at the unison) sticks to him like glue. clarinet should make futile attempts to escape its own shadow, like an insect trying to extricate itself from a spider web. cello joins in the pursuit. . . . pitchless percussion also shadowing, imitating. everyone wanting to get in on the act.[6]

Or hear Chou Wen-chung (b. 1923), a former pupil of Varèse whose Chinese origins allow him to relate what seems new in Ameri-

---

[5] Quoted in "Music Programs and Notes," University of Illinois 1965 Festival of Contemporary Arts, p. 23.

[6] "Work-Notes for *Echoi*," *PNM*, III, 1 (Fall–Winter 1964), 54–61.

can music to some very old Oriental ideas, speaking of his orchestral works *All in the Spring Wind* (1953) and *And the Fallen Petals* (1954):

> . . . a tonal brushwork in space—with ever-changing motion, tension, texture, and sonority. . . . The ancient Chinese musician believed that each single tone or aggregate of tones is a musical entity in itself and a living spark of expression as long as it lasts. Therefore, it was also believed that the meaning in music lies intrinsically in the tones themselves, that maximum expressiveness can be derived from a succession of tones without resorting to extraneous procedures.[7]

These kinds of ideas have a familiar ring to us who have surveyed American music of the past century. They remind us of Carter's "auditory scenarios, for performers to act out with their instruments." They relate to Cage's ideas of "giving up control so that sounds can be sounds" and to Wolff's concern for "a kind of objectivity, almost anonymity—sound come into its own." They go back to Varèse, who liked to quote a nineteenth-century Polish scientist's definition of music as "the corporealization of the intelligence that is in sounds" (University of Southern California lecture, 1939). They go further back ultimately to Ives and his faith in "the large unity of a series of particular aspects of a subject rather than [in] the continuity of its expression," his "discussions and arguments" among musical protagonists, and the spatially separated, semi-coordinated components of *The Unanswered Question*.

In sum, far from being outlandishly new, the anticlassic, asymmetrical, expressionistic, self-defining architecture of sound in both time and space that is the new American music relates to an older world view of musical expression and to a tradition of American music; it projects—experimentally, in Cage's sense of the word—ahead into the future as well.

---

[7] "Towards a Re-Merger in Music," *Contemporary Composers on Contemporary Music* (New York: Holt, Rinehart and Winston, 1967), pp. 309–15.

Index